MFA HIGHLIGHTS photography

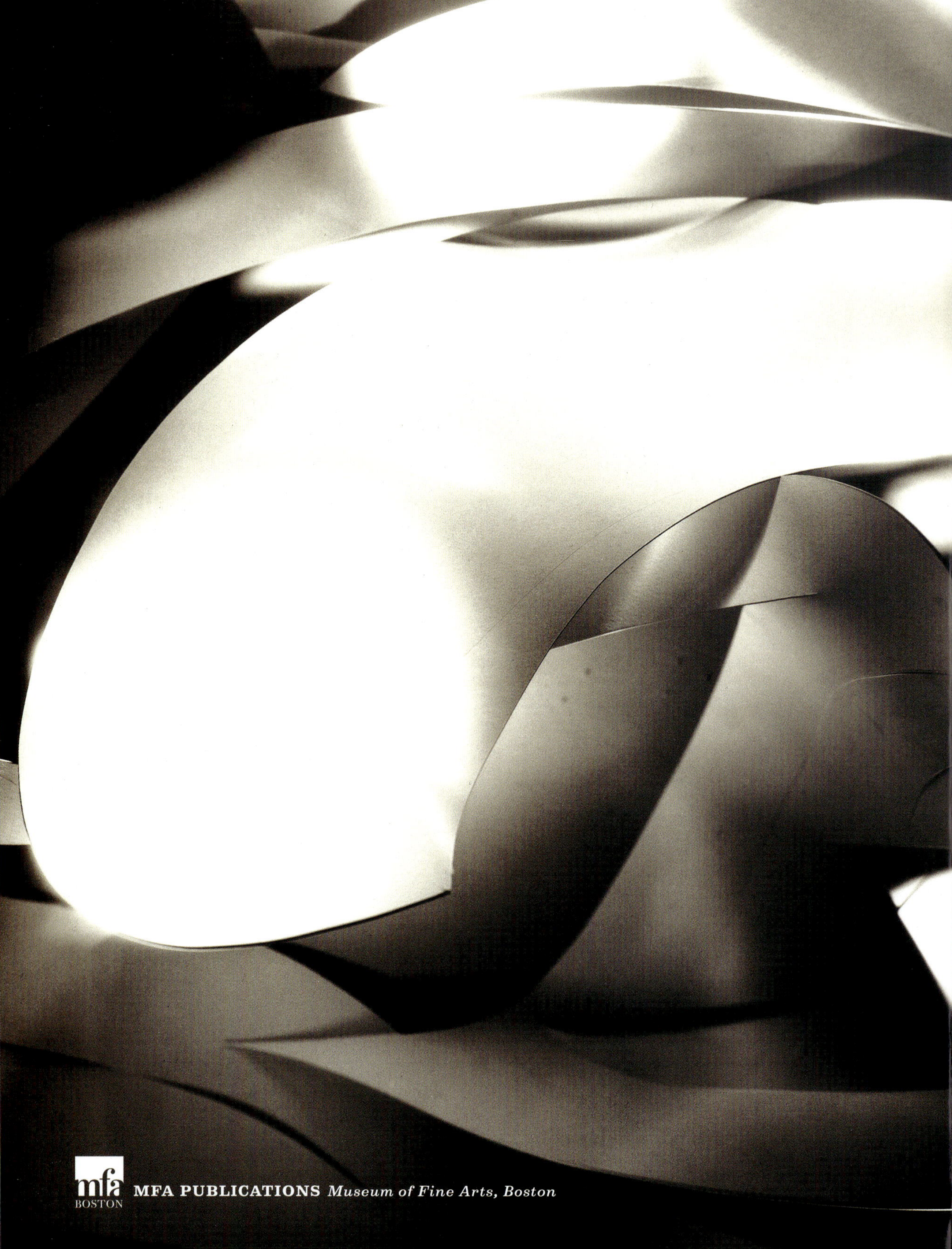
mfa
BOSTON
MFA PUBLICATIONS Museum of Fine Arts, Boston

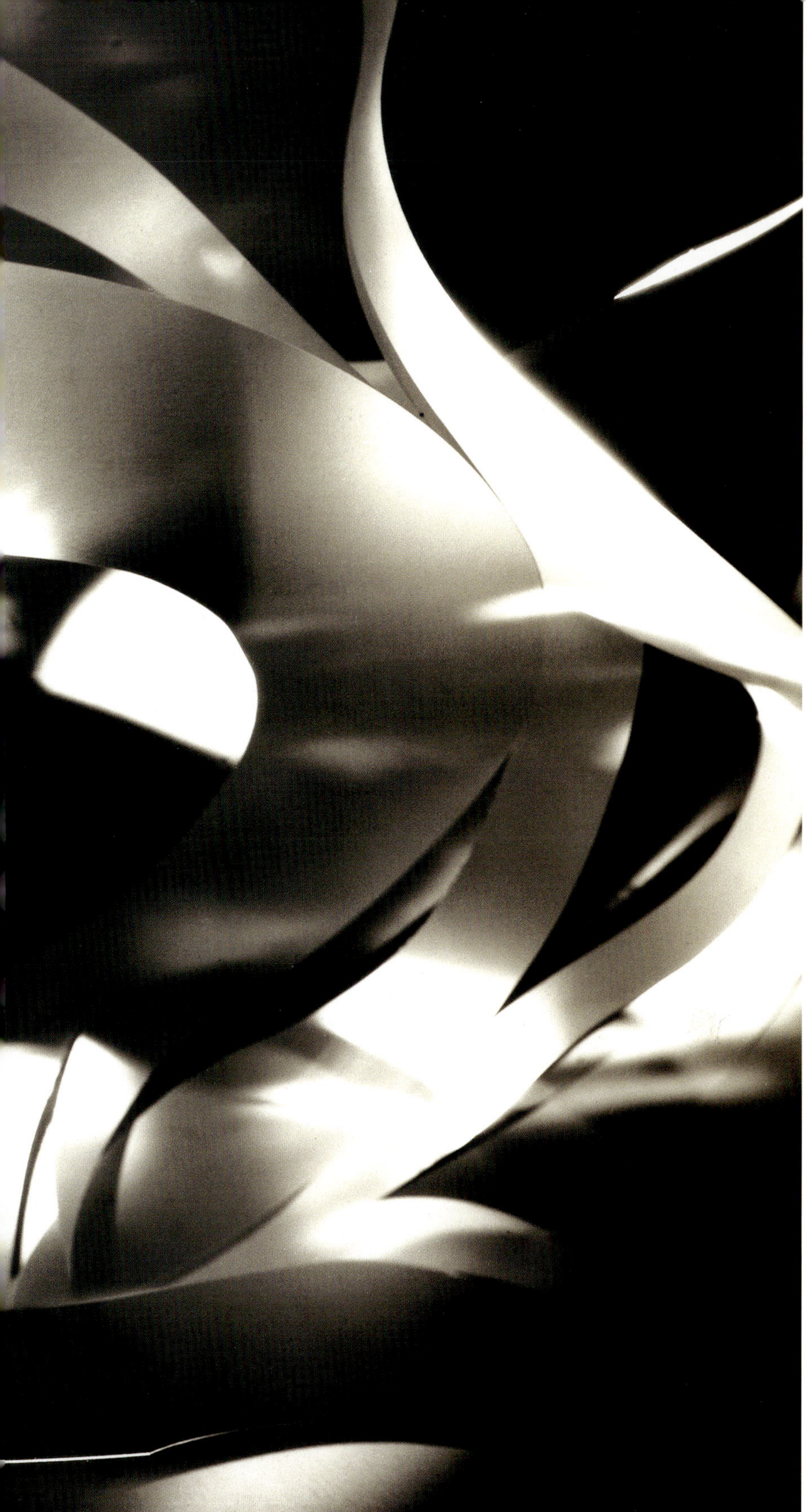

MFA HIGHLIGHTS photography

Anne E. Havinga

Karen E. Haas

Nancy Keeler

Frontispiece: Francis Bruguière, *Cut-Paper Abstraction* (detail), p. 136; pp. 5–6: Edward Weston, *Sand Dunes, Oceano, California* (detail), p. 152

MFA Publications
Museum of Fine Arts, Boston
465 Huntington Avenue
Boston, Massachusetts 02115
www.mfa-publications.org

Library of Congress Control Number: 2007927115
ISBN 978-0-87846-676-4

While the objects in this publication necessarily represent only a small portion of the MFA's holdings, the Museum is proud to be a leader within the American museum community in sharing the objects in its collection via its Web site. Currently, information about more than 330,000 objects is available to the public worldwide. To learn more about the MFA's collections, including provenance, publication, and exhibition history, kindly visit *www.mfa.org/collections.*

For a complete listing of MFA publications, please contact the publisher at the above address, or call 617 369 3438.

All photographs are by the Imaging Studios, Museum of Fine Arts, Boston, unless otherwise noted.

Edited by Sarah McGaughey Tremblay
Copyedited by Jodi M. Simpson
Designed and produced by Terry McAweeney
Series design by Lucinda Hitchcock
Printed and bound at CS Graphics PTE LTD, Singapore

Trade distribution:
D.A.P. / Distributed Art Publishers
155 Sixth Avenue, 2nd floor
New York, New York 10013
Tel. 212 627 1999 Fax 212 627 9484

FIRST EDITION
Printed in Singapore
This book was printed on acid-free paper.

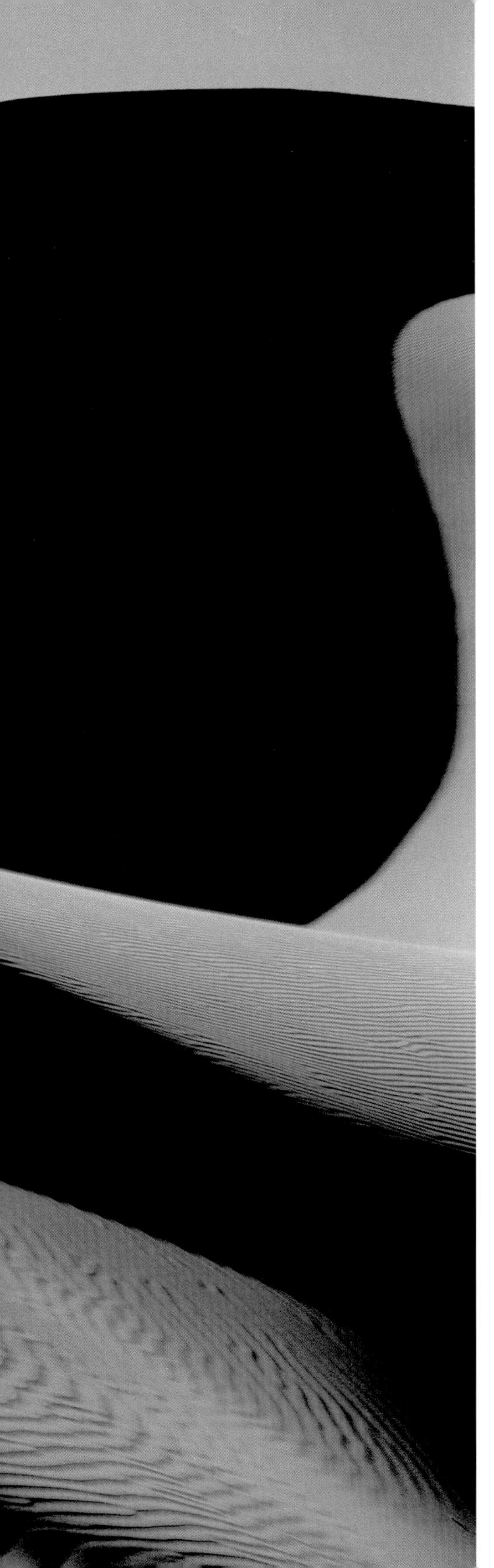

Contents

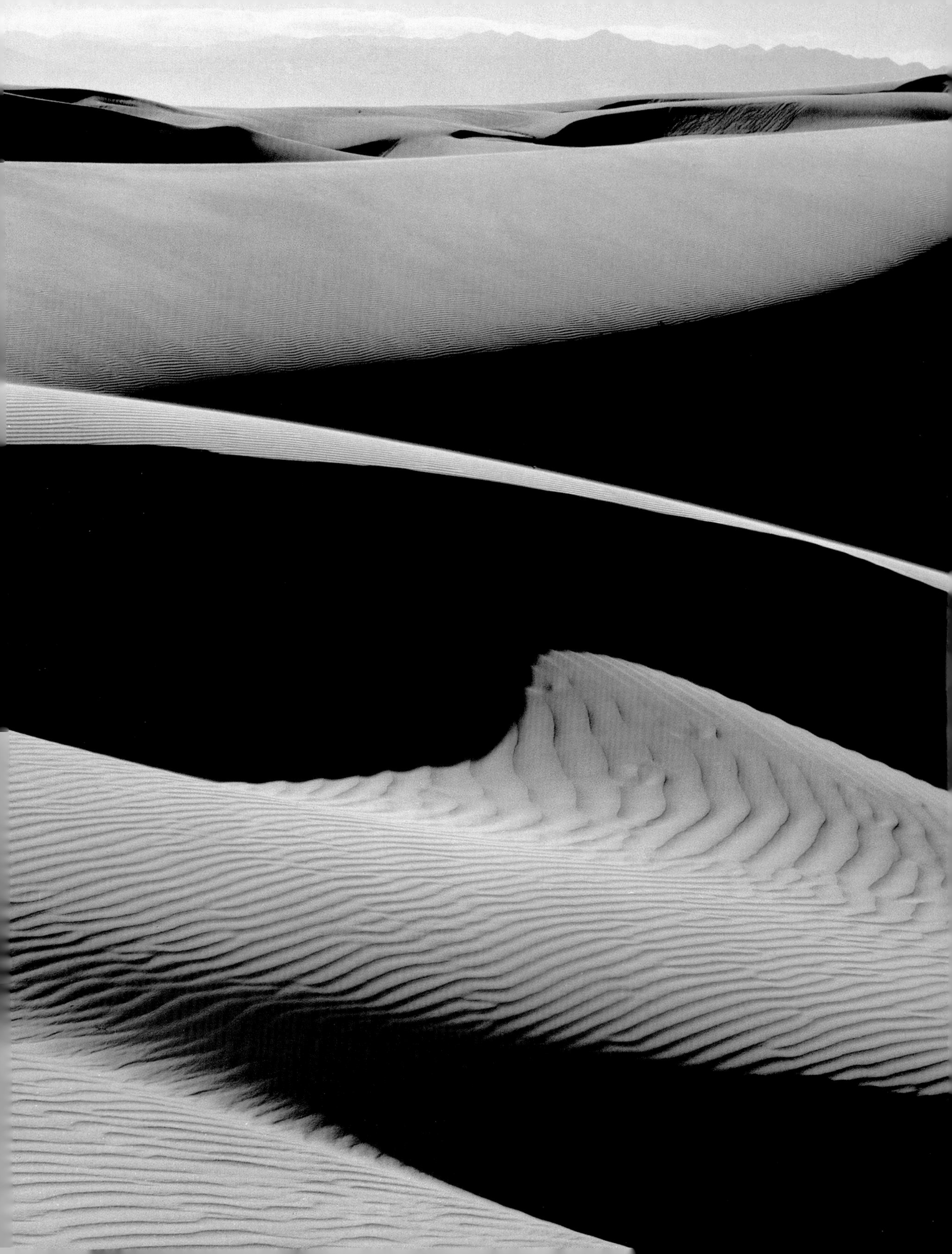

Director's Foreword

Art is for everyone, and it is in this spirit that the MFA Highlights series was conceived. The series introduces some of the greatest works of art in a manner that is both approachable and stimulating. Each volume focuses on an individual collection, allowing fascinating themes — both visual and textual — to emerge. We aim, over time, to represent every one of the Museum's major collections in the Highlights series, thus forming a library that will be a wonderful resource for the understanding and enjoyment of world art.

It is our goal to make the Museum's artworks accessible by every means possible. We hope that each volume of MFA Highlights will help you to know and understand our encyclopedic collections and to make your own discoveries among their riches.

Malcolm Rogers
Ann and Graham Gund Director
Museum of Fine Arts, Boston

Acknowledgments

We are tremendously pleased to publish this overview of the photography collection at the Museum of Fine Arts, Boston. The project has involved a team effort. Several years ago, Clifford S. Ackley, chair of the Department of Prints, Drawings, and Photographs, and Karen Haas, curator of The Lane Collection, collaborated with me in selecting the one hundred images to be highlighted, a challenge since there are so many outstanding photographs in the collection. Karen, in particular, as well as scholar Nancy Keeler, has been integrally involved in all aspects of preparing the publication; I am most grateful for their writing of the bulk of the entries while I was involved with the essay. Among the outside colleagues we consulted, Joanne Lukitsh was particularly helpful. Within the Museum, we thank research assistant Rebecca Senf, who initiated the preparation of the glossary, and Katrina Newbury, the Saundra B. Lane Associate Conservator, who ultimately completed it. All the staff members of the departments of Prints, Drawings, and Photographs and Paper Conservation deserve special thanks, as each of them played a role in the effort, from verifying information, to arranging for works to be photographed, to covering duties so that we could concentrate on our work.

We are grateful to the Museum's Ann and Graham Gund Director, Malcolm Rogers; the Deputy Director, Curatorial, Katherine Getchell; and our publisher, Mark Polizzotti, for envisioning the series of highlights books on the collection to which this volume belongs. At MFA Publications, Sarah McGaughey Tremblay was a most gracious editor. Jodi Simpson and Patty Bergin copyedited and proofread the text, and intern Steve Schirra ensured that their edits were recorded correctly. The beautiful design is by Terry McAweeney, who also orchestrated the production schedule. The funds for creating the digital images of the works of art—carried out by the Museum's team of photographers, especially Damon

Beale and John Woolf—were provided through an endowment established by Katherine Metcalfe and Langdon Wheeler. Haley Shaw and Sionan Burke secured the necessary permissions for reproduction.

We gratefully acknowledge the contributions of all the donors who have nurtured the building of the photography collection through the years, as they have made the Museum's holdings an international resource. The individuals responsible for the wonderful acquisitions represented on these pages are credited alongside the images; the figure illustrations are credited at the back of the book.

It thrills me to be the Museum's first curator solely dedicated to photography, and to take care of the collection that has been tended with such thoughtfulness since the 1960s by Clifford Ackley. Cliff's encouraging presence and wise counsel deserve the sincerest of thanks.

Anne E. Havinga
Estrellita and Yousuf Karsh Curator of Photographs

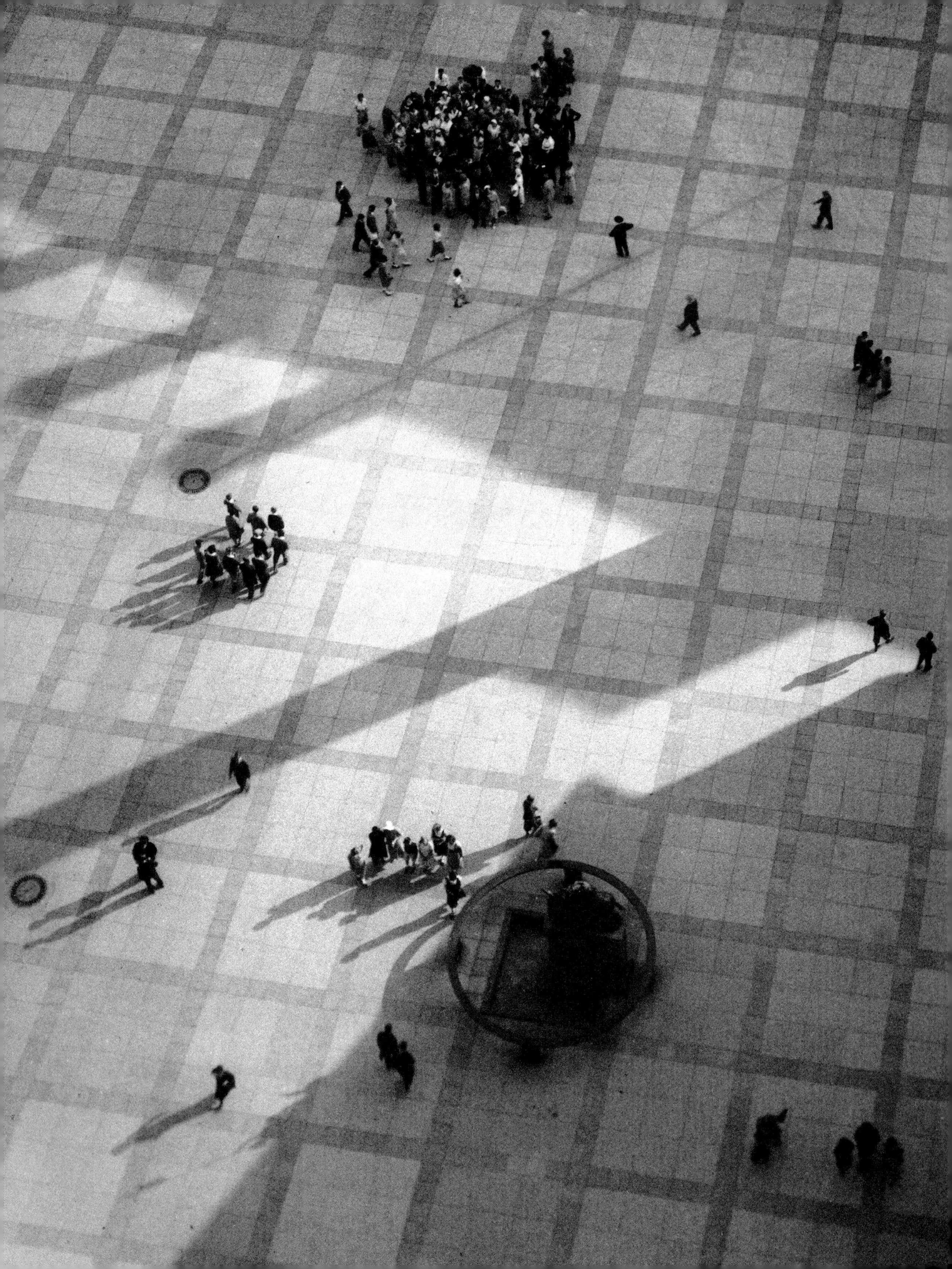

Preserving Memories, Creating Visions: A Brief History of Photography

Anne E. Havinga

The Beginnings and the Announcement of Photography in 1839

The invention of photography grew out of a series of discoveries that occurred over many centuries. The precursor of the camera was the camera obscura, a darkened box or room with a pinhole piercing one side, through which light cast an inverted image of the outside world. In the sixteenth century, camera obscura images were improved when a lens was inserted into the pinhole. By the following century, artists were using portable camerae obscurae as drawing aids, fitting the apparatus with a mirror so they could trace the reflected vision. A century later, painters and draughtsmen also had the option of using a camera lucida, a prism mounted on a rod through which an image could be projected, and then traced, onto a sheet of paper.

After the Napoleonic Wars, an affluent French inventor named Nicéphore Niépce began to experiment with silver, already known to be light sensitive, as a means of securing the image produced by a camera obscura. In 1826, after a decade of trials, Niépce succeeded in creating the first photographic image by inserting a pewter plate coated with a combination of silver halides and bitumen, both of which reacted to light, into a camera obscura. Made after some eight hours of exposure, the image, albeit indistinct, depicted the view out of a window at his family estate.

A year later, Niépce found that Louis-Jacques-Mandé Daguerre, a scenic designer and celebrated inventor of the Diorama (a popular illusionistic spectacle), was pursuing the same goal, and in 1829 they formed a partnership. After Niépce died in 1833, Daguerre continued to refine Niépce's technique, using iodized silver on copper plates. Daguerre discovered by chance that a latent image on the plate could be developed with mercury vapors, and in time he learned that, by immersing the plate in a solution of table salt, he could stop the developing image from becoming overly dark.

After considerable experimentation, Daguerre perfected a method that was reliable and marketable. He announced his breakthrough in early January 1839, calling the small, one-of-a-kind photographic image produced directly in the camera a "daguerreotype." When held at the correct angle, the highly detailed image appeared seemingly by magic, like a mirror of reality, from the silvered sheet of copper. Although painters were anxious that the daguerreotype would mean competition for their work, the public was transfixed by its clarity and detail.

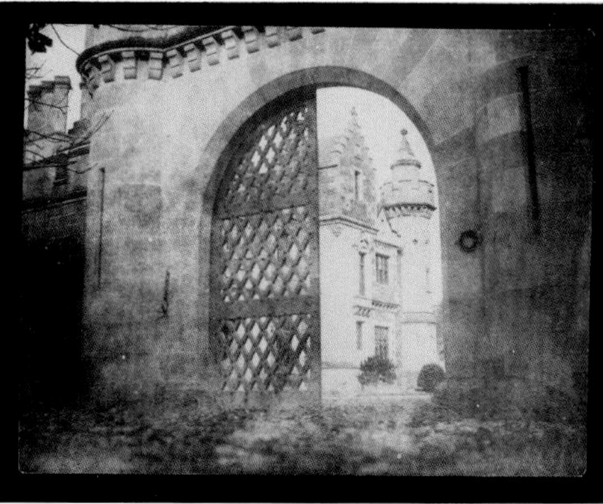

fig. 1 **William Henry Fox Talbot (English, 1800–1877), *Entrance Gate, Abbotsford,* 1844, from *Sun Pictures in Scotland* (1845), salt print from a paper negative**

Meanwhile, in England, the wealthy scientist William Henry Fox Talbot had been striving toward a similar goal. Having struggled in the early 1830s with poor drawing technique (despite the aid of the camera obscura and camera lucida), he speculated: "How charming it would be if it were possible to cause these natural images to imprint themselves durably, and remain fixed upon the paper!"[1]

By the mid-1830s, Talbot was achieving shadowy pictures of simple views through the camera obscura and of plants and lace placed directly on paper that he sensitized with a solution of silver chloride and exposed to sunlight. To solve the problem of tonalities reversing (dark areas appearing light, and light areas reproducing as dark), he used paper that was thin and fairly transparent (later to be called a negative), which he then exposed again onto a second sheet. Unlike the daguerreotype, which produced a unique photographic image, Talbot's process allowed for multiple positives to be made from a single negative. The Englishman publicly announced his photogenic drawings three weeks after the news of Daguerre's invention.

Talbot refined his method over the next few years and named it the "calotype," after the Greek word for "beautiful." From 1844 to 1846, he published his theories on the potential of photography in an important prospectus titled *The Pencil of Nature*, which included a sequence of twenty-four calotype images, and in 1845 he issued *Sun Pictures in Scotland*, illustrated with twenty-three photographic prints (fig. 1). Talbot's negative-positive process marked the beginning of photography as we know it today, for in time its reproducibility gave it greater commercial potential than the unique daguerreotype.

Talbot's experiments stimulated his friend, the eminent scientist Sir John Herschel, to also investigate the photographic process. Herschel had suggested in 1839 that washing photographs in sodium hyposulfite ("hypo") could prevent further chemical reactions and thereby "fix" them. Three years later, Herschel developed the cyanotype (named after the Greek word *cyan*, meaning "deep blue"), which was a photographic print on paper that relied on the use of iron salts instead of silver and produced images that were bluish in tone. Like the calotype, the cyanotype was contact-printed in sunlight. Herschel shared his knowledge with the father of Anna Atkins, the first woman to explore photographic representation. Atkins's subsequent compilations of cyanotype illustrations of algae, ferns, and flowering plants were a pioneering advancement in the recording of scientific specimens.

Seeking to profit from his discovery, Talbot patented his process in England, a move that had the unfortunate effect of inhibiting its development there. Luckily for David Octavius Hill and Robert Adamson, in Edinburgh, Talbot's patents did not pertain to Scotland. Hill, who was a history painter, and Adamson, a young engineer who had learned the calotype process from a friend of Talbot, collaborated to make portraits of clergymen, intellectuals, artists, and the fisherfolk of nearby Newhaven. Hill and Adamson understood that good pictorial design depended less on precision of detail than on a balance of light and dark tones.

The Daguerreotype in the United States at Midcentury

Despite the good results of Talbot, Atkins, and Hill and Adamson, relatively few individuals pursued negative-positive photography during the 1840s. The images of early calotypes appear to stain the top layer of the paper fibers, giving them a soft, indistinct appearance, and many viewers in the mid-nineteenth century found the crystal-clear image of the daguerreotype far more appealing. Furthermore, Daguerre made his process available to the public with fewer restrictions than Talbot. Daguerre also promoted his method through the manufacture of cameras and materials, and he authorized operators to demonstrate it in Europe and abroad. By the early fall of 1839, the daguerreotype had started to spread in the United States, and Daguerre sent his agent François Gouraud to demonstrate the technique to the public in New York, Boston, and Providence, Rhode Island.

The most difficult obstacle for early daguerreotypists was the lengthy exposure time the technique required. This was complicated by factors such as the amount of available light—which in turn depended on the weather, the time of day, and the season—as well as the quality of the lens, the preparation of the plate, and the skill of the photographer. A rapid sequence of technical improvements shortened exposure times from a range of eight to fifteen minutes in early 1839 to as little as ten seconds by the fall of 1840.

Daguerre's invention was successful in his own country, but it flourished in the United States. Its detailed, unromanticized recording of sitters' appearances was well suited to a populace deeply invested in realism and straightforwardness. The daguerreotype's brilliance made it precious to the beholder, and its uniqueness made it irresistible. In a short period of time, daguerreotypists set up studios across the country to create handheld photographic portraits that replaced the painted miniature. Many of these establishments were elaborately decorated and situated on the upper floors of buildings in which windows or a skylight could offer strong, clear light. Primarily middle-class customers ordered the small, relatively inexpensive portraits. The likenesses often became cherished mementos of loved ones who had died, moved west, or enlisted in the Civil War.

The finest daguerreotype artists in the States established themselves in major cities to appeal to an elite clientele. Among the most prominent were Albert Sands Southworth and Josiah Johnson Hawes, who formed a partnership in Boston in 1843 and produced many exquisitely crafted large-plate daguerreotypes. Photographing a great number of the mid-nineteenth century's most renowned American political and intellectual figures—including Ralph Waldo Emerson, Henry Wadsworth Longfellow, and Daniel Webster—Southworth and Hawes became known for the naturalism of their characterizations, their varied lighting, and their careful posing of sitters. They also investigated photographing outdoors, making a number of landscapes that challenged them to overcome the difficulties posed by the uncontrollable factors of light, temperature, and humidity.

Developments in Negative-Positive Photography in the 1850s

Daguerreotypes were spectacular images, but their uniqueness and fragility ultimately led to their demise. Although a daguerreotype offered an affecting experience for a viewer holding one in his or her hand, its reflective surface made collective viewing difficult. By the early 1850s, new pioneers were making advances with Talbot's negative-positive process, and the daguerreotype was gradually being eclipsed. In 1851, the French photographer Gustave Le Gray published a practice of waxing the paper before sensitizing and exposing it to improve the precision and tonal range of the resulting negative (this also made it possible to prepare the paper days ahead). In that same year, the Englishman Frederick Scott Archer devised a method to bind the light-sensitive material to glass with collodion. Archer's method required exposing and processing the glass plate before the wet collodion dried, but it dramatically shortened exposure times and greatly improved clarity.

Another Frenchman, Louis-Désiré Blanquart-Evrard, introduced albumen-coated paper, which by 1855 had become the dominant photographic printing material (not to be replaced until about 1890, when photographers began making platinum and then gelatin silver prints). Coating paper with albumen (egg white), offered a smoother transition of tones and even greater detail. Blanquart-Evrard also standardized photographic printing, making it possible to produce large numbers of prints of uniform quality, which boosted the commercial promise of the medium. Photography still required unwieldy cameras, hand-prepared materials, and the training that came with experience, but these improvements made the negative-positive process increasingly viable.

Artist-Photographers in Mid-Nineteenth-Century France

Many of the most important figures involved with negative-positive photography in the 1850s were active in France, beyond the reach of the copyright restrictions that Talbot had imposed in England. Of these individuals, a number—including Le Gray, Henri Le Secq, Charles Marville, and Charles Nègre—were trained as painters and therefore were interested in exploring photography's potential for pictorial expression. They were influenced by the Romantic realism of artists such as Eugène Delacroix and Gustave Courbet and of writers such as Victor Hugo and Gustave Flaubert.

These photographers discovered that the success of an image made with the camera depended in large part on the quality of its rendering of atmospheric light and shadow. Recognizing also that they could improve their albumen prints in the darkroom, they masked out unwanted areas and enhanced others through chemical toning. To heighten the effect of his remarkable seascapes of the mid-1850s, for example, Le Gray frequently added dramatic clouds by means of a separate negative and printed the ocean views on a scale that was impressively grand for his time.

The great achievements of the early French photographers are partly owed to the generous sharing of information and work that occurred during the meetings of the Société Héliographique (established in January 1851 and renamed a few years later the Société Française de Photographie). Members of this association included highly regarded figures in the arts and sciences in addition to photographers, and the organization's weekly journal *La Lumière* (Light) published serious critical analyses of photographers' efforts and the artistry of their accomplishments.

Another advantage for these French photographers was the early support from public and private commissions. One of the most ambitious official projects was initiated in 1851 by the state's Commission des Monuments Historiques, which invited five photographers—Edouard Baldus, Hippolyte Bayard, Gustave

Le Gray, Henri Le Secq, and Auguste Mestral—to undertake a photographic survey of the country's Romanesque and Gothic architecture. This endeavor, generally referred to as the Mission Héliographique, was fueled by fervent nationalistic sentiment. It built on a compilation of about three thousand lithographic prints of similar subjects called the *Voyages Pittoresques*, which had been initiated in 1820. One of the goals of the project was to indicate the state of preservation of historic sites so the government could assess the need for restoration.

The French were also eager to photographically record their beloved capital, Paris. Baldus was hired in the mid-1850s to document the vast building of the new Louvre (linking the old building with the Tuileries palace), an assignment for which he eventually made more than two thousand images. Charles Marville spent much of his career recording the efforts of Napoleon III's civic planner, Baron Georges-Eugène Haussmann, to modernize the city; his efforts were rewarded in 1862 when he was named the official photographer of Paris.

Midcentury Photography in England

In 1851, when the celebrated Great Exhibition was held at the Crystal Palace in London to showcase the technological achievements of the age, seven hundred photographs from six nations were displayed. So impressive were the daguerreotypes from the United States and the negative-positive photographs from France that the British felt somewhat outdone, and a concerned group of Londoners approached Talbot to relax the restrictions imposed by his copyright.

Among this group of lobbyists was Roger Fenton, a young painter and lawyer who, while studying painting in Paris, had learned the process of photography and had been impressed by the community of French photographers. In 1853, Fenton helped create an English organization, the Photographic Society of London (eventually renamed the Royal Photographic Society of Great Britain), and served as its first secretary. The society nurtured the exchange of ideas and attracted the interest of Queen Victoria and her husband, Prince Albert. Although Fenton found England less forthcoming than France when it came to patronage, he secured a number of significant projects: photographing the landscape of England, Scotland, and Wales, recording the battlefields of the Crimean War, making portraits of the royal family, and documenting the collections of the British Museum.

There is a general difference between most French and English photographs of the 1850s and 1860s: whereas French photographers more often commemorated the magnificence of their historic patrimony in monumental images filled with painterly atmosphere, their counterparts in England were captivated by the camera's ability to capture the picturesque details of the rural landscape. Benjamin Brecknell Turner, one of the early English amateurs who learned directly from Talbot and licensed his process, recorded exquisite scenic views of the rustic countryside that evoked feelings of humbleness and truthfulness, qualities greatly admired by his countrymen (fig. 2).

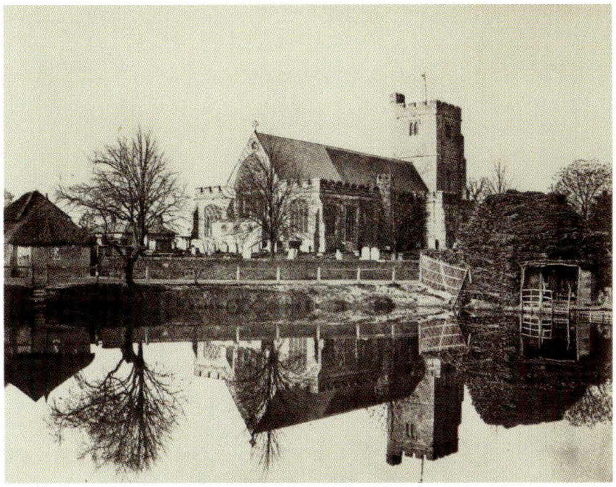

The contrast between the two styles was noted at the time. As Fenton described in 1852: "The French pictures are of cities, fortresses, churches, palaces—the living triumphs or the decaying monuments of man's genius and pride," while the English ones are "representations of the peaceful village; the unassuming church, among its tombstones and trees; the guarded oak, standing alone in the forest; intricate mazes of tangled wood, reflected in some dark pool . . . shocks of corn . . . the wild upland pass . . . or the still lake."[2]

fig. 2 **Benjamin Brecknell Turner (English, 1815–1894),** ***Hawkhurst Church, Kent*****, 1852, albumen print from a paper negative**

Making Photographs for Profit in the 1850s and 1860s

By the 1850s, the prospects of negative-positive photography as a commercial tool were abundantly clear. A wide range of photographic portraits, from crude likenesses taken by the inexperienced to well-crafted portrayals by professionals, were obtainable in many urban centers. For example, Mathew Brady, who had opened his first successful portrait businesses in New York and Washington, DC, in the 1840s, became famous in the following decade for the likenesses in his Gallery of Illustrious Americans and for the large so-called Brady Imperials of distinguished citizens, including President Abraham Lincoln, that his studios issued. Brady went on to create a profitable business during the Civil War, documenting military officers and the aftermath of battles with a hired team of photographers.

Working in Paris, André Adolphe Eugène Disdéri patented a process in 1854 whereby a camera affixed with multiple lenses could produce a negative with four, six, or eight views, which he cut down and printed as images that could be affixed to visiting-card-size mounts. The success of Disdéri's *cartes-de-visite*, executed with a studio of assistants, stimulated the opening of similar establishments in many cities across Europe and the United States, and a craze for these small-format likenesses lasted for several decades.

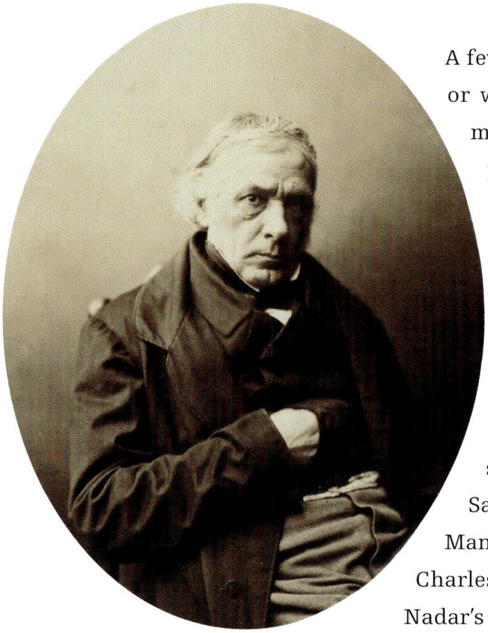

A few portraitists preferred working alone or with just a few assistants in order to maintain control over the quality of their production. The caricaturist and journalist Gaspard Félix Tournachon, for instance, who went by the name "Nadar," worked in this manner. Scheduling only a few sittings per day, he specialized in carefully composed, beautifully lit portraits of well-known men and women of Paris. Many of his sitters were friends, including the actress Sarah Bernhardt, the artists Edouard Manet and Eugène Delacroix, and the writer Charles Baudelaire.

fig. 3 **Gustave Le Gray (French, 1820–1884), *Portrait of Victor Cousin*, about 1856, albumen print**

Nadar's contemporary Gustave Le Gray made a small number of similarly insightful portraits that focused on the personalities of his sitters, as can be seen in his characterization of the highly regarded philosopher and minister of education Victor Cousin (fig. 3). Pictures of prominent citizens were so lucrative in these years that some photographers—Etienne Carjat, for example—issued portraits in a variety of sizes, from small prints intended for reproduction on magazine pages to mammoth plates meant for public display.

Like the computer boom of the late twentieth century, photography in its early years held the promise of huge fortunes. One avenue that camera practitioners explored in the industrializing nineteenth century was the improvement of manufacturing and business methods. The French textile-designers-turned-photographers Adolphe Braun and Charles-Hippolyte Aubry, for instance, each made photographs of flowers for the use of artists and designers—in effect, models that would not wilt—during the 1850s and 1860s (fig. 4). While Aubry directed more effort toward the artistic arrangement of his bouquets, Braun focused on developing his business. His company continued to sell large numbers of topographical views and reproductions of works of art into the twentieth century.

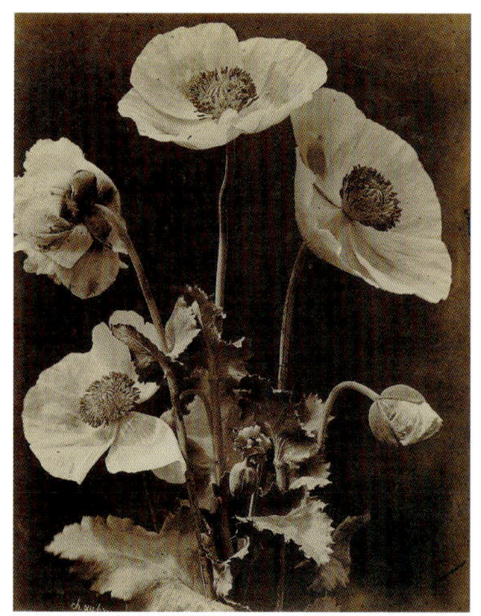
fig. 4 **Charles-Hippolyte Aubry (French, 1811–1877), *Poppies*, about 1864, albumen print**

Louis-Rémy Robert, head of the painting and gilding workshop at the Sèvres porcelain factory, used the camera to record and advertise his company's finest pieces. While his photographs were exhibited at the 1855 Exposition Universelle in Paris to illustrate the quality of the factory's workmanship, it is clear upon close scrutiny that they were also made with an eye for the camera's ability to interpret painted and sculpted form.

Innovative Amateurs in France, Britain, and the United States in the 1860s–1870s

Throughout photography's history, a number of important advancements were made by amateurs who probed the medium's expressive possibilities primarily for pleasure. In France, Adalbert Cuvelier and his friends helped inspire a fashion in the 1850s for *clichés-verre*, which produced images from hand-drawn glass negatives and were used by the Barbizon painters in the circle of Camille Corot. Eugène Cuvelier, son of Adalbert, made not only *clichés-verre* but also sensitive photographs of the landscape around his northern hometown of Arras and in the vast Forest of Fontainebleau, where he settled in 1859. The poetry of his images of woodland trees, pathways, and clearings echoes the painted imagery of Corot, Charles-François Daubigny, and Théodore Rousseau and provides an informative example of the dialogue between painting and photography in this period.

The Englishwoman Julia Margaret Cameron took up photography in 1863 when she was in her late forties and the last of her children had left home. Cameron composed images that celebrated family, religion, and intellectual accomplishment. Emulating Old Master paintings, she often experimented with dramatically bold close-ups and selective focus. Her effort, as she wrote in a letter to her friend Sir John Herschel, was to "ennoble Photography and to secure for it the character and uses of High Art by combining the real & Ideal & sacrificing nothing of Truth by all possible devotion to Poetry & beauty."[3] To her critics, Cameron's method seemed overly fervent in intention and careless in technique, but the expressiveness of her images had an enormous influence on photographers, from the Pictorialists of the late nineteenth century to a number of practitioners of the medium today.

In the United States during this period, the physician and writer Oliver Wendell Holmes made a small number of albumen prints depicting genre scenes around his home in Cambridge, Massachusetts. When held to the eye, the popular stereoscopic viewer he invented dramatically enhanced two nearly identical mounted photographic images, which revealed themselves—seemingly by magic—in three-dimensions. The articles Holmes wrote in the late 1850s and early 1860s for the *Atlantic Monthly*, in which he promoted negative-positive photography as a tool for educating the masses, signaled the end of the daguerreotype era in the States.

Early Photographs of Exotic Lands

As early as the 1840s, photographs were enabling people to experience the wonders of distant sites about which they otherwise could only have dreamed. In subsequent decades, entrepreneurs armed with cameras rushed to fulfill armchair travelers' thirst for images, facing long journeys to regions where severe climatic conditions often made their work arduous. In the late 1840s and early 1850s, Maxime Du Camp, John Beasley Greene, Auguste Salzmann, and Félix Teynard photographed archeological sites throughout the Middle East, returning to publish albums of their work. Egypt and the Holy Land, in particular, captured the public's imagination. By the end of the 1850s, the entrepreneur Francis Frith dared to lug oversize 16 x 20 inch glass plates to document the archeological monuments of Egypt and Palestine. The grandeur and the detail of Frith's images set a standard for tourists' experiences of the region.

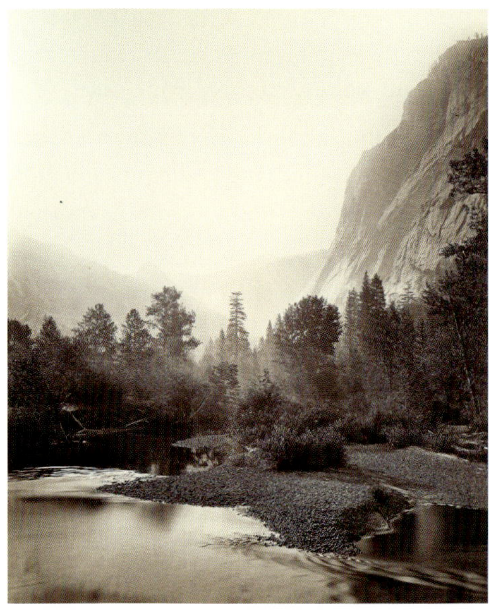

fig. 5 Carleton E. Watkins (American, 1829–1916), *Mount Starr King, Yosemite, No. 69*, 1865–66, albumen print

American photographers who took part in their country's exploration of the western frontier included Carleton Watkins, who as early as 1861 brought a mammoth-plate camera to Yosemite Valley to make images of the breathtaking landscape (fig. 5). His photographs of mountains, forests, waterfalls, and lakes, as well as those by Eadweard Muybridge (who later became known for photographic studies of animal and human locomotion), evoke the sublime paintings of the country's western landscape by artists of the period such as Albert Bierstadt.

A number of photographers of the American West joined government expeditions. Timothy O'Sullivan followed the geological exploration of the Fortieth Parallel in 1867. William Henry Jackson worked for the Union Pacific Railroad and then attached himself to the surveys led by Ferdinand V. Hayden; his images of Yellowstone, made in 1870, were used to lobby Congress for its establishment as a national park.

The establishment of railway networks in the third quarter of the nineteenth century brought travelers within closer reach of far-off destinations, making travel for leisure common among the upper classes. In time, more and more photographers established firms near extraordinary sites in order to sell commemorative views to these travelers. Tourists would purchase such photographs and assemble them into souvenir albums of their journeys.

A Redefining of Style in the Late Nineteenth Century

By the 1870s, a wider range of cameras had been developed, and the new gelatin dry plate, which could be purchased ready-made, not only eliminated the need for last-minute chemical preparations but also allowed for shorter exposures. An ever-increasing number of people were taking up photography, which led serious practitioners to worry that the future of their occupation was being threatened by unsophisticated amateur snapshooters. Photographers at the forefront of the profession thus began to develop aesthetic guidelines for their work.

In 1889, the Englishman Peter Henry Emerson published a book titled *Naturalistic Photography for Students of the Art*, in which he encouraged colleagues to use differential focus to create what he perceived to be a more realistic "truth to Nature." Emerson documented rural laborers in East Anglia, the region of southeast England in which he lived, using the newly developed platinum printing process, which gave his prints a silvery gray tonality (fig. 6). His pictures honored the traditions of rural life, much as the work of the Barbizon artists had done outside of Paris a few decades earlier, and his soft light and atmosphere was related to the internationalization of the French artistic movement Impressionism.

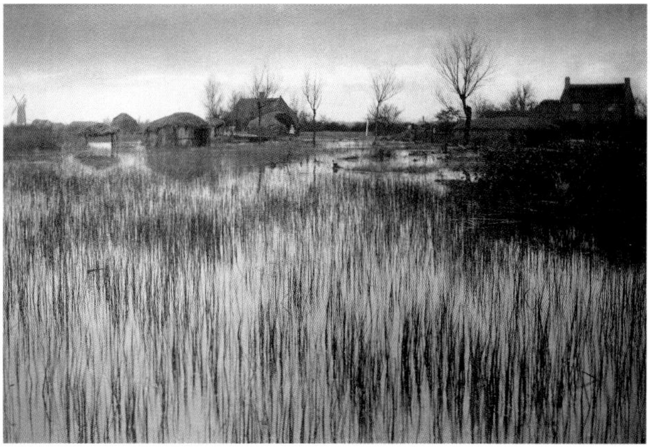

fig. 6 **Peter Henry Emerson (English, 1856–1936), *A Rushy Shore*, 1886, from *Life and Landscape on the Norfolk Broads* (1886), platinum print**

Emerson's ideas helped stimulate the rise of Pictorialist photography, the predominant international photographic style at the turn of the century that saw itself as a movement against a conventional photographic mainstream. The Pictorialists banded together in major cities on both sides of the Atlantic to form societies that served as forums for the sharing of ideas and venues for showing their work. They familiarized themselves with trends in painting and were fascinated by Impressionism, Naturalism, Symbolism, Japonisme, and the Arts and Crafts movement. Pictorialists believed that they could elevate the status of photography if their images had the tonal subtlety of prints and drawings. They used soft focus and enthusiastically manipulated their negatives and retouched their prints to increase their images' poetic effect. Many of these photographers printed in platinum, but some made use of the newer, pigment-based process called "gum bichromate," which yielded broad charcoal-like or crayon-like tones and allowed the possibility of printing in other colors. On occasion, these photographers even issued their images on decorative papers that were textured or colored.

One of the most important Pictorialists was the American Alfred Stieglitz, who as an engineering student in Berlin during the 1880s became interested in exploring the camera's ability to record naturalistic effects. Stieglitz founded the Photo-Secession, the United States' Pictorialist association, in 1902 and supported the work of leading photographers across the country and abroad through personal encouragement as well as through his exhibitions and journals. His aim, to foster creativity by sharing his passion for art and photography, was typical of a number of turn-of-the-century artists. American Pictorialists devoted to educating others ranged from Gertrude Käsebier, who like others took on apprentices, to F. Holland Day, who transported poor immigrant youths to the Swiss-style chalet he had built on the coast of Maine so they could experience art and nature. Clarence H. White established several photography schools, first a summer program in 1910 near Day's place in Maine, and then, in 1914, a year-round program in New York that he named the Clarence H. White School of Photography. White's school was the first real institution dedicated to the formal instruction of the medium in the United States.

Documentary Photography at the Turn of the Twentieth Century

The idyllic world of the Pictorialists did not appeal to all serious photographers working around 1900. Jacob Riis and Lewis Hine were drawn to the camera as an instrument to reveal social inequity. These photographers printed their work in gelatin silver, which produced images with a glossy, reflective surface and became the dominant black-and-white printing process of the twentieth century. In 1890, Riis published his photographs in his book *How the Other Half Lives: Studies among the Tenements of New York*. Hine, who made more than five thousand negatives for the National Child Labor Committee, used his images to promote his cause through lectures, exhibitions, and publications. The compelling nature of Hine's work helped guide Congress to establish a series of child labor regulations and safety laws for all workers.

Other photographers, including the Philadelphian William Herman Rau, sought to capture something of the reality of modern life at the turn of the century. In the late 1880s and 1890s, Rau was the official photographer of the Lehigh Valley Railroad and the Pennsylvania Railroad. Some of his railroad images possess an immediacy and graphic boldness—displayed in the head-on rush of the tracks in *Main Line West of Cove* (fig. 7), for example—that

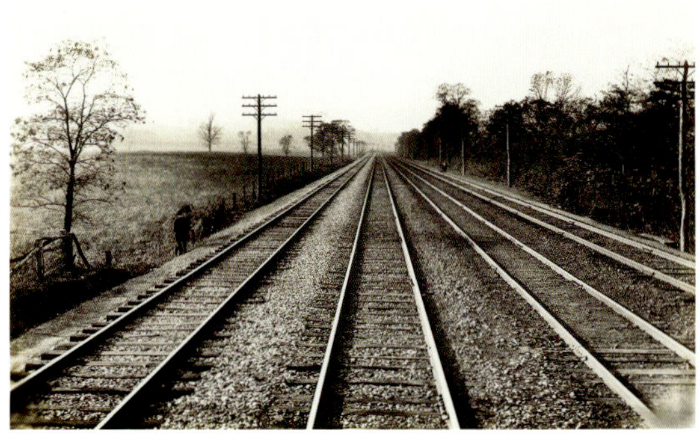

fig. 7 **William Herman Rau, (American, 1855–1920), *Main Line West of Cove*, about 1893, gelatin silver print**

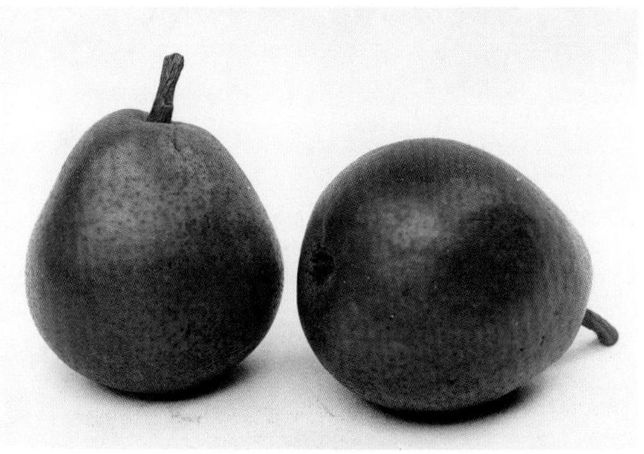

fig. 8 **Charles Jones (English, 1866–1959), *Pear, Beurre Superfine*, 1895–1910, gelatin silver print**

looks forward to the dynamism of photographic imagery of the twentieth century.

Focusing on a very different type of subject, the English photographer Charles Jones made images around this same time that are protomodernist in their formalism. He worked as a gardener on various estates, most notably Ote Hall, in Sussex. Jones's lovingly crafted close-ups emphasize abstract shape and design. They also reveal his appreciation for the vegetables, fruits, and flowers that were the products of his labors (fig. 8).

Meanwhile, in France, Eugène Atget roamed the picturesque streets and parks of Paris and its environs with his camera. Earning his living by selling his photographs to artists, architects, decorators, publishers, and libraries, Atget thought of himself not as a photographer but as an "author-producer." His images, taken from about 1890 until the 1920s, reveal an aesthetic sensibility that seems to extend beyond pure description, in part because they are infused with the photographer's passion for art, history, and French literature. Atget's subtle, expressive vision became a touchstone for many photographers in the twentieth century.

Technological Advances around 1900

Major developments in equipment and practice, in place by the 1890s, increasingly democratized the medium. In 1880, the halftone printing process, by which images were reduced to a pattern of dots of varying sizes that blended when viewed by the human eye, was introduced. Halftones made it possible to reproduce images photomechanically in ink, alongside text, with a printing press, which meant that photographs could easily be included in newspapers, journals, and books. In 1888, George Eastman marketed the first Kodak box camera, a handheld black box with a fixed-focus lens, sold loaded with a roll of film. The original models produced about one hundred circular snapshots, two and a half inches in diameter. Once the film was exposed, the purchaser simply shipped the camera back to the company for developing, printing, and reloading.

Although the initial Kodak lens had a fixed focus and could be used only in bright outdoor light, amateur photographers were suddenly able to record, with convenience, aspects of their daily lives. The French photographer Jacques-

Henri Lartigue, for example, received a camera as a boy from his father and charmingly chronicled the well-to-do lifestyle of his family, photographing kite-flying, automobile racing, and fashionable Parisian women.

In time, leading photographers including Stieglitz were smitten with the new handheld camera, which was more portable and less conspicuous than the large camera and tripod they had been using. Additionally, the camera was waterproof and could be tilted or held close to the subject to create fresh compositions. The negatives were small, but they could be enlarged for greater presence. Now that the developing process was much less expensive, photographers were also more willing to crop images, allowing further opportunities for expression.

Alfred Stieglitz and American Modernist Photography in the New Century

Stieglitz positioned himself as the central champion of artistic photography, from the Pictorialist movement of the 1890s to the modernist movement of the 1920s. He promoted the medium as an art form and advanced the work of photographers through his journals *Camera Notes* and *Camera Work* and in his New York exhibition spaces known as the Little Galleries of the Photo-Secession (later named 291) and An American Place. He also introduced modern European painting and sculpture to the American audience, exhibiting or publishing the work of the avant-garde European artists Constantin Brancusi, Henri Matisse, Pablo Picasso, and Auguste Rodin and the American painters Arthur Dove, Marsden Hartley, and Georgia O'Keeffe. Stieglitz lived at a time of increasing urbanization and technological change, and through his life and work, he provided an example of the way in which a photographer might live and represent the twentieth-century modern experience. His overbearing personality caused a number of his advocates to part ways with him, but his influence on the course of photography and American art in the first half of the twentieth century was monumental.

The development of the modernist aesthetic in photography can be traced through the course of Stieglitz's own images. From the beginning, he was interested in recording daily life, which, unlike many of his Pictorialist photographer friends, he captured in images that tended to be descriptive rather than metaphorical. When he settled in New York in 1890, Stieglitz deliberately chose the urban environment as his subject. A number of his New York images investigated the handheld camera's ability to register effects of light and weather. He printed them not only in platinum and gelatin silver but also in the form of photogravures, using an ink-based printing process invented early in the history of the medium.

By the end of the first decade of the twentieth century, the Pictorialists gradually had become dissatisfied with what they perceived as the artifice of their style. Stieglitz, as the leading figure in the field, introduced them to the revolutionary forms of abstraction that European artists were adopting to creatively translate the three-dimensional world into the two-dimensional picture plane. As early as 1907, he began to replace the atmospheric effects of the city with a new attention to sharply focused, unmanipulated images that emphasized the formal relationships of abstract shapes. Many of the Pictorialist photographers who were Stieglitz's friends also moved toward a deliberately straight vision in the 1910s and 1920s.

Stieglitz's acquaintance with the new European artistic movements had been nurtured largely through his protégé Edward Steichen. In the early years of the century, this young American, who was initially interested in both painting and photography, spent time in Paris where he befriended a number of artists of the avant-garde. Steichen supported Stieglitz's activities by designing the cover for the journal *Camera Work*, which debuted in 1903, and, in 1905, by offering his studio at 291 Fifth Avenue for Stieglitz's first gallery. Once a chief Pictorialist, Steichen went on to be a leading figure in the photographing of fashion and advertising; he also served as a director of photography for the military during both world wars, and, in 1947, he was named head of the photography department at the Museum of Modern Art in New York.

Stieglitz, meanwhile, developed the idea of making an extended series of photographs of one person, a "portrait in time" with each image expressing a facet of the individual's physiognomy and personality. He executed this plan with Georgia O'Keeffe, the artist with whom he began a passionate relationship in 1916. Stieglitz made hundreds of photographs of O'Keeffe between 1917 and 1937, depicting not only various sides of his sitter but also the intensity of their relationship. The images also speak to Stieglitz's ideas about the modern twentieth-century woman.

In the last issue of *Camera Work* (1917), Stieglitz featured the photographs of Paul Strand. The early portraits that Strand had taken on the streets of New York City had caught Stieglitz's eye, as did Strand's dynamically cropped, close-up abstractions of household still lifes, made in the summers of 1915 and 1916. Strand, in turn, made a number of insightful portraits of his wife, Rebecca, that parallel Stieglitz's photographs of O'Keeffe (fig. 9).

By 1917, Stieglitz had also become aware of the photography of two other modernists, Morton Schamberg and Charles Sheeler, painters who had been inspired by avant-garde European art on their own travels overseas in 1909. Sharing a studio in Philadelphia

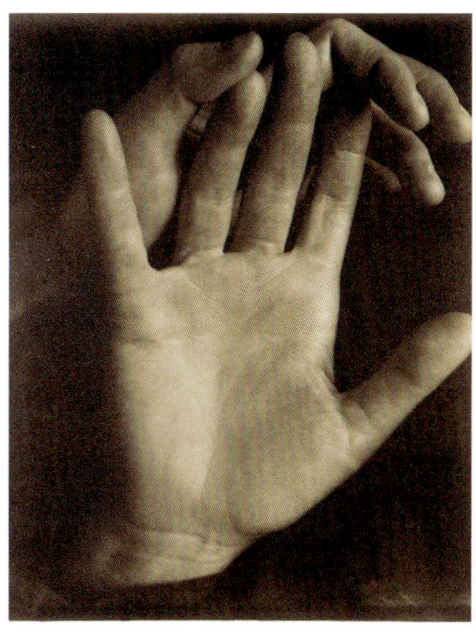

fig. 9 **Paul Strand, (American, 1890–1976), *Rebecca's Hands*, 1923, palladium print**

on their return to the States, Schamberg and Sheeler began to earn their living through photography. Schamberg worked mainly as a portraitist but also made a small number of photographic still lifes and city views. In 1916 and 1917, Sheeler executed an eloquent series of images of an eighteenth-century farmhouse the two friends rented in Bucks County, Pennsylvania, before photographing, on commission, the Ford Motor Company plant outside Detroit a decade later (see fig. 25). The monumental pictures that he made on these projects have become bold symbols of utilitarian structure.

The New Photographic Vision in Europe between the Wars

The first manifestation of the modernist photographic vision in Europe took place in Germany. Working in Cologne, August Sander began, around 1910, to make a systematic catalogue of portraits of the German people according to social type and occupation. The highly detailed photographs in his visual inventory—ranging from farmers and prosperous businessmen to artists and the unemployed—describe not only the social status of these people but also their individuality.

Meanwhile, photographers associated with the Neue Sachlichkeit (New Objectivity) movement created images of intense realism in their effort to describe the material world. One of the best-known figures working in this style was Albert Renger-Patzsch, who created precisely focused photographs that capture the subtle, fundamental beauty of architectural, industrial, and organic forms (fig. 10). About 1930, both he and Karl Blossfeldt, another Neue Sachlichkeit photographer who specialized in plant forms, published sequences of their austerely elegant images in carefully designed and influential books.

fig. 10 **Albert Renger-Patzsch (German, 1897–1966), *Trees in Winter*, 1926, gelatin silver print**

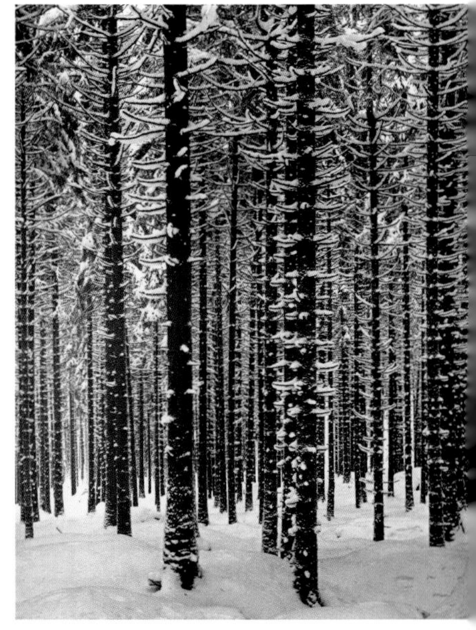

In contrast to the straightforwardness of Renger-Patzsch's and Blossfeldt's images, another sector of European artists chose to explore experimental abstraction in their pursuit of a modernist photographic vision. Led by the American expatriate Man Ray and the Hungarian-born László Moholy-Nagy, these artists advocated an unconventional style of modernism inspired by Cubism, Surrealism, Futurism, Constructivism, and Dadaism.

Living in Paris in the early 1920s and supporting himself through fashion photography and portraiture, Man Ray by chance made a series of photograms—shadowy, cameraless photographs produced by placing an object or objects on a piece of light-sensitive paper or film and exposing them to light. He named these images "rayograms" and went on to experiment with a variety of darkroom techniques such as solarization, double exposure, and combination printing. Many of Man Ray's visual effects were made through chance and intuition, and the resulting images were intentionally surreal and hallucinatory.

Moholy-Nagy arrived in Berlin in 1920, and like Man Ray he began to explore experimental techniques to develop a new photographic language. He advocated tilting the camera, composing aerial views and close-ups, and making photomontages and photograms. From 1923 to 1928, Moholy-Nagy developed his artistic ideas at the Bauhaus school. Founded in 1919 and located first in Weimar, then Dessau, and then Berlin before being closed by the Nazis in 1933, the Bauhaus promoted a radical revisionist curriculum that sought to fuse art and industry for the modern age. Moholy-Nagy was also an influential force in the organization of "Film und Foto," a comprehensive exhibition of photography held initially in Stuttgart in the spring of 1929, to which he contributed ninety-seven of his own photographic works. This important international show included approximately one thousand photographs in total and celebrated the avant-garde vision that by this time was widespread in Europe, the United States, and the Soviet Union.

A group of Czech photographers working during this period created their own lyrical brand of modernism. Josef Sudek became known as the "poet of Prague" for his impressionistic images of the streets of his city, introspective studio still lifes, views through his garden window, and panoramic landscapes. Jaromir Funke photographed evocative geometric abstractions using shadows, mirrors, and reflections, while Frantisek Drtikol experimented with light, shadow, and cut-outs to create Art Deco–like effects in his stylized photographs of the female nude.

As the Nazis rose to power, the vanguard of European artistic experimentation was forced to shut down. The photographers who stayed in Germany during the war felt obliged to either change their style or continue their work quietly. For example, August Sander focused more intently on his delicate recordings of the landscape near the village in the Westerwald where he lived. Hans Bellmer, who had begun in the mid-1930s to make disturbing photographic fantasies portraying female dolls, fled from Germany to Paris, where there was a more sympathetic audience for his work.

After the war, a number of European photographers revived some of the ideas of Bauhaus abstraction. In Germany in the 1950s, photographers associated with Subjektive Fotografie (Subjective Photography) made abstract views of aspects of nature and industrial subjects, as well as images created through chemical manipulation in the darkroom. Marta Hoepffner, for example, created original images in both black-and-white and color that were boldly experimental for their time (fig. 11). A number of these German photographers—including Peter Keetman, Siegfried Lauterwasser, Toni Schneiders, and Otto Steinert—were part of the so-called Fotoform group, linked because they exhibited their work together in this period. Another European photographer advancing the ideas of abstraction at midcentury was Mario Giacomelli, who focused on interpreting village scenes, the people, and the landscape around his hometown of Senigallia, Italy. Giacomelli's poetic images, like those of the German photographers, have a spatial flatness and are printed in strongly graphic tones.

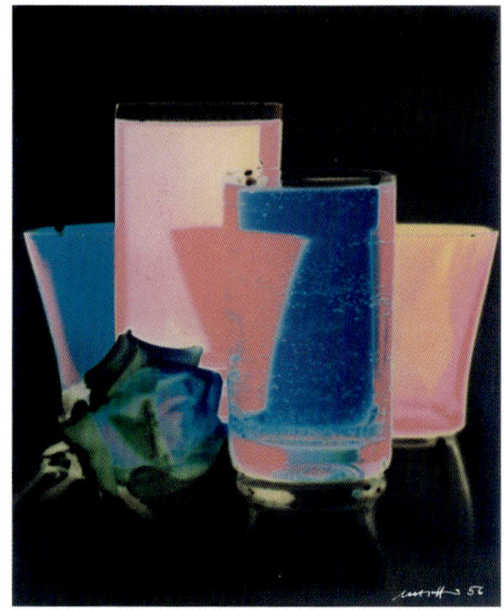

fig. 11 **Marta Hoepffner (German, 1912–2000), *Glasses with Rose*, 1956, color carbro print, solarized**

The Surrealism of Everyday Life, 1930s

Besides the Surrealist abstractions of Man Ray and Moholy-Nagy, a number of photographers working primarily in Europe began, around 1930, to explore the camera's ability to capture unusual visual juxtapositions in the world around them. These individuals photographed details of everyday life in a photojournalistic style. Brassaï (born Gyula Halász, in Transylvania) settled in Paris and called his work a search for "the magic beneath the surface of reality" (fig. 12).[4] André Kertész, who also photographed in Paris, and later in New York, used a similar approach in creating his lyrical interpretations of modern urban life.

Henri Cartier-Bresson's photographs were also infused with elements of Surrealism. He traveled around the world photographing what he eventually called the "decisive moment," which he defined as "the simultaneous recognition, in a fraction of a second, of the significance of an event as well as of a precise organization of forms which give that event its proper expression."[5]

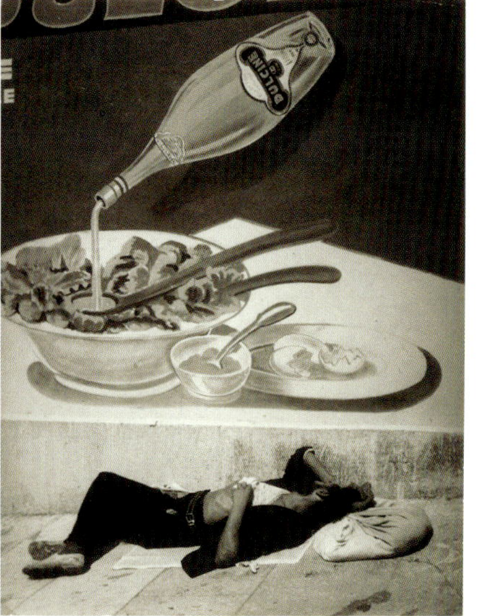

fig. 12 **Brassaï (Gyula Halász), (French, born in Hungary, 1899–1984), *Sleeping Tramp in Marseilles*, 1935, gelatin silver print**

These photographers were among the first to use the new Leica, a small handheld camera introduced in the mid-1920s that used 35 mm roll film and a range of lenses. Favored for its lightness and maneuverability and its ability to stop action without attracting attention, this camera compelled photographers to be alert to what they saw through the viewfinder. It also allowed them to take a sequence of pictures in rapid succession that could later be edited to find the best image. Other small cameras with fast film—such as the Rolleiflex, which had a square format instead of a rectangular one and attracted a loyal following due to its waist-level viewfinder—were available soon after.

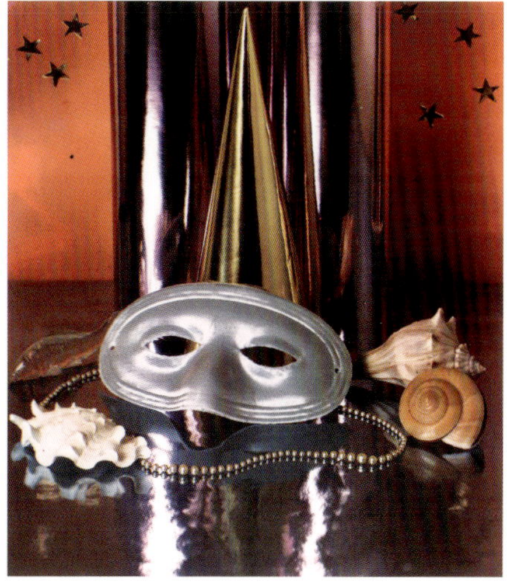

fig. 13 **Paul Outerbridge, Jr. (American, 1896–1958),** ***Still Life: Mask with Shells and Pearls*****, 1936–38, color carbro print**

By the 1930s, color had begun to enter photography's expanding repertoire. Practitioners had been searching for a practical way to produce color photographs since the early years of the medium, and for a long time the best they could do was to hand-tint their images after printing. In 1907, the Lumière brothers in France patented a complex system involving the distribution of dyed potato-starch granules on a glass plate, making transparencies they called "autochromes" that resulted in fragile, unique images on glass plates. During the 1930s, a number of photographers started to create three-color carbro prints, using a process developed from the late-nineteenth-century carbon print. The color carbro technique was laborious, involving three separate negatives with red, green, and blue filters that were printed sequentially, but viewers found the permanence and richness of the shades very appealing. Anton Bruehl, Nickolas Muray, and Paul Outerbridge made many advertising images in this manner (fig. 13). While the process's color attracted magazine publishers, photographers also loved it for its Surrealist look.

The Camera as Social Witness during the American Depression

When the American photographer Berenice Abbott settled in New York in 1929, after having lived for a decade in Paris, she brought with her the archive of Eugène Atget photographs that she had acquired after the Frenchman's death, and set about using her camera to document New York (fig. 14). Whereas Atget had been drawn to vestiges of the past, Abbott sought to represent the exciting metropolis of the present, with its skyscrapers, motorized vehicles, and multitude of signs. Despite her knowledge of the European avant-garde, she chose a realist documentary style that was more in keeping with the predominant photographic taste of her homeland as it was about to enter a devastating phase of economic depression.

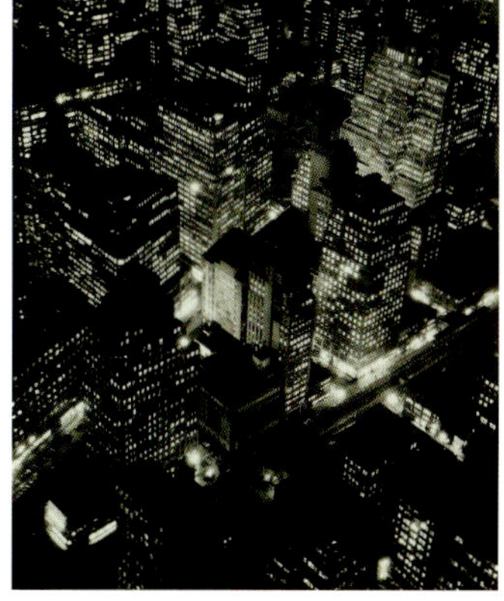

fig. 14 **Berenice Abbott (American, 1898–1991),** ***New York at Night*****, 1932, gelatin silver print**

The photographer Walker Evans, who had also spent time in Europe and whom Abbott befriended upon her return, was likewise moving toward a documentary style. Setting out to photograph the richness of American vernacular culture, Evans understatedly and poetically recorded the hardships of human life. A list of goals that he drafted for one of his editors in 1934 reveals his sensitivity and his incisive wit:

> American city is what I am after. . . .
> People, all classes, surrounded by bunches of the new down-and-out.
> Automobile and the automobile landscape.
> Architecture, American urban taste, commerce, small scale, large scale, the city street atmosphere, the street smell, the hateful stuff, women's clubs, fake culture, bad education, religion in decay.
> The movies.
> Evidence of what people of the city read, eat, see for amusement, do for relaxation and not get it.
> Sex.
> Advertising
> A lot else, you see what I mean.[6]

Depression-era documentary photography in the United States was issue driven and socially conscious. Walker Evans was one of the first hires of Roy Stryker, the director of the Resettlement Administration, a government program instituted to record the dislocation of life during the period. Renamed the Farm Security Administration in 1937, this organization sought to gather photographic evidence of the living conditions of citizens and the need for New Deal reform. Stryker commissioned a number of photographers besides Evans, including Dorothea Lange, Gordon Parks, Arthur Rothstein, and Ben Shahn. These photographers traveled the country, especially in the South and West, working to give visual testament to the struggles of the unfortunate.

In New York, a group of photographers followed a parallel mission in their depiction of the poorer neighborhoods of their city. Morris Engel, Jerome Liebling, Walter Rosenblum, Aaron Siskind, and others founded the Photo League in 1936. A center for photography and intellectual companionship, the Photo League continued Lewis Hine's firmly held belief in the camera's ability to make visual records that, over time, could foster change.

The Natural Landscape and the f.64 Photographers

California photographers developed their own unique ideas about modernism in the early twentieth century. Heirs to the landscape imagery of William Henry Jackson, Timothy O'Sullivan, and Carleton Watkins, they directed their lenses toward aspects of nature and the wilderness.

The subject matter of Edward Weston's photographs became increasingly organic after the mid-1920s. In 1927, he began making the bold close-ups of shells and vegetables that have become icons in the history of the medium. In 1932, he joined forces with a group of San Francisco Bay Area photographers, including Ansel Adams, Imogen Cunningham, and Willard Van Dyke, to form a loosely knit organization they called "Group f.64," after the aperture setting on their large-format cameras that permitted the sharpest focus and greatest depth of field. These photographers trained their cameras on the expressive patterns of nature found in mountains, plants, rocks, and trees.

Adams, who is thought to have suggested the name of the f.64 group, built a long, influential career by creating images that convey his deeply reverential feeling for the pristine mountains of the American West. The disciplined craftsmanship of Adams's work became a standard for countless American photographers of the twentieth century. Many took his Yosemite workshops and read his books, in which he taught his theory of previsualizing an image and how to use his Zone System technique to calculate exposure and development.

Expanding Opportunities in the Commercial Realm after the First World War

It became increasingly possible for committed photographers to earn their living by means of the camera. Fortunately this coincided with a growth of opportunities in advertising and the media. Students trained at the Clarence H. White School of Photography in New York, for example, were specifically taught to apply the principles of modernist design to the commercial work that they might undertake. Photographic images made by graduates of White's school and their contemporaries appeared on a wide range of marketing materials, from small labels on spark plug boxes to enormous billboard advertisements overlooking new highways.

Edward Steichen became the central figure in this field in the United States when he obtained the influential position of chief photographer at Condé Nast Publications in 1923. The expansion of fashion and lifestyle magazines in this period coincided with the burgeoning economic prosperity of the decade. Photographing fashions and the fashionable for *Vogue* and *Vanity Fair*, Steichen redirected the advertising aesthetic away from its softly romantic Pictorialism toward a look of crisp geometric modernism.

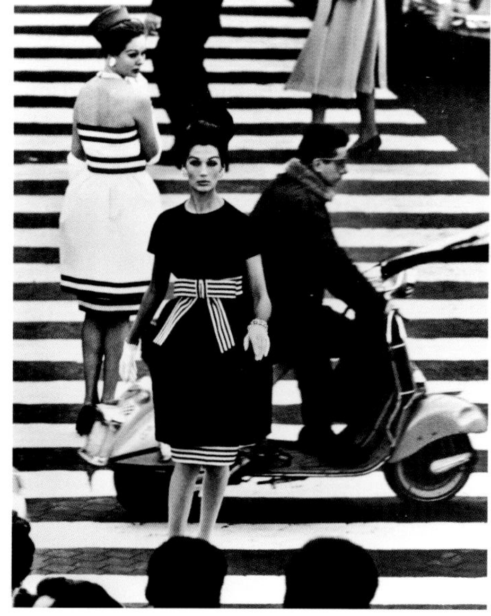

fig. 15 **William Klein (American, born in 1928), *Simone + Nina, Piazza di Spagna, Rome*, for *Vogue*, 1960, printed later, gelatin silver print**

The fashion magazine *Vogue* and its main competitor, *Harper's Bazaar*, contributed much to photographic style in the middle decades of the century. Their innovative editors and art directors published images that represented avant-garde aesthetic ideas, featured in elegantly uncluttered layouts that enhanced their content's allure. Richard Avedon, Erwin Blumenfeld, Louise Dahl-Wolfe,

William Klein, and Irving Penn, to name a few, were challenged by the parameters within which they were required to be creative in their effort to make eye-catching images of women in fashionable dress (fig. 15). Since there were few other arenas for viewing photographic work around that time, fashion magazines provided a valuable forum for photographers to learn about each other's work.

The Rise of Photojournalism in the 1930s

Photojournalists were as excited as the fashion and advertising photographers about the new opportunities available for their work, as newspaper and magazine editors around the world avidly pursued photographic images for their publications. News events and feats of human accomplishment were particularly sought after. The Russian press photographer Ivan Shagin, for instance, recorded the inflating of an enormous balloon designed to reach the stratosphere (fig. 16).

Weegee, one of the most famous newspaper photographers in the United States, recorded sensational news-making scenes for the New York tabloid press in the 1930s and 1940s. He was born Usher Fellig in a territory of Austria (now part of Ukraine), and acquired his "Weegee" nickname—inspired by the *ouija* board game—because he had a seemingly clairvoyant ability to predict locations of crimes and catastrophes (in fact, he listened to a short-wave police radio in his car). He worked mainly at night, and his candid images of criminals and victims caught in the electric flash of his camera reveal the dark side of city life (fig. 17).

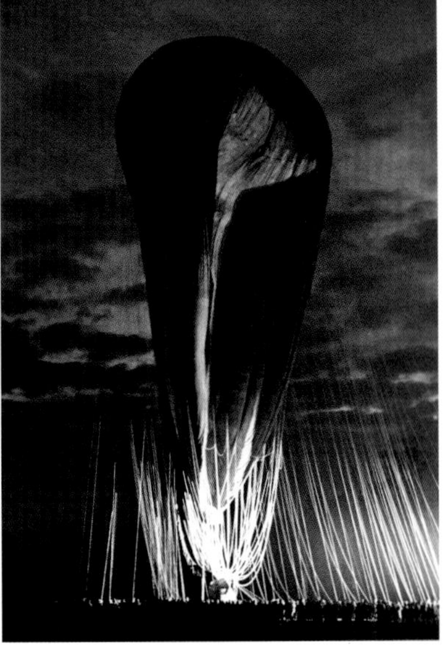

fig. 16 **Ivan Mikhaylovich Shagin (Russian, 1904–1982),** ***A Stratostat before Take-Off into the Stratosphere*****, 1933, gelatin silver print**

The ability to transmit an image by telegraph, which came into practice in the mid-1930s, was central to the growth of photographic magazines. A number of the decade's publications that reported real-life stories, from historic events to human interest, were virtually overnight successes. None had more influence than the American magazine *Life*, which was first published in 1936 and in short order circulated to millions of subscribers.

Magazine editors provided tremendous opportunities for photographers. When war broke out in Europe in the late 1930s, legendary figures such as Robert Capa and Margaret Bourke-White took great risks to obtain pictures close to the conflict. Photojournalists produced not only candid images but also sequences of pictures intended to tell a whole story at a glance and to entertain as well as be newsworthy. *Life* magazine launched the careers of many of their contributors, including Yousuf Karsh, whose famous portrait of British prime minister Winston Churchill (see fig. 26) established this Turkish-Armenian immigrant to Canada as the most successful portraitist of the world's statesmen, scientists, artists, writers, and movie stars.

The power of the editors at *Life* and other magazines, however, sometimes created problems for these suppliers of images. Editors defined the story, wrote the captions, and freely cropped submissions without feeling obliged to consult the creator of the work. Editors also determined whether a story was to be illustrated in black-and-white or color, and with the introduction of 35 mm color film in the mid-1930s, they frequently demanded that images be submitted in color. Feeling a loss of control over their work, photographers founded cooperatives, or photo agencies, to protect their rights. One of the earliest and best known was Magnum, founded in 1946 by Henri Cartier-Bresson, Robert Capa, and several others. These organizations stocked photographers' images and negotiated on their behalf. Such agencies are still active today, protecting the rights of photographers including James Nachtwey and Sebastião Salgado, whose images of poverty, famine, and war seem to transform horrible human tragedy into images of absurdist beauty.

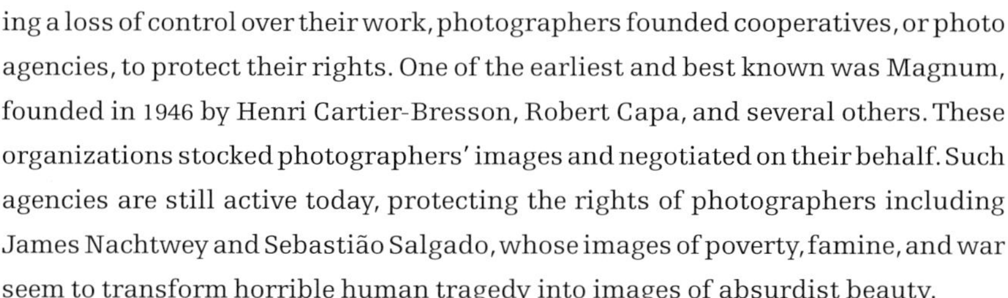

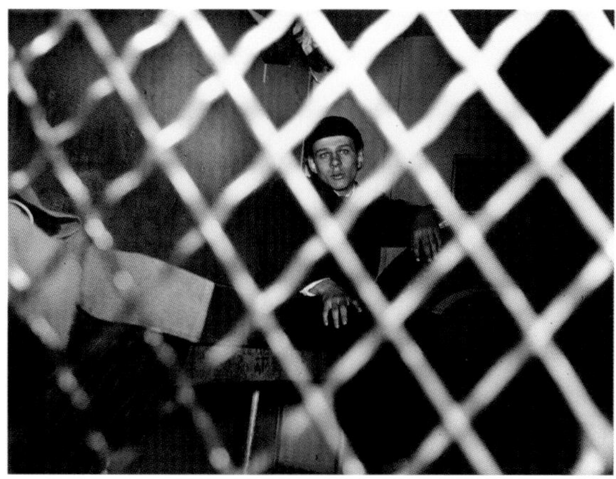

fig. 17 Weegee (Usher Fellig) (American, born in Austria, 1899–1968), *Frank Pape, Sixteen-Year-Old Boy Who Strangled a Four-Year-Old Child to Death*, 1944, gelatin silver print

The photojournalist aesthetic influenced a cadre of street photographers from the 1930s on. In New York, for example, Helen Levitt bought a Leica after seeing the photographs of Cartier-Bresson and started photographing people, especially children, in her city. The lyrical images she made express both the pleasures and the travails of childhood. Similarly, Lisette Model, a war refugee from Europe, roamed the streets documenting the hectic bustle—people walking briskly, singing in bars—of New York life.

Collecting and Teaching Photography in the United States at Midcentury

In the period between the wars, art institutions in the United States began to take a serious interest in incorporating photography into their collections and programming. As early as 1924, the Museum of Fine Arts, Boston, accepted a group of pictures into its collection as a gift from Alfred Stieglitz—one of the first serious acquisitions of photography by a major museum. In 1937, the newly established Museum of Modern Art in New York initiated an exhibition program, accompanied by a series of publications. In 1955, Edward Steichen's "The Family of Man," the enormously popular MoMA exhibition depicting the common human experience, traveled to venues around the globe; its bestselling catalogue brought an awareness of the artistry of the medium into people's living rooms.

American institutions of higher learning also began to incorporate photographic instruction into their curricula in the middle decades of the twentieth century. Schools benefited from the immigration of European artists and intelligentsia during World War II. In 1937, László Moholy-Nagy was invited to open a design school in Chicago, which directed American photography down a fresh experimental path. Calling his institution the New Bauhaus, then the Chicago School of Design, and finally the Institute of Design, he developed a program that encouraged students to think less about a documentary approach and more about theoretical issues, such as how to use the camera as a tool for abstraction.

Moholy-Nagy hired several groundbreaking teachers, including György Kepes, a fellow Hungarian, and Arthur Siegel, who had been an early student of the school. After Moholy-Nagy's death in 1946, the program continued to be a force through the influential teaching of Harry Callahan and Aaron Siskind. These photographers maintained an emphasis on formal abstraction and on conveying a personal expression in one's images. The great impact of the Institute of Design's approach was spread when Callahan, and then Siskind, left in the early 1960s and 1970s to teach at the Rhode Island School of Design.

Minor White, who taught at various schools in San Francisco, Rochester, and Boston from the mid-1940s to the mid-1970s, also owed a great deal to the aesthetic set forth in Chicago. He had been inspired early on by Stieglitz's cloud photographs, the *Equivalents*, and as a result photographed commonplace fragments—forms in nature and urban environments, reflections of light—as symbols of metaphoric feeling. White taught his students to think about making pictures that were meditative and spiritual. He also transmitted his ideas as the longtime editor of the serious photography journal *Aperture*, which he helped found in 1952 and with which he was involved until 1975.

New Directions in the 1950s

In the postwar era, young photographers working in the United States were disenchanted with the times and initiated a new aesthetic course. They focused their lenses on the unflattering aspects of American culture and on the psychological isolation of people in urban settings. Several of these photographers made rough, sometimes blurred images that revealed the influence of stream-of-consciousness filmmaking. One was William Klein, a New Yorker who had been living in Paris and returned to his native city in 1954, when Condé Nast's art director Alexander Liberman expressed interest in his work. With funding supplied by Liberman's office, Klein spent a year creating an intense photographic diary of the street life of the city. The result was a group of images that came across as provocatively abrasive; fearing a strong reaction, *Vogue* dared not publish them.

About the same time, the Swiss-born photographer Robert Frank, who had moved to the United States in the late 1940s, started down a similar visual path. With a Guggenheim grant that he received in 1955, Frank spent two years traveling around the country and photographing people in diners, parades, factories, cars, buses, parks, and other public arenas. The photographs he made reveal the ironies he observed in the popular perception of the United States as a place of contentment and prosperity.

Klein and Frank barely knew each other, even though they clearly shared a similar aesthetic attitude and, on occasion, photographed at the same events. Neither found an immediate audience for his images in this country, and so they turned to Europe to publish their work. Klein's *Life is Good and Good for You in New York* was issued in France in 1956, and Frank's *The Americans* appeared there as well, in 1958.

Despite the initial skepticism, *The Americans* was published in the United States (with an introduction by Jack Kerouac) in 1959. The complex poetry of the images in this book eventually went on to have a profound effect on American photographers of the next generation. Meanwhile, Klein's photographs, which did not become well known in his homeland, were influential in Europe (his book won the acclaimed Prix Nadar in France) and also in Japan, where photographers such as Shomei Tomatsu and Daido Moriyama looked to Klein's example when they set out to portray their own ambivalence toward the postwar changes in their country's culture (fig. 18).

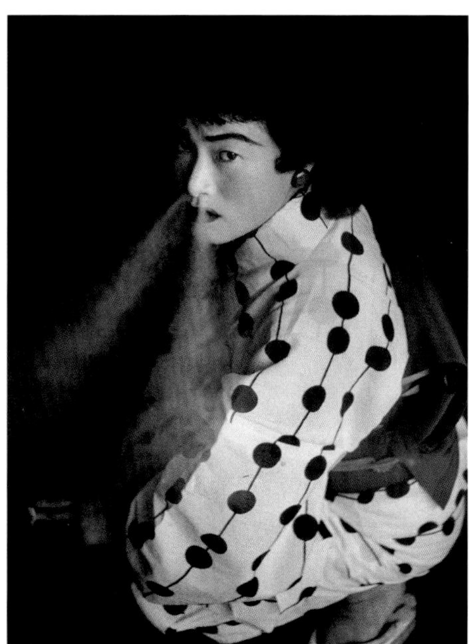

fig. 18 **Shomei Tomatsu (Japanese, born in 1930), *Prostitute, Nagoya*, 1958, printed in 2003, gelatin silver print**

Since early in the history of the medium, photographers had assembled their images in books in order to present them to the largest possible audience. By the middle of the twentieth century, having one's work published in a book became the primary goal of dedicated practitioners. Efforts such as Brassaï's *Paris de Nuit* (1933), Walker Evans's *American Photographs* (1938), and André Kertész's *Day of Paris* (1945) provided models, as did Cartier-Bresson's commercially successful 1952 *Images à la Sauvette* (published in English as *The Decisive Moment*). Gradually, museums joined in by beginning to produce substantive catalogues. In the next few decades, virtually every photographer of standing had been or was involved in the publication of a book.

American Photography in the 1960s and 1970s

The 1960s marked a broad crisis of confidence across modern culture. In the United States, the Vietnam War, political assassinations, racial conflict, the women's movement, and student protests were traumatizing events that made citizens question the mores of society. The upheaval of the 1960s also led to a transformation in photographic style. Photographers explored the cultural contradictions from a personal and frequently cynical point of view. For example, Diane Arbus began making unsettling portraits of people she encountered in and around New York (fig. 19). She was able to present the eccentrics whom she sought out—nudists, transvestites, midgets, the mentally disabled—as sympathetic and familiar, and when she documented "normal" subjects—suburbanites, for example—she managed to make them appear fascinatingly intriguing.

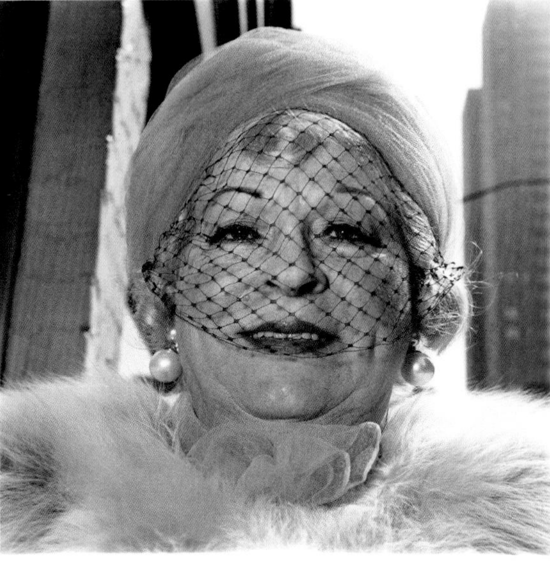

fig. 19 **Diane Arbus (American, 1923–1971), *Woman with a Veil on Fifth Avenue, NYC*, 1968, gelatin silver print, printed by Neil Selkirk**

Garry Winogrand and Lee Friedlander also investigated the ambiguity of everyday life from a documentary perspective. Winogrand photographed the social landscape using close viewpoints and tilted horizons. Friedlander, who continues to photograph today, is particularly interested in the visual layering of buildings, signs, cars, advertisements, and sculpture in the picture plane. These photographers built on the work of Robert Frank as well as on the surrealism apparent in photographic work since the 1920s. Their pictures were grouped with Arbus's in the influential "New Documents" exhibition at MoMA in 1967, and the title of the show became the term associated with the three photographers' work.

In contrast, the freedom of the 1960s led photographers such as Jerry Uelsmann, Duane Michals, and Lucas Samaras to create pictures that looked inward, centering on memory and dreams. Uelsmann combined images in the darkroom to achieve his symbolic photomontages, while Michals photographed humorous staged narratives of personal fantasy. Samaras made expressive self-portraits using the new SX-70 instant Polaroid print, often manipulating emulsions during development or slicing his prints to heighten their hallucinatory impact. The American Robert Cumming further developed these ideas in the next decade; he constructed elaborate set-ups and made seemingly documentary images that conveyed his own witty musings on themes related to art and illusion. William Wegman, a school friend of Cumming's, worked in a related manner when making his whimsical posed portraits of Weimaraner dogs, which poke fun at the seriousness of formal portraiture.

In the 1970s, counterculture groups became a focus for a few photographers of the American social scene, including Larry Clark, Bruce Davidson, and Danny Lyon. Part of the intensity of their work derives from the fact that these photographers were sometimes complicit in the behavior that they were photographing. In the 1980s, Nan Goldin documented issues of gender and drug use in the relationships of her closely knit circle of bohemian friends. Eventually published as *The Ballad of Sexual Dependency*, Goldin's photographic diary was initially presented as a slide show screened in New York clubs and alternative art spaces.

A number of innovative landscape photographers working in the United States in the 1970s turned away from the prevailing images of the pristine wilderness epitomized in the work of Ansel Adams. Some of these photographers—Robert Adams, Frank Gohlke, Nicholas Nixon, Steven Shore, and others—chose to create seemingly neutral documents of the broadening impact of man on the land around him. The work of these individuals was shown with that of like-minded others in an influential 1975 exhibition at George Eastman House in Rochester, New York, and the exhibition's title, "New Topographics," became the name for their style of photography.

The Increasing Acceptance of Color

Although by the 1960s inexpensive color film had largely replaced the average person's black-and-white snapshots, it was still rare for most dedicated photographers to think of color photography as a serious medium. Color was closely associated with the less-respected commercial end of the field, and chromogenic prints, which were the standard type of color prints, were prone to discoloration over time and were expensive to make. In addition, color was perceived to distract most photographers from formalist concerns in their compositions.

Eliot Porter had been one of the few to break with convention when he took up color in 1939 and decided to specialize in it. Porter believed that color provided a more complete description of the natural landscape that was his chosen subject. He primarily used dye transfer, a process known for its saturated and stable hues. His photographic approach, like that of Ansel Adams, tied in perfectly with the environmental movement of the 1960s. Both Porter's and Adams's images frequently appeared in books published at the time by the Sierra Club.

By the 1960s and 1970s, as motion pictures were being regularly produced in color and color television sets were increasingly common, a new generation of

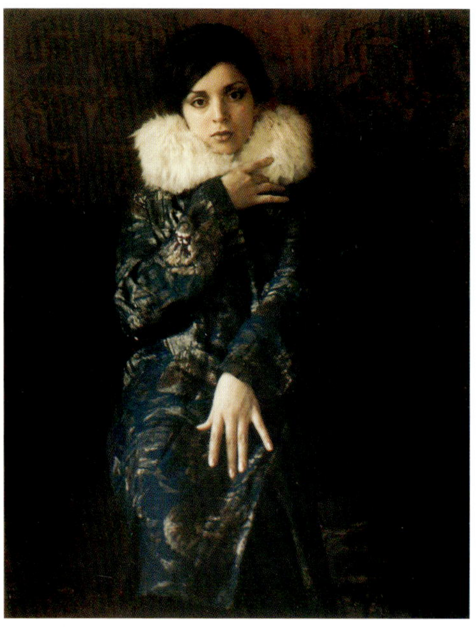

fig. 20 **Marie Cosindas (American), *Ellen*, 1965, dye transfer color print from a Polaroid original**

young photographers delved into the aesthetic issues of color. The Boston photographer Marie Cosindas explored the luxurious density of the early Polaroid color process to create deeply colored portraits and still life arrangements (fig. 20). The painterly tones in her images relate to the work of the Old Masters, and their wealth of textures suggests an expressive richness.

Another important figure in the advancement of color photography was William Eggleston. Working in Memphis, Tennessee, Eggleston became interested in carefully orchestrating the color elements in his dye-transfer compositions. By the early 1970s, he was making eloquent images of banal American objects, such as children's tricycles. The casual, snapshot-like appearance of his pictures belies the deliberateness with which they were crafted.

Photographers also learned that color could be used to intensify a work's emotional impact. During vacations on Cape Cod with his family starting in 1976, Joel Meyerowitz made luminous images of the landscape with a large 8 x 10 camera, which he printed as chromogenic prints. Published in his book *Cape Light* (1978), Meyerowitz's work helped attract popular attention to the artistic potential of color photography.

Museum acknowledgment of the significance of these and other photographers' efforts signaled an acceptance of color as a serious medium. By the 1980s, many, if not most, photographers worked in color. One recent example is the work of the contemporary British artist Martin Parr, whose ironic interpretations of our consumerist society feature a highly saturated, bright palette (fig. 21).

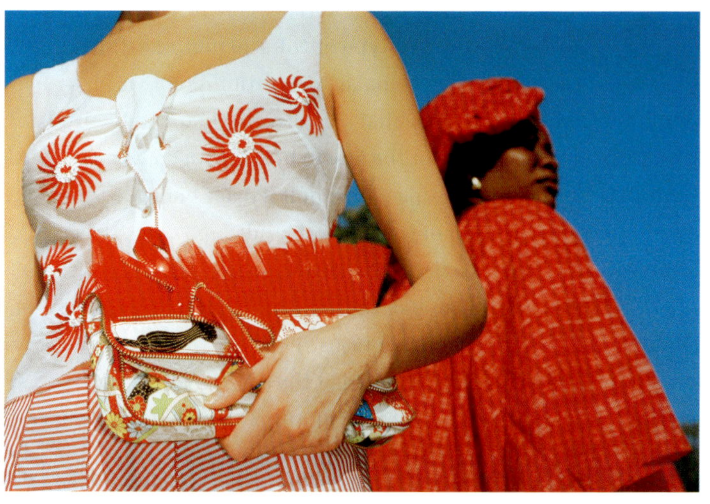

fig. 21 **Martin Parr (English, born in 1952), *Dakar*, 2001, Lambda print**

The Expanding Relationship between Photography and Other Media

Since its inception, photography has enjoyed a rich interplay with the arts of painting, printmaking, and drawing. In the early years, camera practitioners modeled their images on already established pictorial conventions, while artists working in traditional media looked to photographs to find fresh ways of representing the world. Since this time, the mingling of media has encouraged methods of photomechanical printing, such as photoetching, photolithography, photogravure, and more recently, photosilkscreen.

The 1960s saw a dramatic increase in the incorporation of photographic imagery in the visual arts. For many of the artists of this period, photography became another tool for expression, one that could be altered or adapted to painting and printmaking techniques. The Pop artists Andy Warhol, Robert Rauschenberg, and others silkscreened photographic images onto their canvases, and Chuck Close, Richard Estes, James Rosenquist, and Ed Ruscha incorporated a variety of camera-related imagery in their art making (fig. 22).

By the 1980s, a broader crossover existed between photography, painting, and printmaking. Some people no longer thought of themselves strictly as photographers but rather as artists in a larger sense who happened to work with images made with a camera. This was particularly true for the makers of oversize images, who felt that an enlarged scale described a subject more fully and enhanced a picture's impact. A major influence on the trend toward large photographic prints was the work of Bernd and Hilla Becher, whose monumental images of water towers, blast furnaces, and other industrial forms revived the ideas about heightened description advanced by the Neue Sachlichkeit photographers earlier in the century. Their grid-like works also related to current minimalist and conceptualist trends in painting and sculpture. Teaching at the Düsseldorf Art Academy from the mid-1970s to the mid-1990s, the Bechers inspired a generation of German photographers including Andreas Gursky, Candida Höfer, Thomas Ruff, and Thomas Struth.

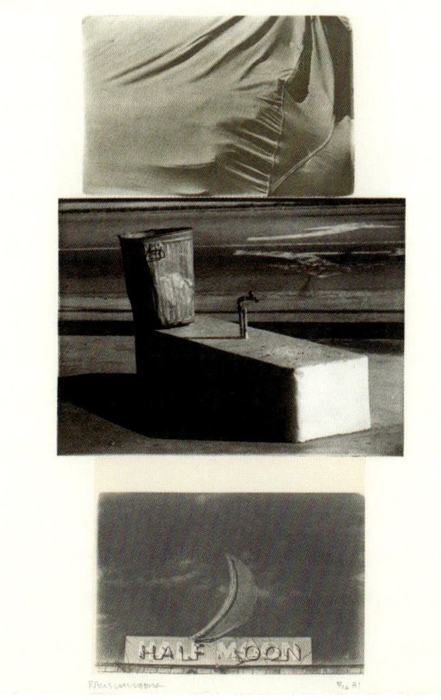

fig. 22 **Robert Rauschenberg (American, born in 1925),** ***The Razorback Bunch (Etching IV)*****, 1967–69, photoetching printed from five plates**

Today, there is also an interesting exchange between photographs made for commercial purposes and photography as personal expression. Many highly successful commercial photographers have tried to maintain a personal aesthetic in their professional work. Herb Ritts, for example, has become known for images of celebrity and fashion that combine classic formalism with a heightened sensuality. Like Ritts, other photographers are now making large-scale prints of their work for exhibition in museums. As institutions take commercial photography seriously, the barriers between these two segments of the field will continue to fall away.

The Impact of Digital Photography since 1990

The invention of digital photography caused a veritable revolution in the field. When digital cameras first came on the market in the early 1990s, images could be recorded instantaneously by means of electronic data rather than as light-exposed and chemically developed film. Suddenly, photographers working for newspapers and magazines discovered that they no longer needed a darkroom and could easily supply images through telephone lines. Since then, the chemical-based photographic technology has become rapidly outmoded, and the digital technology has been radically changing how everyone—artists and amateurs alike—makes and stores photographic pictures.

Digital images can be produced either from a digital camera or from images captured by a 35 mm or other film-based camera and scanned into a computer. Once the image is digitized, an artist is able to tweak small areas or dramatically alter the image's content using software. For example, the contemporary German photographer Loretta Lux, who trained as a painter and is now a successful photographer using digital equipment, modifies elements in her photographs of children to transform them into beings from an enchanted world. This capability marks a significant difference from traditional photographic methods, in which improving an image required handwork in the darkroom that could often be seen on the finished print. While there were serious questions about ink stability in the first generation of digital photography, in recent years the pigmented inks that are often used to print digital images have been improved to make the colors more permanent.

The predominance of digital image making and the printing flexibility it offers caused a backlash among artists longing for the craftsmanship of historic photographic processes. This trend had already started in the 1960s, well before the digital era, when a number of photographers delved into long-ignored approaches to image-making—using pinhole cameras, for instance, and making platinum and cyanotype prints—largely in reaction to the preponderance of gelatin silver prints at that time. The late-1990s investigation into antiquated, or alternative, methods marks photographers' interest in making images that comment on the nature of the photographic process itself. In this manner, Sally Mann used ninteenth-century techniques for her large metaphorical landscapes of the South, and Adam Fuss explored metaphysical themes in his recent photograms and daguerreotypes. Even Abelardo Morell's photographs of camera obscura overlays of the outside world on the walls of rooms evoke historical image making (fig. 23). These artists' works have set up a dialogue between the past and present in the medium.

Early in the history of photography, the daguerreotype was referred to as "the mirror with a memory," and all photographs—whether daguerreotypes, albumen prints, gelatin silver prints, digital prints, or camera images printed by other means—preserve moments excerpted from the passage of time. With each passing generation, photography's technology has been transformed and its purposes have diversified. Photographs offer a viewing experience that no other means of art making can provide, and the immediacy of this experience is what makes them so compelling. These basic characteristics of photography have ensured its vital and enduring presence, from the medium's inception to well into the future.

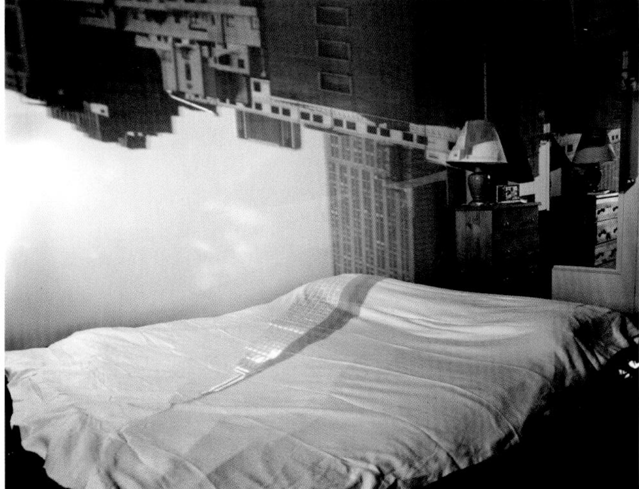

fig. 23 **Abelardo Morell (American, born in Cuba in 1948), *Camera Obscura Image of the Empire State Building in Bedroom*, 1994, gelatin silver print**

1 William Henry Fox Talbot, *The Pencil of Nature* (London: Longman, Brown, Green, and Longmans, 1844), unpaginated.

2 Roger Fenton, "On the Present Position and Future Prospects of the Art of Photography," *Journal of the Society of Arts*, December 24, 1852, quoted in Gordon Baldwin et al., *All the Mighty World: The Photographs of Roger Fenton, 1852–1860* (New York: Metropolitan Museum of Art, 2004), 10.

3 Quoted in Colin Ford, *The Cameron Collection: An Album of Photographs Presented to Sir John Herschel* (Wokingham, England, and New York: Van Nostrand Reinhold, 1975), 140–41.

4 Brassaï, *Camera in Paris* (Paris: Edition Arts et Métiers Graphiques, 1949), quoted in Andrew Roth, ed., *The Book of 101 Books* (New York: PPP Editions in association with Roth Horowitz, 2001), 76.

5 Henri Cartier-Bresson, *The Decisive Moment* (New York: Simon and Schuster, 1952), preface.

6 Walker Evans to Ernestine Evans, February 1934, draft of a letter in the collection of the J. Paul Getty Museum, quoted in Maria Morris Hambourg et al., *Walker Evans* (New York: Metropolitan Museum of Art, 2000), 57.

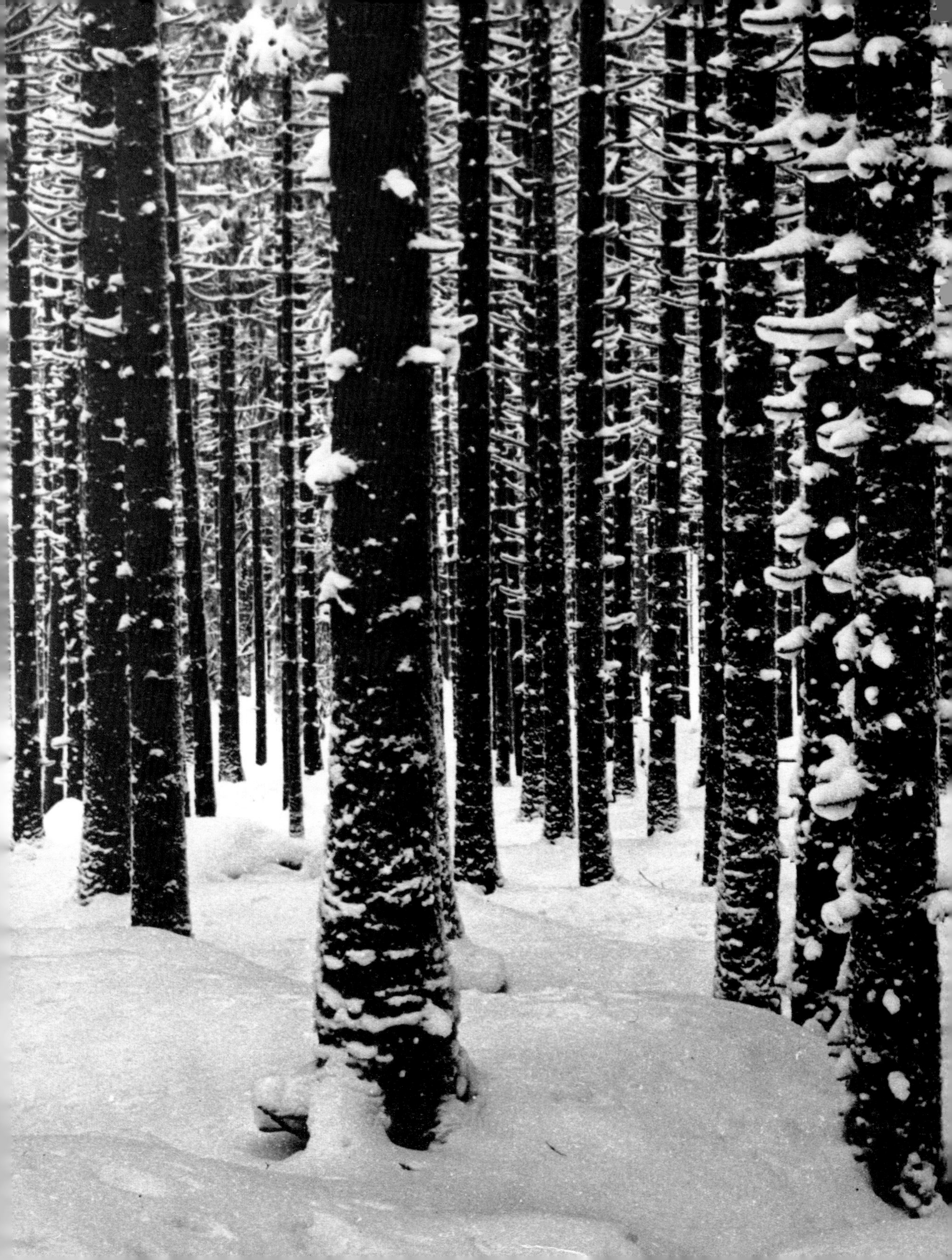

Collecting Photography at the Museum of Fine Arts, Boston

Anne E. Havinga

The Museum of Fine Arts, Boston, was one of the first art museums to establish a photography collection, beginning in 1924 with the gift by Alfred Stieglitz of twenty-seven of his photographs. Soon thereafter, Stieglitz's landscapes and portraits were shown in selections from the Museum's collection, alongside Old Master etchings and engravings by Rembrandt and Dürer. In 1950, four years after Stieglitz's death, his wife Georgia O'Keeffe donated thirty-five more of his photographs (fig. 24) and placed seven of his portraits of her on loan (the Museum ultimately acquired these, in 1995, from the Georgia O'Keeffe Foundation). O'Keeffe carefully selected these photographs to complement the initial group, so that the two installments provided a balanced overview of the influential photographer's career. These acquisitions also supplied a foundation on which to build and stimulated gifts of photographs by Stieglitz's friends Clarence H. White and Frederick H. Evans, as well as by Paul Outerbridge. In the 1940s, the collection was further augmented by the donation of an archive of more than one hundred daguerreotypes by the Boston firm of Southworth and Hawes, given by the son of Josiah Johnson Hawes.

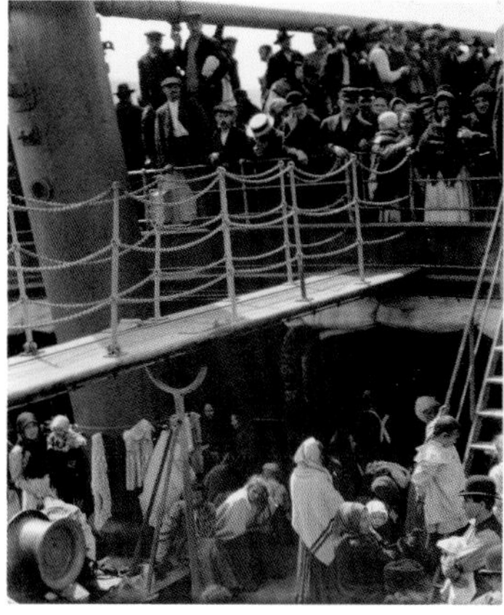

fig. 24 **Alfred Stieglitz (American, 1864–1946), *The Steerage*, 1907, gelatin silver print**

The MFA made its first photographic purchases in the 1960s, at which time most museums were only beginning to take an interest in photography. The initial acquisition, in 1967, was a group of five Edward Weston photographs. The Museum soon made further significant purchases, and the collection rapidly grew to span the whole history of the medium. Purchase grants awarded by the Polaroid Foundation in the 1970s and 1980s fostered the acquisition of work by living photographers, including Walker Evans. In 1978, the trustees made the commitment to purchase twenty-two Paul Strand photographs, and the Department of Prints and Drawings was consequently renamed the Department of Prints, Drawings, and Photographs. Since the 1970s, the Museum has also received a substantial number of nineteenth-century photographs, early photomechanical prints, and photographically illustrated books from a dedicated anonymous friend.

In the 1980s, the MFA initiated a series of exhibitions from the modernist photography collection of William and Saundra Lane. Owner of a Massachusetts plastics-manufacturing company, William Lane had collected the paintings of Stuart Davis, Arthur Dove, John Marin, Georgia O'Keeffe, Charles Sheeler, and others before turning to photography in the 1960s. In 1965, the Lanes purchased Sheeler's photographic estate (fig. 25), which inspired them to acquire extensive collections of works by Ansel Adams, Imogen Cunningham, and Edward Weston. In 1990, they offered a major gift of paintings to the Museum. Since William Lane's passing in 1995, Saundra Lane has continued to expand her photography collection and to be generous in sharing it with the MFA. Among her recent gifts are a group of eleven photographs, including Ansel Adams's *Surf Sequence* (p. 155), Morton Schamberg's *Rooftops* (p. 114), and Edward Weston's *Charis, Lake Ediza* (p. 72). In 2003, she funded the acquisition of the Sonja Bullaty and Angelo Lomeo Collection of Josef Sudek Photographs, a major archive of the Czech modernist's work. The MFA's photography program has benefited greatly from the deep resources of The Lane Collection, which is now largely housed at the Museum and is overseen by the Curator of The Lane Collection, a position that Saundra Lane established in 2001.

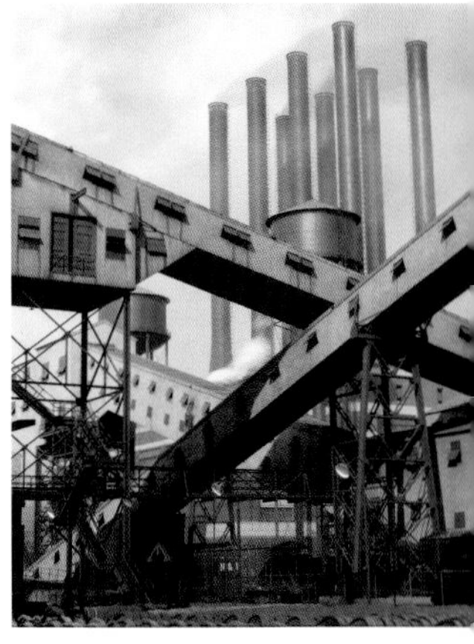

fig. 25 **Charles Sheeler (American, 1883–1965), *Criss-Crossed Conveyors—Ford Plant*, 1927, gelatin silver print, The Lane Collection**

The MFA's first endowed fund for photography acquisitions, the Horace W. Goldsmith Foundation Fund for Photography, was created in 1997. This fund has enabled the Museum to acquire a substantial number of works, especially by living photographers. Although the collection continues to grow through purchases, donation remains a significant method of acquisition. In 1994, the MFA received an additional sixty-seven daguerreotypes by Southworth and Hawes. A 1999 exhibition of photographs by the pioneering mountaineer, cartographer, and explorer Bradford Washburn resulted in a gift of eighty-five views. In 2001, the Boston collector Richard Germann donated more than one hundred turn-of-the-twentieth-century photographs and photographically illustrated books. In 2006, an extensive album of cyanotypes by the artist Arthur Wesley Dow was acquired, through combined purchase and gift, from Philio Wigglesworth Cushing and Henry Coolidge Wigglesworth. Over the years, monetary donations from numerous other friends of the Museum have made possible the purchase of important photographs for the collection.

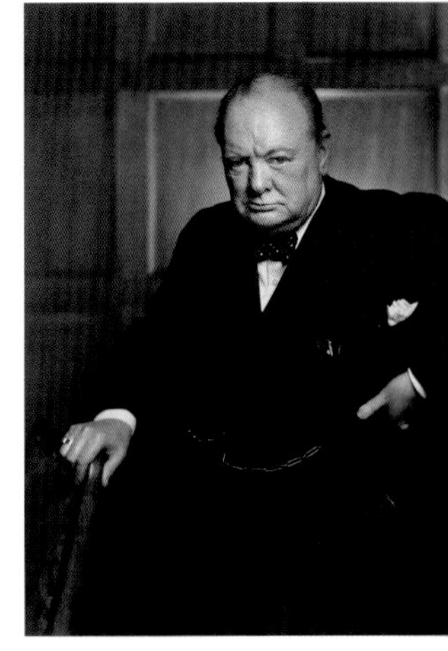

fig. 26 **Yousuf Karsh (Canadian, born in Turkish Armenia, 1908–2002), *Winston Churchill*, 1941, gelatin silver print**

The first curator solely responsible for photographs was appointed in 2001. The position was endowed in 2006 through the generosity of Mrs. Estrellita Karsh, widow of the portrait photographer Yousuf Karsh, who moved to Boston from Ottawa in the mid-1990s (fig. 26). Karsh felt great affection for the MFA, for he was apprenticed in the 1920s to the Boston photographer John Garo and spent time learning from the painted portraits hanging in the Museum's galleries. Karsh and his wife initiated a photography lecture series in 1997 and a prize for promising photography students at the School of the Museum of Fine Arts in 1999, making the MFA a center for the discussion and creation of fine art photography.

The photography collection has been shaped by all of these influences. The strengths in the Stieglitz holdings have inspired the curators to develop specific themes such as hands, trees, and close-up portraits, which can now be shared with visitors in wide-ranging variety. The collection increasingly spans the history of the medium, although it does not yet represent every acknowledged master. Besides the Southworth and Hawes, Stieglitz, and Strand material and access to The Lane Collection, the MFA also has rich holdings of large-scale nineteenth-century American landscapes, turn-of-the-century Pictorialism, and European modernism. It has focused of late on augmenting the collection of mid-twentieth-century American, European, and Japanese photography and, thanks to the infusion of new funds, on broadening the representation of contemporary work. The current strategy is to add depth to the collection through the acquisition of significant photographs, as well as to develop new areas of interest, such as fashion and celebrity photography. To this end, the Museum has recently welcomed large gifts of photographs by Yousuf Karsh and Herb Ritts (fig. 27). In 2007, the Herb Ritts Foundation generously contributed funds to support the institution's first gallery dedicated to the medium, which will open as part of the current expansion. When not on view in exhibitions, the MFA's photography collection can easily be viewed by appointment in the Morse Study Room of the Department of Prints, Drawings, and Photographs.

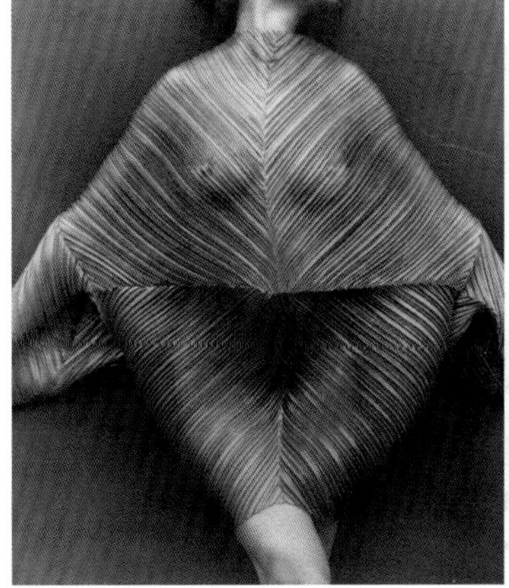

fig. 27 **Herb Ritts (American, 1952–2002),** ***Wrapped Torso, Los Angeles*****, 1989, platinum print**

This volume is meant to provide a sampling of the range and depth of the collection, which now numbers nearly five thousand works. Rather than organizing the material chronologically, we have grouped the images into loosely defined themes, pairing the photographs to encourage consideration of the variety of approaches to similar subject matter adopted by the creative individuals who have been inspired to make art with the camera.

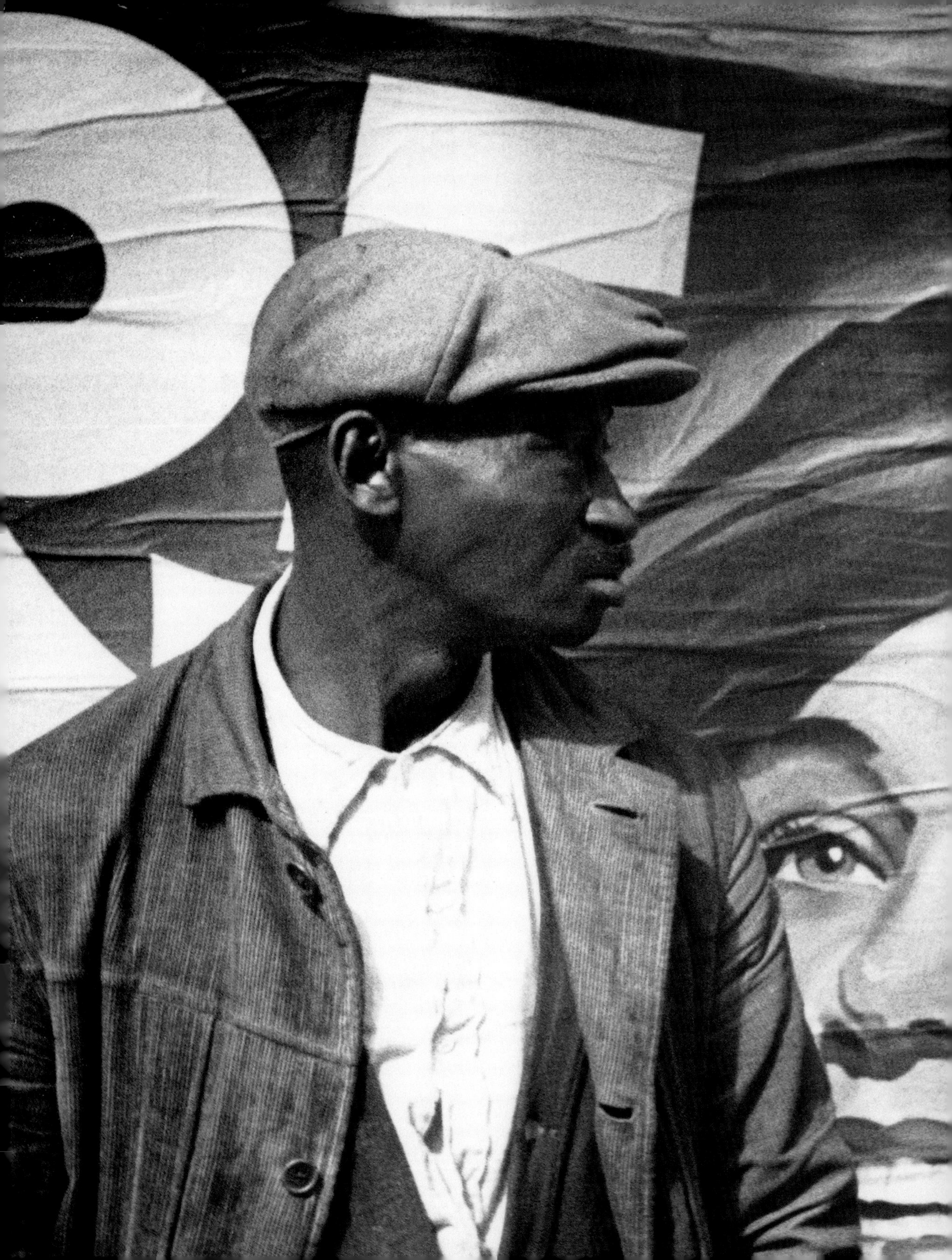

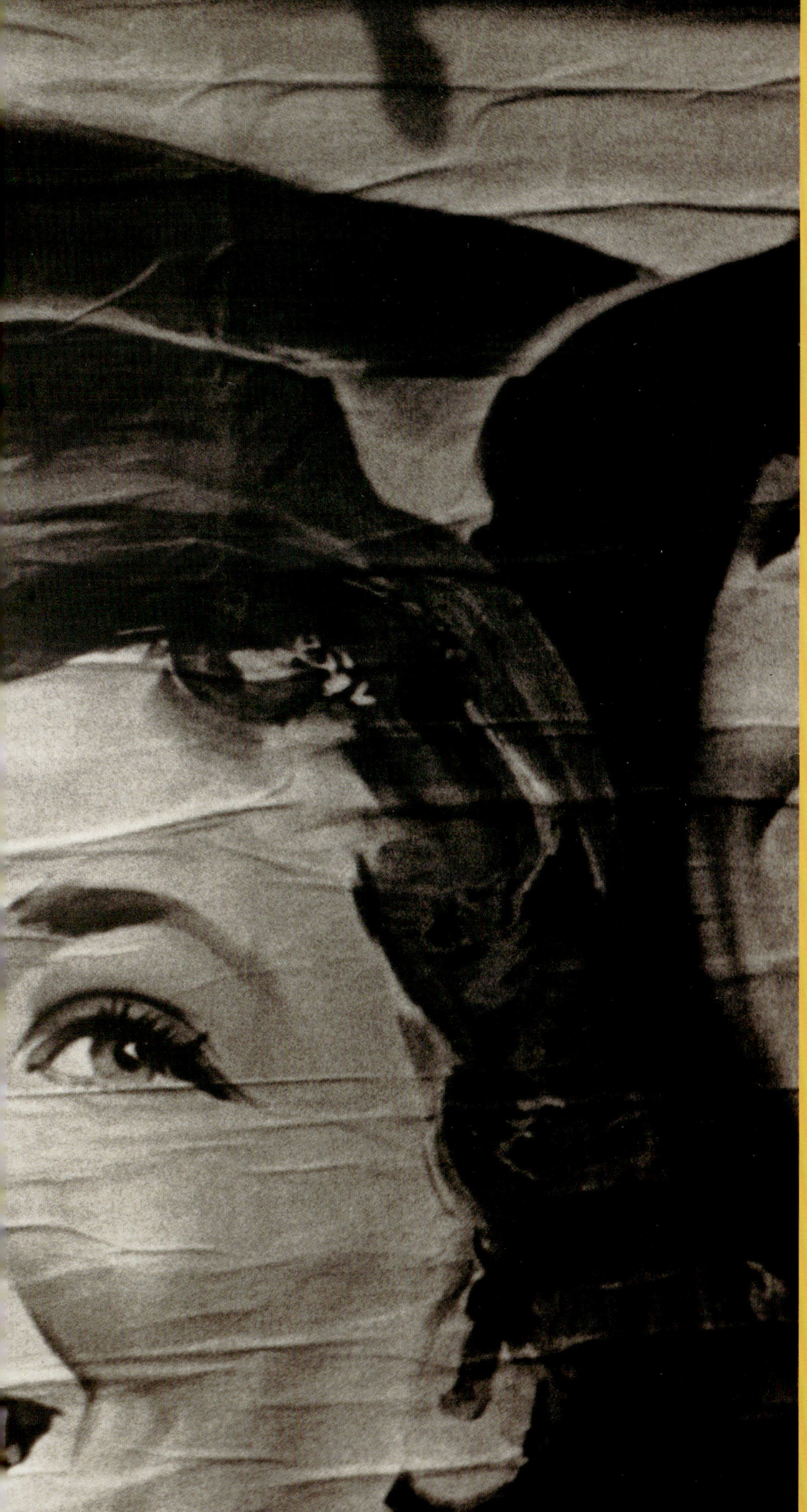

1 FACE AND FIGURE

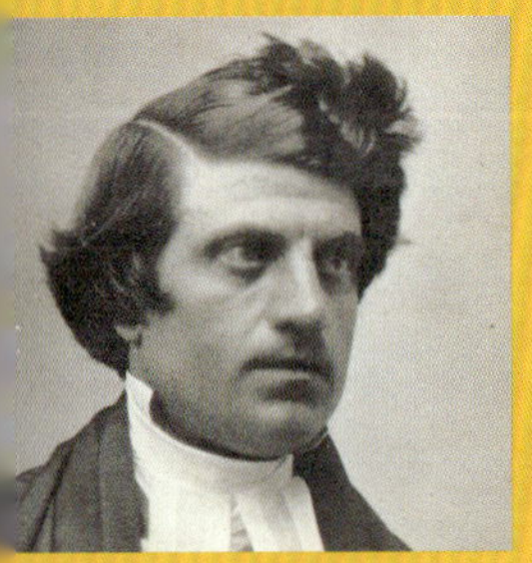
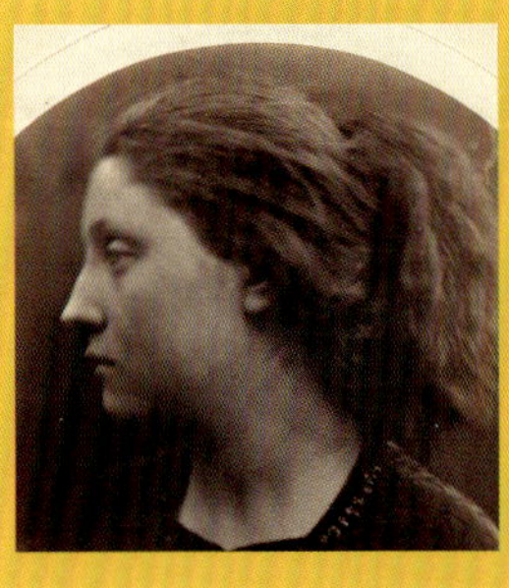
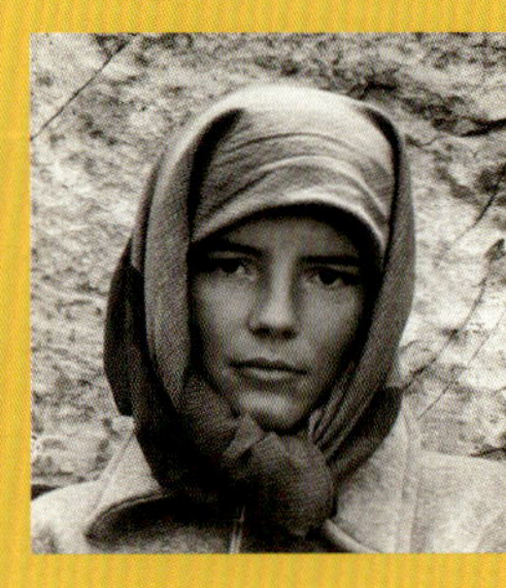
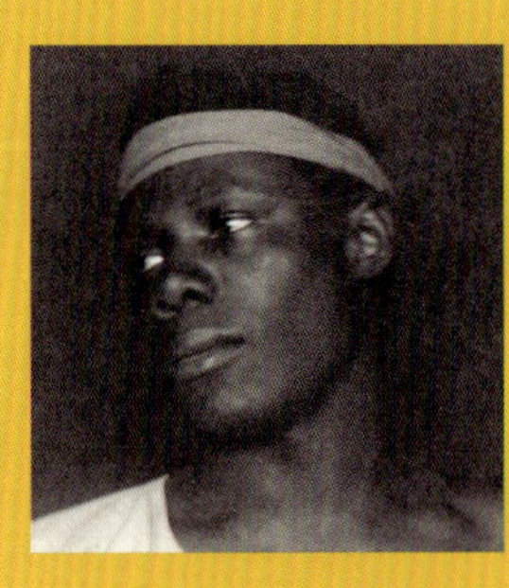
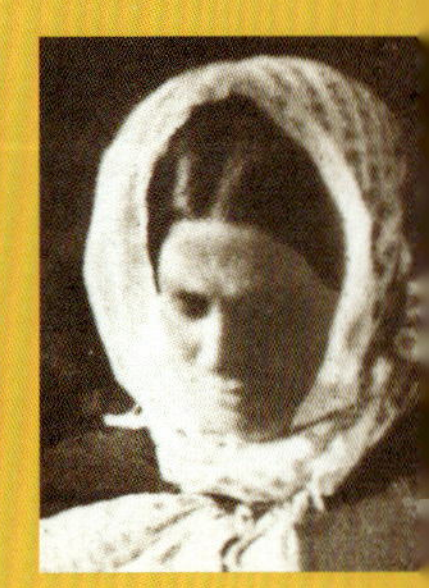

Face and Figure

From early times on, photographers, like artists working in other media, have sought to interpret the human face, an individual's gestures, or physical bearing. While the lengthy exposure times that initially were the norm yielded blurred results, by the early 1840s the fact that sitters had to remain still for only a matter of seconds made photographic portraiture a feasible pursuit. Of the formats that were available then, the daguerreotype was particularly well suited to recording a person's appearance. The breathtaking detail and realism of the unique portraits produced by Daguerre's method on smooth, silvered plates astonished the world. In the 1850s, the negative-positive photographic process, which was by then replacing the daguerreotype, offered new opportunities. While it took until that decade for photographs printed on paper to attain pristine clarity, multiples could be made and the images more easily shared and sold. This process could also more conveniently record human activity outdoors.

The camera became the perfect tool for portraiture, as it produced images that communicated a person's likeness in precise detail. This capability encouraged camera users of various levels of skill to make portraits—of the famous, the unknown, the rich, the poor, family members, friends, and themselves—with energy and a great range of purpose and style. They produced formal and informal depictions, full-length portrayals and close-ups, literal and symbolic representations.

Photographers with a deep visual understanding have long recognized that a truly successful likeness should suggest meaning beyond mere factual description. To this end, many attempted to convey something about a sitter's personality, inner feelings, mood, social position, or the circumstances in which he or she lived. In the last hundred years, it has become increasingly common for artists also to make photographic images that address, in metaphorical terms, the process of art making itself. Whether relying on the force of exact description or the evocation of atmosphere and allusion, the images reproduced on these pages illustrate the creative choices photographers have made when directing their lens toward the human face and figure.

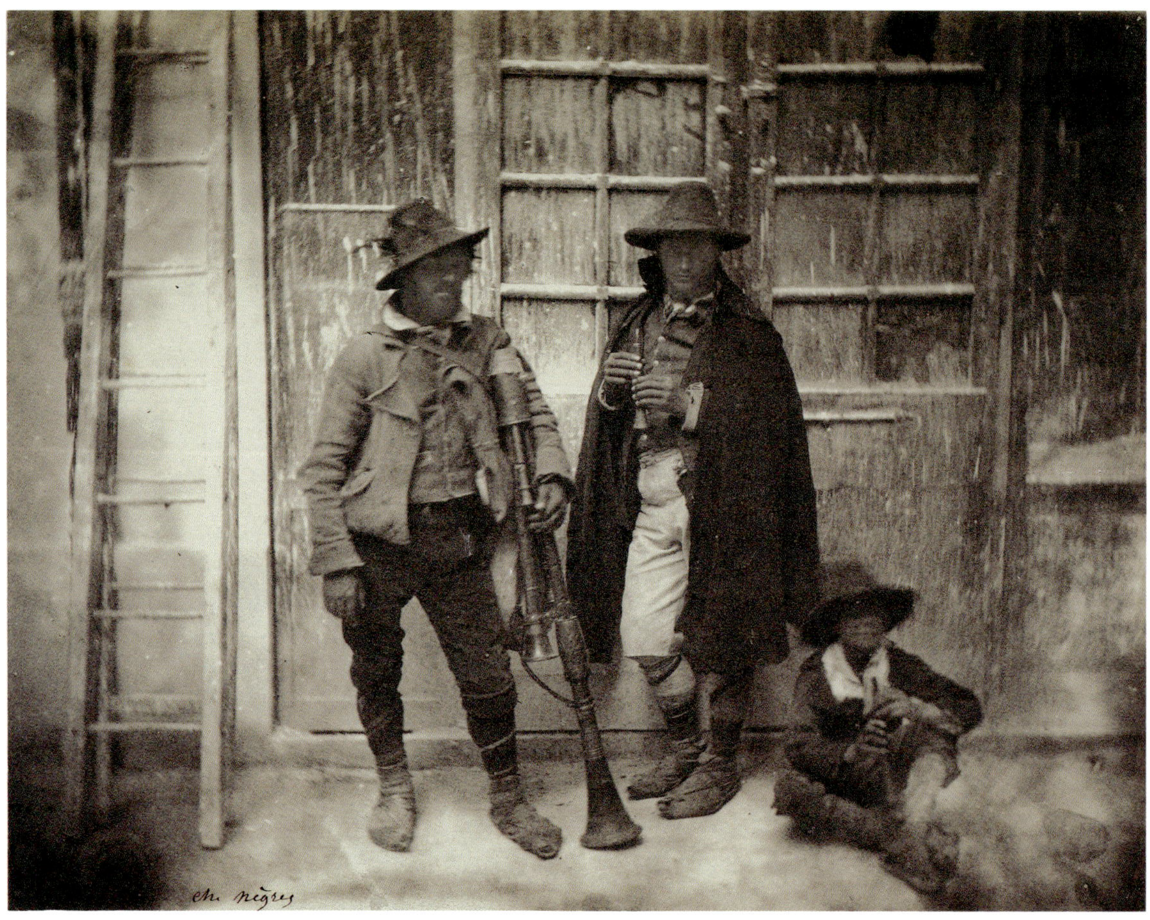

Charles Nègre (French, 1820–1880)

Trois Pifferari (Three Pipers), 1853–54

Salt print from a wet collodion negative

15.9 x 20.2 cm (6 ¼ x 7 15/16 in.)

Charles H. Bayley Picture and Painting Fund and Museum purchase with funds donated by Saundra B. Lane 2002.334

Charles Nègre belonged to the first generation of artist-photographers in France. His training as an artist informed all of the works in his large and varied oeuvre, perhaps especially his studies of the street people of Paris and their occupations, long a favorite subject of printmakers. His genre scenes, which were posed because of the protracted exposures, are pioneering examples of street photography, depicting familiar types such as ragpickers, chimney sweeps, and stonemasons. Exotic Italian pipers, shown here at rest in a palpitating light, had a strong presence in the artistic and musical imagination of the day. Nègre's salted paper print lends a soft, pictorial effect to the details of their instruments, costume, and physiognomy.

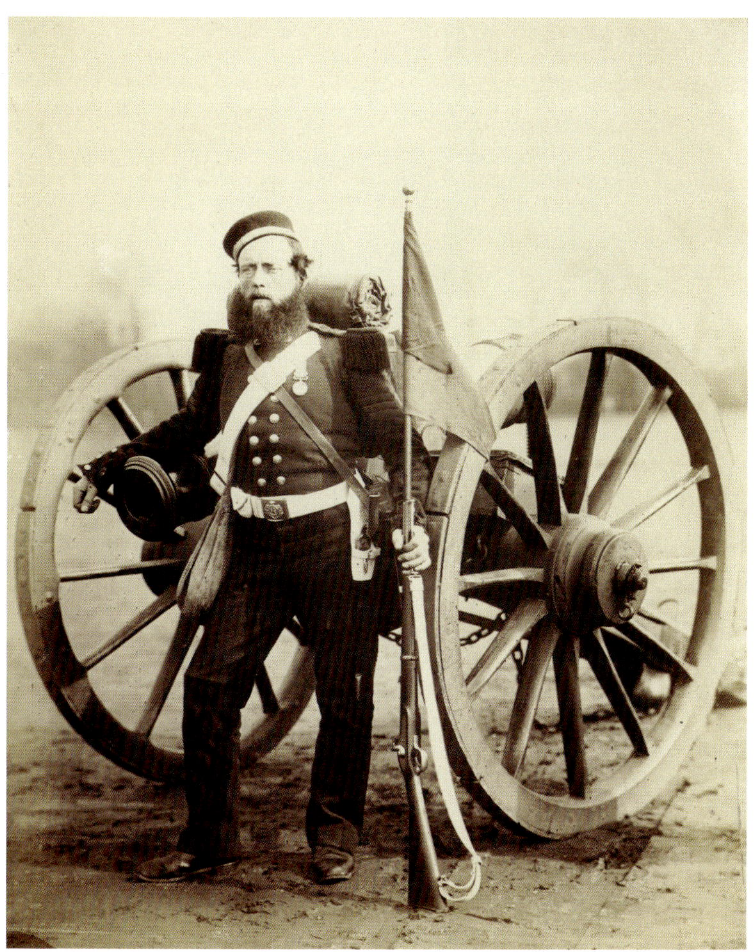

Robert Howlett (English, 1831–1858)

Sergeant William Russell, 5th Battalion, Royal Artillery, 1856

Albumen print

23.5 x 18.6 cm (9 ¼ x 7 ¼ in.)

Sophie M. Friedman Fund 1992.513

Robert Howlett was one of Britain's earliest professional photographers. His wide-ranging practice included portraiture, landscape photography, and studies for painters. Commissioned in 1856 by Queen Victoria to make portraits of the heroes of the Crimean War, he posed Sergeant William Russell standing between the massive wheels of an artillery wagon, his arm draped over the cannon. In his left hand, Russell holds upright his rifle and a flag, probably his company colors. His face looks stricken but proud, and he wears a hero's medal on his chest. The manly realism and sophisticated composition make this image more than an individual portrait: Howlett has created an icon of the British Empire's military strength and the bravery of its men.

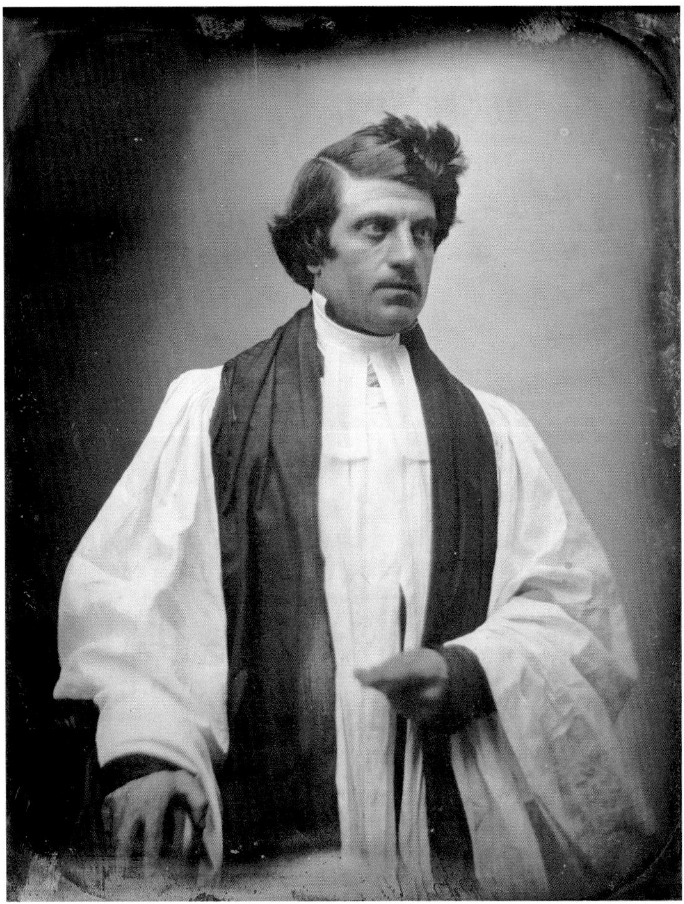

Albert Sands Southworth (American, 1811–1894)
Josiah Johnson Hawes (American, 1808–1901)
Reverend William T. Smithett, 1853
Daguerreotype; 21.9 x 16.6 cm (8⅝ x 6 9/16 in.)
Gift of Edward Southworth Hawes in memory of his father Josiah Johnson Hawes 43.1391

The early history of photography is distinguished by several remarkable partnerships. In Edinburgh, the painter David Octavius Hill and the engineer Robert Adamson brought Talbot's calotype, or paper negative, process to an artistic summit. Meanwhile, in Boston, the team of Albert Sands Southworth and Josiah Johnson Hawes mastered a style of daguerreotype portraiture that defined the spirit and idealism of a generation of accomplished Americans.

The quiet dignity of this portrait of Elizabeth Johnstone, from Hill and Adamson's documentary series on the Scottish fishing village of Newhaven, is due in part to certain characteristics of the calotype process. The grainy paper negative eliminated excessive detail and shaped a monumental figure out of broad areas of light and shadow. Showing the strain

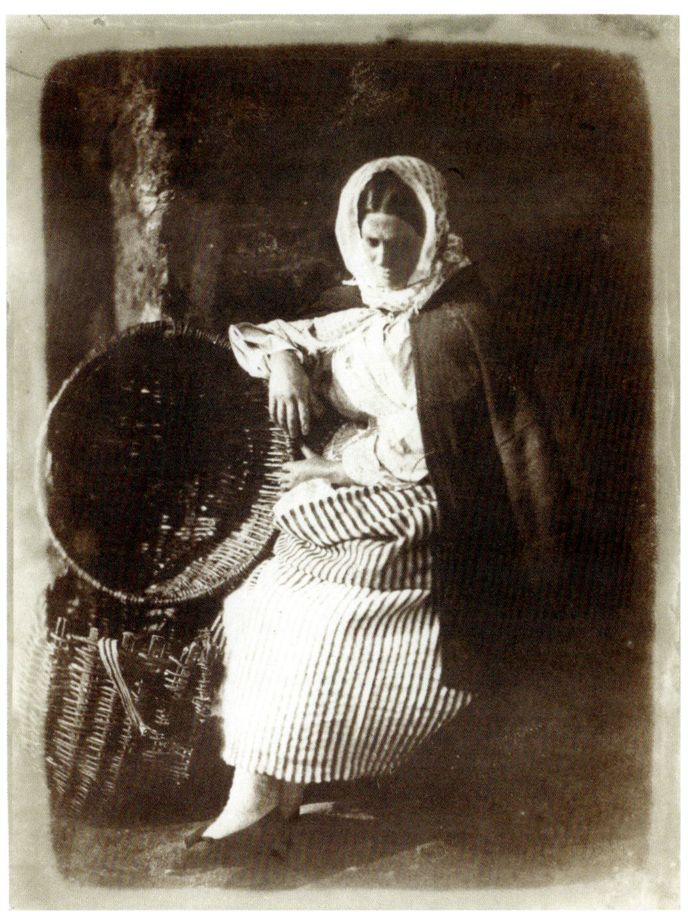

David Octavius Hill (Scottish, 1802–1870)
Robert Adamson (Scottish, 1821–1848)
Elizabeth Johnstone, "Seated Newhaven Fishwife," about 1845
Salt print from a paper negative
21.3 x 15.9 cm (8 3/8 x 6 1/4 in.)
Purchased with funds donated by David Bakalar 1974.469

of the long exposure, the sitter supports herself against the stack of picturesque baskets, her eyes downcast. Her sculptural serenity is enlivened by the conflicting stripes of the skirts and aprons of her regional costume, an effect repeated in the sparkling pattern of the rough woven baskets.

Southworth and Hawes similarly exploited the qualities of their chosen technique, using the mirror-like sharpness and detail of the daguerreotype to portray the clear vision and idealistic fervor of the Reverend Smithett. Here, every detail counts, from Smithett's wild hair to the tense grip of his right hand. His intent gaze looks beyond the picture, and the crisp white and black of his surplice and stole highlight a powerful, upright body that emanates confidence and certainty in that distant vision.

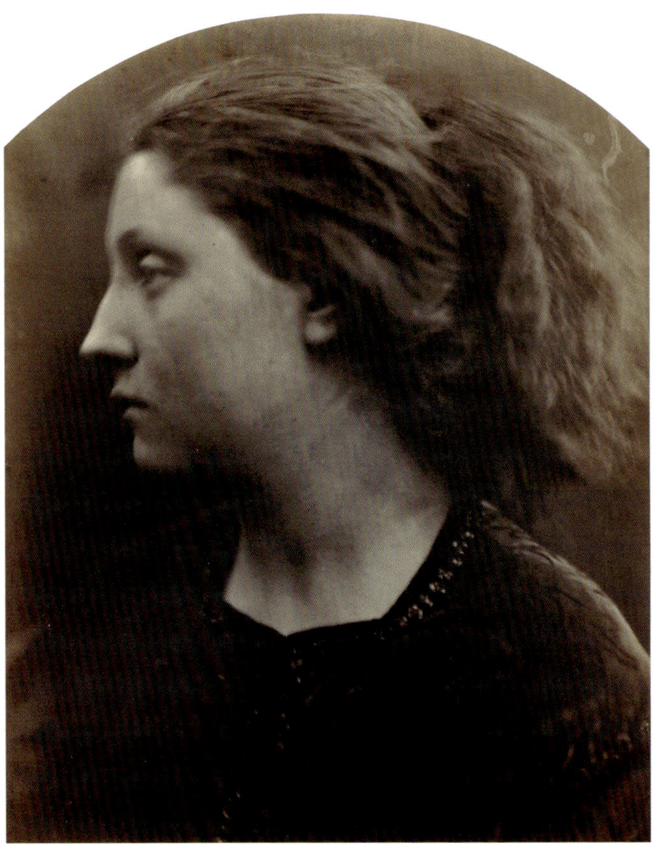

Julia Margaret Cameron

(English, born in India, 1815–1879)

Adriana, 1866

Albumen print; 36.1 x 28.1 cm (14 3/16 x 11 1/16 in.)

Sophie M. Friedman Fund 1987.499

Julia Margaret Cameron took up photography at the age of forty-eight and became known for her portraits of notable Victorians, inspired by Old Master and Pre-Raphaelite painting. Family members, friends, and servants also served as her models for theatrical compositions based on stories from the Bible, poems by Tennyson, and even works of popular literature. In this portrait, the house servant Mary Hillier represents Adriana, the disappointed heroine of a serial novel published in 1866. Cameron admired her striking profile and often used this composition to represent women of strong character, such as Sappho and Psyche. The sculptural lines of Hillier's features stand out against the thick, dark mass of her hair and the rich velvet of her gown, emphasizing the purity and seriousness of the wrongėd woman.

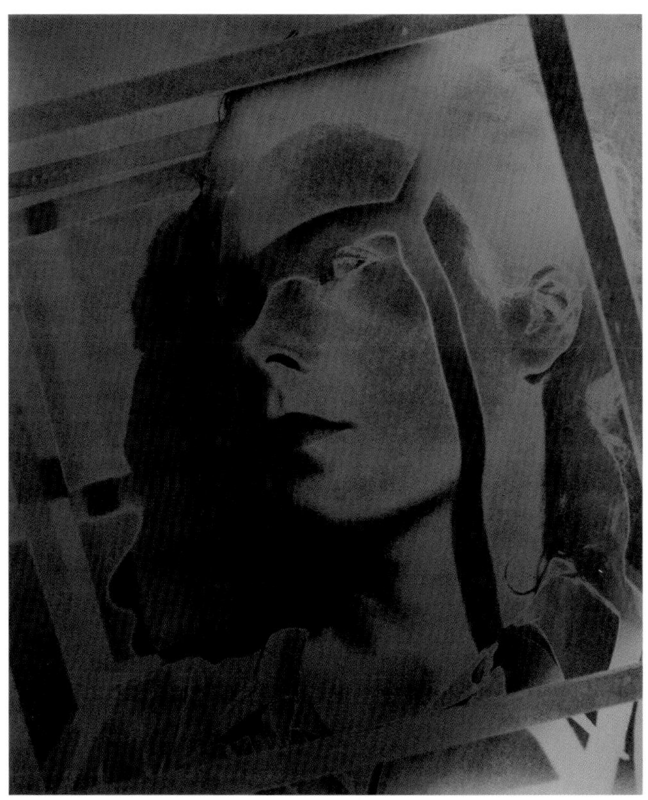

György Kepes (American, born in Hungary, 1906–2001)
Juliet's Shadow Caged, 1939, printed in 1940
Gelatin silver print, solarized; 34.9 x 27.9 cm (13¾ x 11 in.)
Sophie M. Friedman Fund 1984.147

György Kepes, professor of visual design at the Massachusetts Institute of Technology for nearly thirty years, began his teaching career in 1937 at Chicago's New Bauhaus, which was founded by his teacher and Hungarian compatriot László Moholy-Nagy. This institution, where experimental techniques including photograms, photomontages, and solarization were encouraged, became one of the most influential modern schools of photography in the United States. In *Juliet's Shadow Caged*, the model's head is enclosed in a cubic frame and casts an exaggerated shadow due to raking light from a high angle. The picture is broken up, like sections of stained glass, by the barlike shadows of the frame. With its narrow tonal range of silvery grays, the solarized image seems eerie and otherworldly, passing into the surreal dimension suggested by the title.

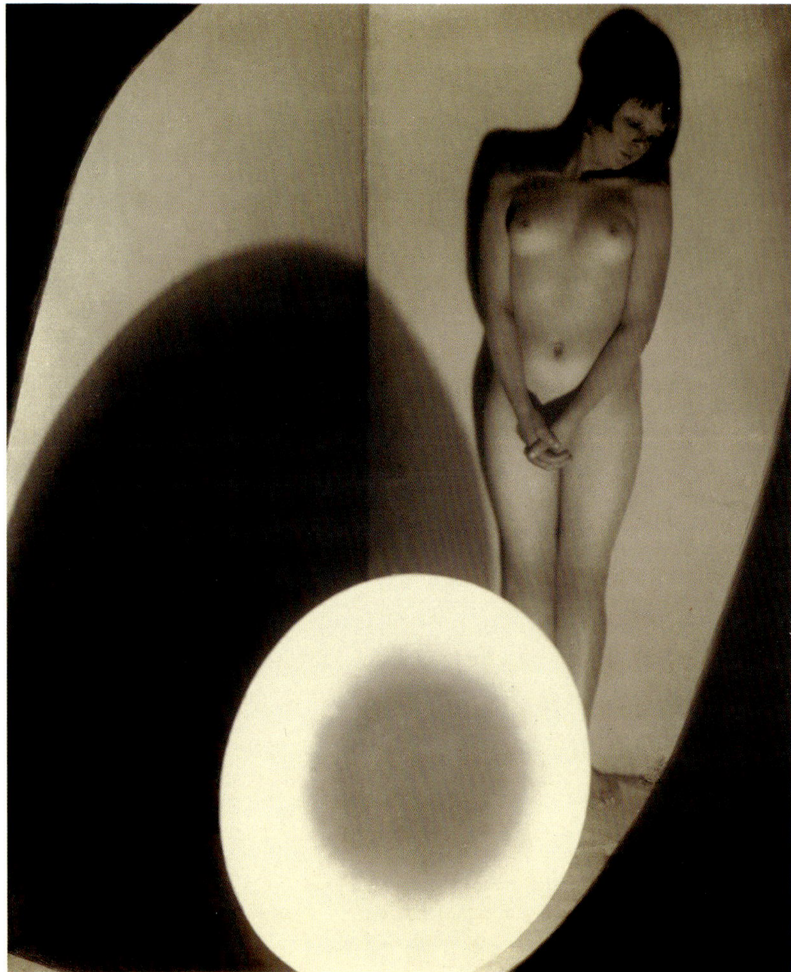

Frantisek Drtikol (Czechoslovakian, 1883–1961)

Nude in Corner behind Disk, 1920–30

Carbon print; 27.6 x 22.5 cm (10⅞ x 8⅞ in.)

Sophie M. Friedman Fund 1984.420

Frantisek Drtikol's and Bill Jacobson's photographs of the nude body illustrate the ongoing influence of contemporary art movements on photographic creation. Drtikol, who in his youth had been inspired by Art Nouveau, had embraced Art Deco ideals by the 1920s. This photograph represents his movement toward abstraction in his depiction of the nude model. He began, he stated, to "use the body as a decorative object, positioning it in various settings and lights." Employing a simple disk as a prop, the artist layered violent contrasts of light and shadow like a collage. The model becomes simply another element in the geometric composition, her body distorted by deep shadows created with dramatic, harsh lighting.

The influence of color-field, or stain, painting is evident in the large scale, abstractness, and flatness

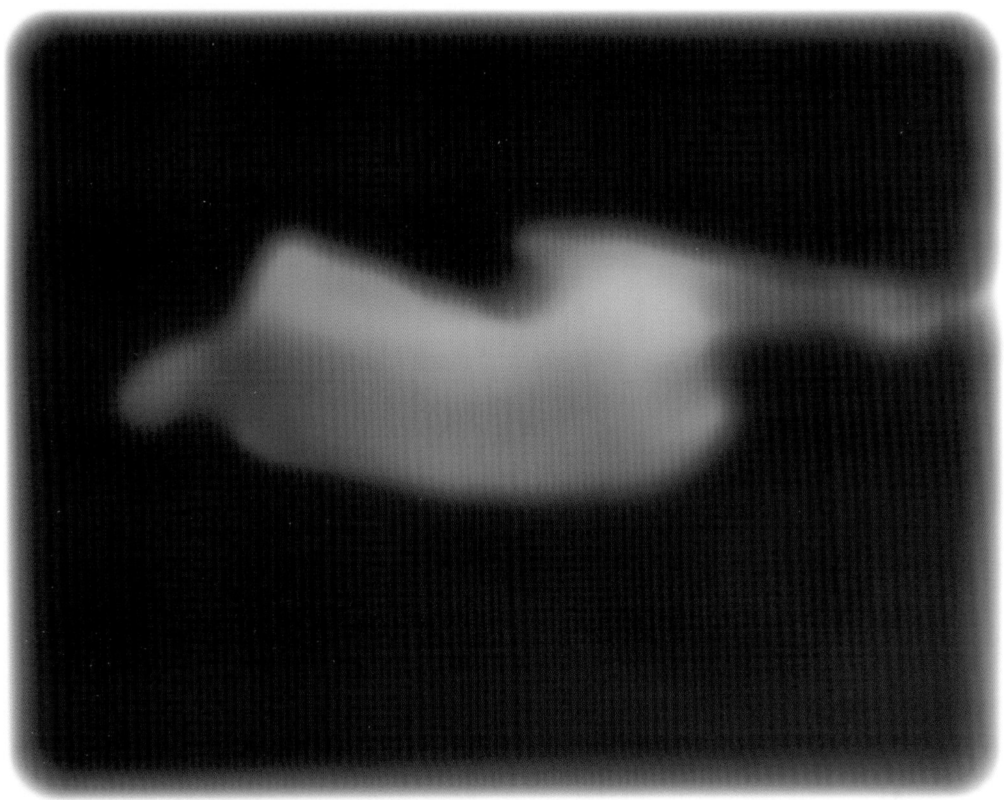

Bill Jacobson (American, born in 1955)

Song of Sentient Beings #1617, 1995

Gelatin silver print; 101.6 x 127 cm (40 x 50 in.)

Museum purchase with funds donated by

Mrs. George R. Rowland, Sr. 2000.584

of Jacobson's nude. The ghostly shape floating in blackness is barely recognizable as a human body. As evanescent as smoke or fog, the out-of-focus image makes reference to earlier photographic movements such as spirit photography, with its ectoplasmic forms, and soft-focus Pictorialism. Jacobson, who was overwhelmed by the impact of the AIDS epidemic on the artistic community, alludes to the fragility of the human body. His blurred technique removes the subject from reality and places it within the realm of dream or fading memory, raising the question of whether the photograph is a representation of reality or a work of human imagination.

The London photographer Frederick H. Evans and the Bostonian F. Holland Day, like other Pictorialists working around 1900, advocated for the making of artistically expressive photographs. They developed personal approaches to the medium through their careful control of composition, tone, and atmosphere. Evans, who earned his living as a bookseller until 1898, is best known for his images of cathedrals and chateaux in England and France. Day, who had published fine art books before turning to photography, specialized in portraits as well as religious studies and symbolic male nudes.

The two men became acquainted about 1890 and were active correspondents. Visiting Evans in London in 1901, Day modeled an Arab costume he had recently purchased in Algiers. The fine platinum print Evans produced attests to his skills as a craftsman and his appreciation for poetic detail. The portrait captures Day's elegant demeanor and predilection for theatricality.

The second image also makes clear Day's attraction to exotic appearances. The Boston photographer's dozen or so portraits of the artist and model J. Alexander Skeete posed as a noble African leader reveal the humanitarian interest that Day took in racial difference. In these portraits, the photographer endeavored to capture a particularly subtle range of black, gray, and white tones. This example, showing the sitter's head and chest bathed in soft light, is one of Day's most tender renditions of Skeete.

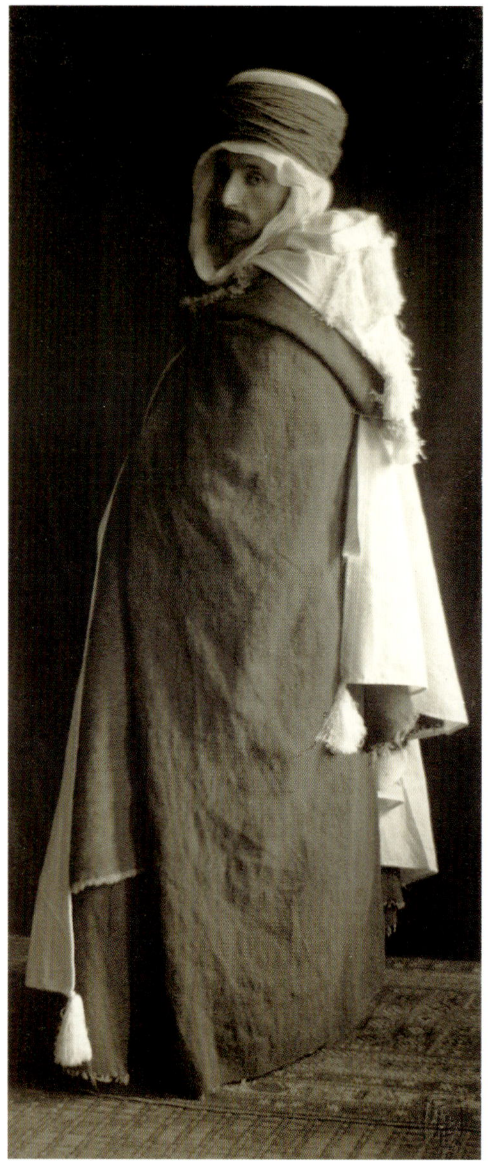

Frederick H. Evans (English, 1853–1943)

Portrait of F. Holland Day, 1901

Platinum print; 24.3 x 9.8 cm (9 9/16 x 3 7/8 in.)

Gift of David Bakalar 1974.50

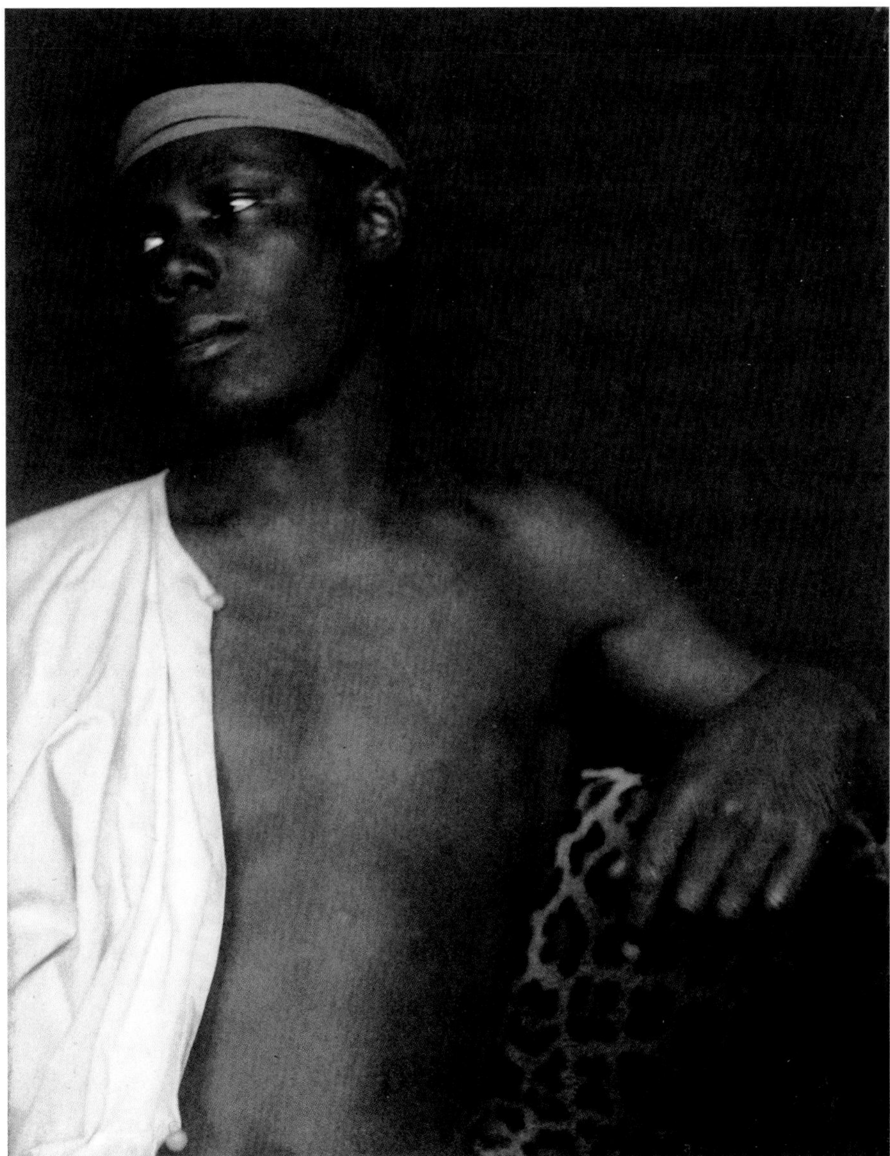

F. Holland Day (American, 1864–1933)

Nubia, about 1896–97

Platinum print; 16.1 x 12.3 cm (6 5/16 x 4 13/16 in.)

Charles H. Bayley Picture and Painting Fund 2002.620

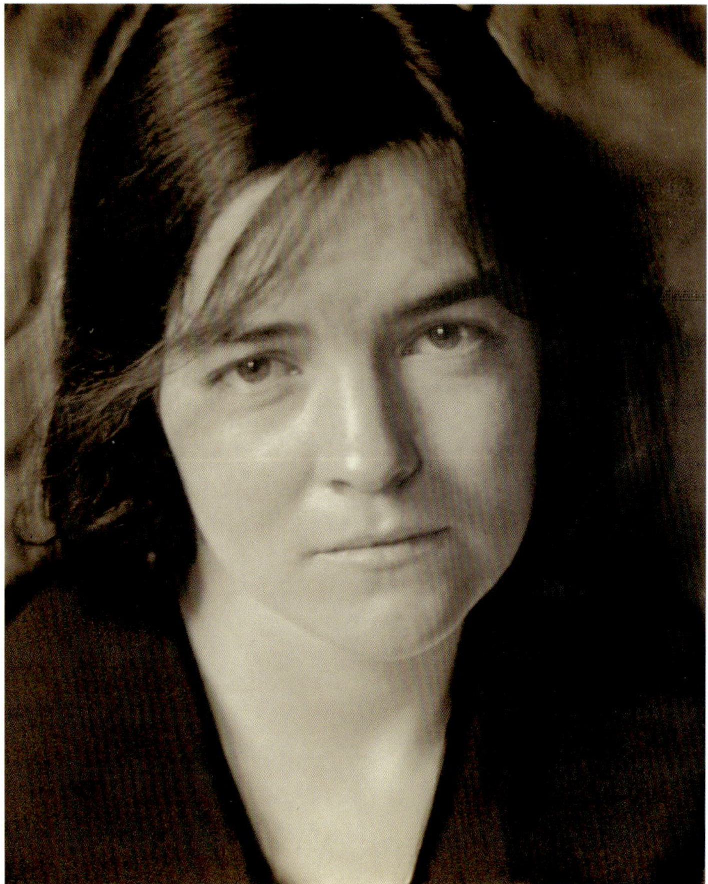

Edward Steichen (American, born in Luxembourg, 1879–1973)

Dana, about 1923

Palladium and gum bichromate combination print

25.4 x 20.3 cm (10 x 8 in.)

Museum purchase with funds donated

by Virginia Herrick Deknatel 2001.11

From its very beginnings, photography has been recognized as an ideal tool for recording the likenesses of friends and loved ones. The most compelling portraits often reflect the relationship between the artist and sitter. Like Alfred Stieglitz, whose images of Georgia O'Keeffe may have inspired the look of this sensitive palladium portrait, Edward Steichen took a series of intimate portraits of a woman he was close to, Dana Desboro. This pensive picture of the beautiful young actress who later became his second wife was made not long after the two first met in 1923. Dana's dreamy expression and tousled hair are skillfully rendered in soft, natural light in a style very different from the glamorous artifice of Steichen's studio portraiture and fashion-magazine work of the period.

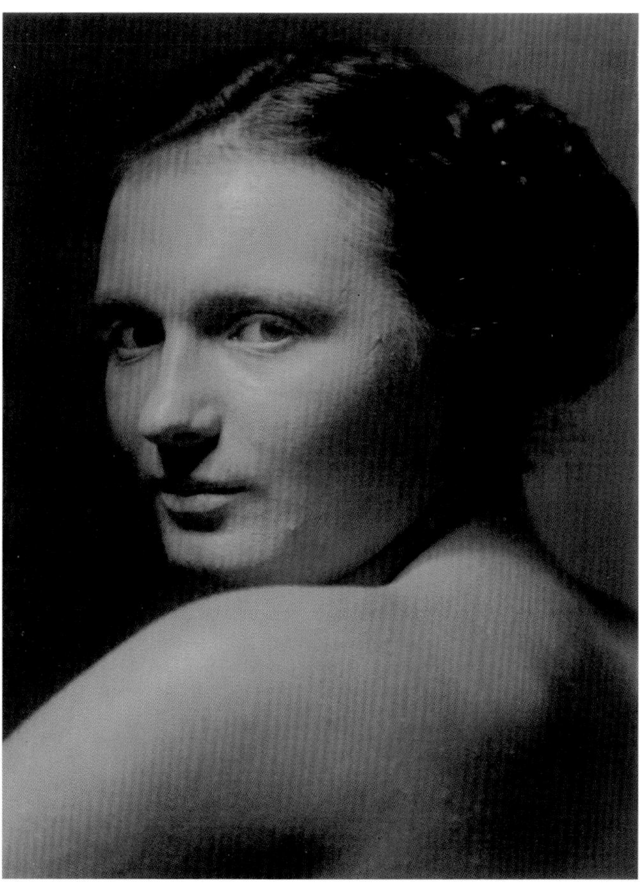

Josef Sudek (Czechoslovakian, 1896–1976)

Milena, 1942

Bromoil print; 18.1 x 13.3 cm (7 ⅛ x 5 ¼ in.)

The Sonja Bullaty and Angelo Lomeo Collection

of Josef Sudek Photographs

The Saundra B. Lane Photography Purchase Fund 2003.166

Josef Sudek is not often thought of as a photographer of people, but he did occasionally make portraits, nearly always of his small circle of close friends. Milena Vildova was a dancer and actress living in Prague who sometimes attended the musical evenings Sudek hosted in his studio to listen to recordings of his favorite classical composers. In his stunning bromoil print, Sudek has captured Vildova's expressive face just as she turns to look back over her shoulder, with light gently playing across her features. During World War II, Sudek made fewer of his better known landscapes of the city and its surrounding countryside, focusing instead on more personal subjects such as this—portraits, quiet interiors, and simple still lifes arranged on his windowsill.

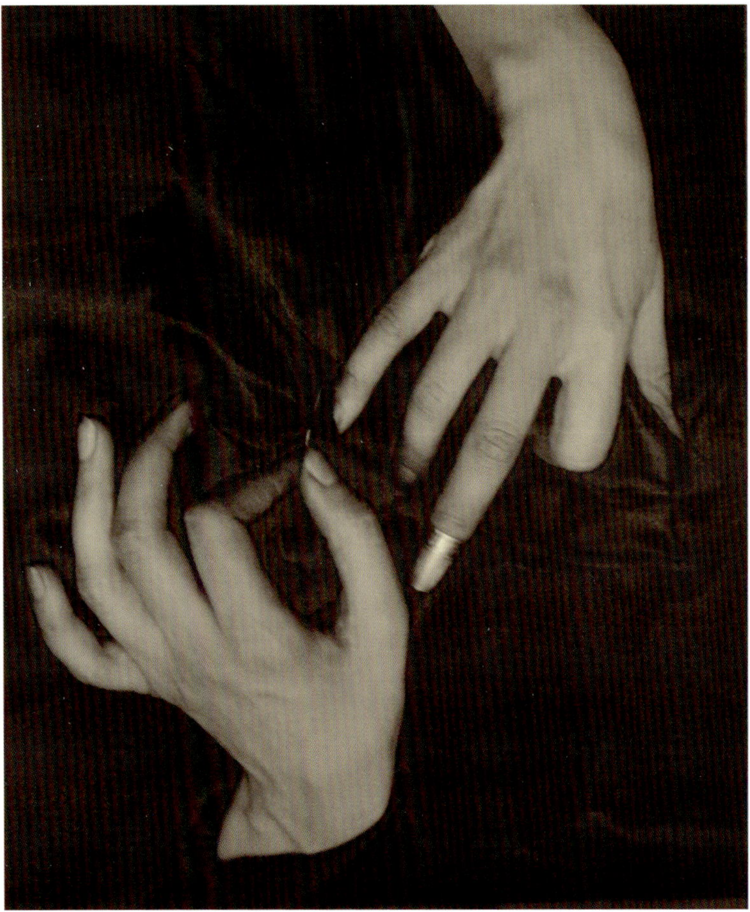

Alfred Stieglitz (American, 1864–1946)

Georgia O'Keeffe, A Portrait (8), 1919

Palladium print, solarized; 23.5 x 18.4 cm (9 ¼ x 7 ¼ in.)

Gift of Alfred Stieglitz 24.1728

Sometimes the most revealing and evocative photographic portraits are not images of faces at all. Alfred Stieglitz's photograph of the painter Georgia O'Keeffe, whom he met in 1916 and married in 1924, is part of a groundbreaking series of several hundred portraits he made of her over twenty-some years. This cropped view of her hands posed elegantly with a silver thimble is characteristic of these often fragmentary portrayals, which together Stieglitz felt captured her essence in a way that no single image ever could. Indeed, many years after her husband's death, O'Keeffe claimed: "When I look over the photographs Stieglitz took of me . . . I wonder who that person is. It is as if in my one life I have lived many lives."

Unlike Stieglitz's highly refined portrait of O'Keeffe, Tina Modotti's closely cropped picture of a worker's dusty hands conveys the realities of hard work. In 1923, the Italian-born film actress accompanied her lover, photographer Edward Weston, to Mexico City,

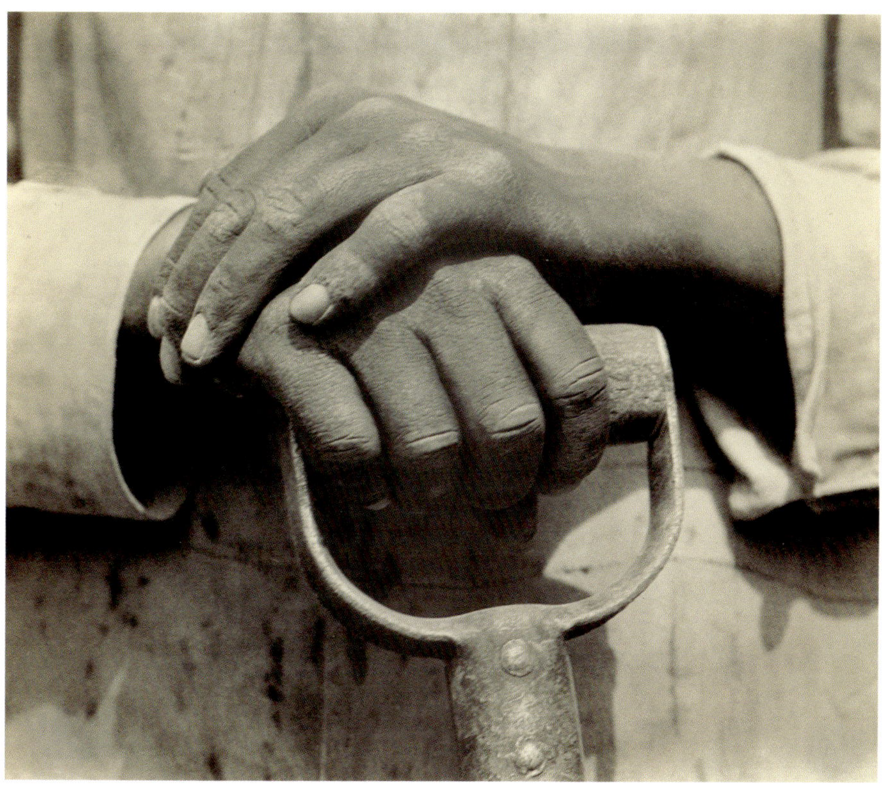

Tina Modotti (American, born in Italy, died in Mexico, 1896–1942)
Worker's Hands, Mexico, 1927
Gelatin silver print; 19.2 x 21.7 cm (7 9/16 x 8 9/16 in.)
Sophie M. Friedman Fund 1985.813

where Weston taught her to use a large-format camera. She worked as his studio assistant, quickly mastering the technique and making striking portraits, close-up images of flowers, and still lifes of her own. Modotti's compassion for the indigenous culture and political struggles of the Mexican people led her to join the Communist Party in 1927 and to focus on socially concerned subjects, using her camera as a tool to document the proud faces and weathered hands of the peasant laborers, artisans, and revolutionaries of her adopted country.

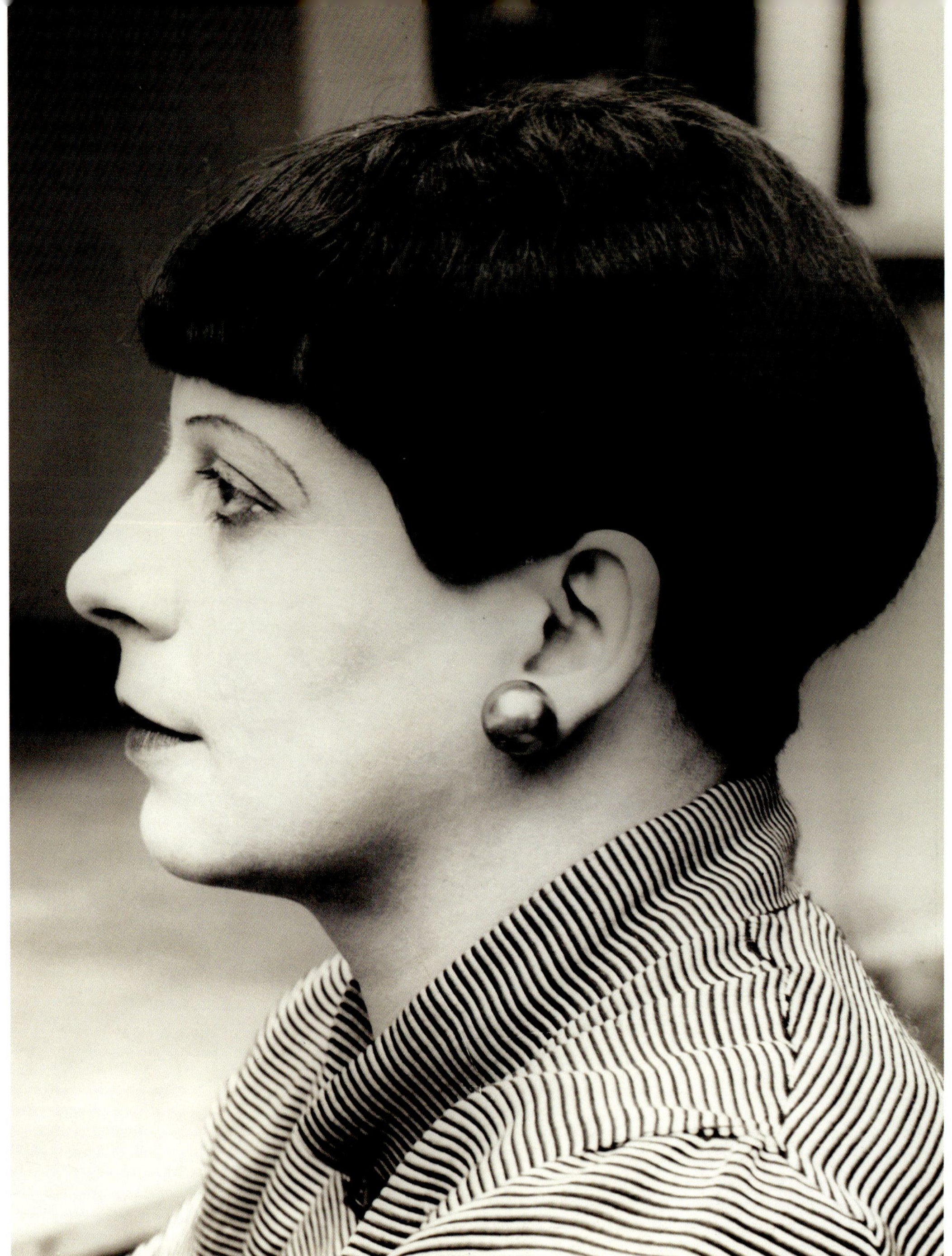

Lucia Moholy (née Schultz) (English, born in Prague, active in Germany, 1894–1989)

Florence Henri, Paris, 1927

Gelatin silver print; 40.3 x 29.8 cm (15 7/8 x 11 3/4 in.)

Sophie M. Friedman Fund 1986.249

Lucia Moholy, wife of László Moholy-Nagy, was the most important woman photographer at the Bauhaus during the 1920s, and her example influenced several other young women there to experiment with the medium. Her work included documentary images of objects produced by Bauhaus artists and of the school's sleek modernist buildings, designed by Walter Gropius. She is best known for her portraits, such as this one of her student Florence Henri, which she described as related to her architectural and product photography in their rigorously objective approach. Moholy would typically take headshots of her subjects from several different angles—strictly frontal, profile, obliquely from above, and three-quarter view—against plain backgrounds, in this case perfectly capturing the graphic contours of Henri's black cap of hair and white powdered face.

In 1946, Harry Callahan was hired to teach at Chicago's Institute of Design (the so-called New Bauhaus) by László Moholy-Nagy, who was then the school's director. Self-taught as a photographer, Callahan found the camera the ideal tool for artistic experimentation and regularly used it to record aspects of his private life. His wife Eleanor was his favorite subject for more than fifteen years. He sometimes photographed her from a great distance and other times at extremely close range, as in this starkly unsentimental study in white. Eleanor's arms raised above her head hide her dark hair and form a pale frame around her face, giving her a slightly startled and strangely androgynous appearance.

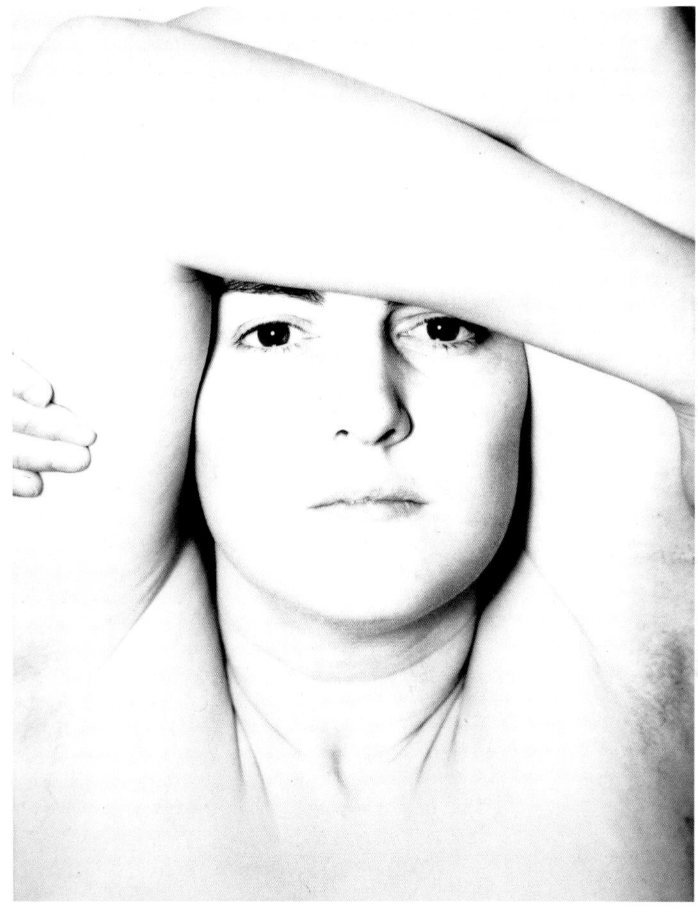

Harry Callahan (American, 1912–1999)

Eleanor, about 1947

Gelatin silver print; 11.6 x 8.3 cm (4 9/16 x 3 1/4 in.)

Gift of Barbara and Gene Polk 2003.810

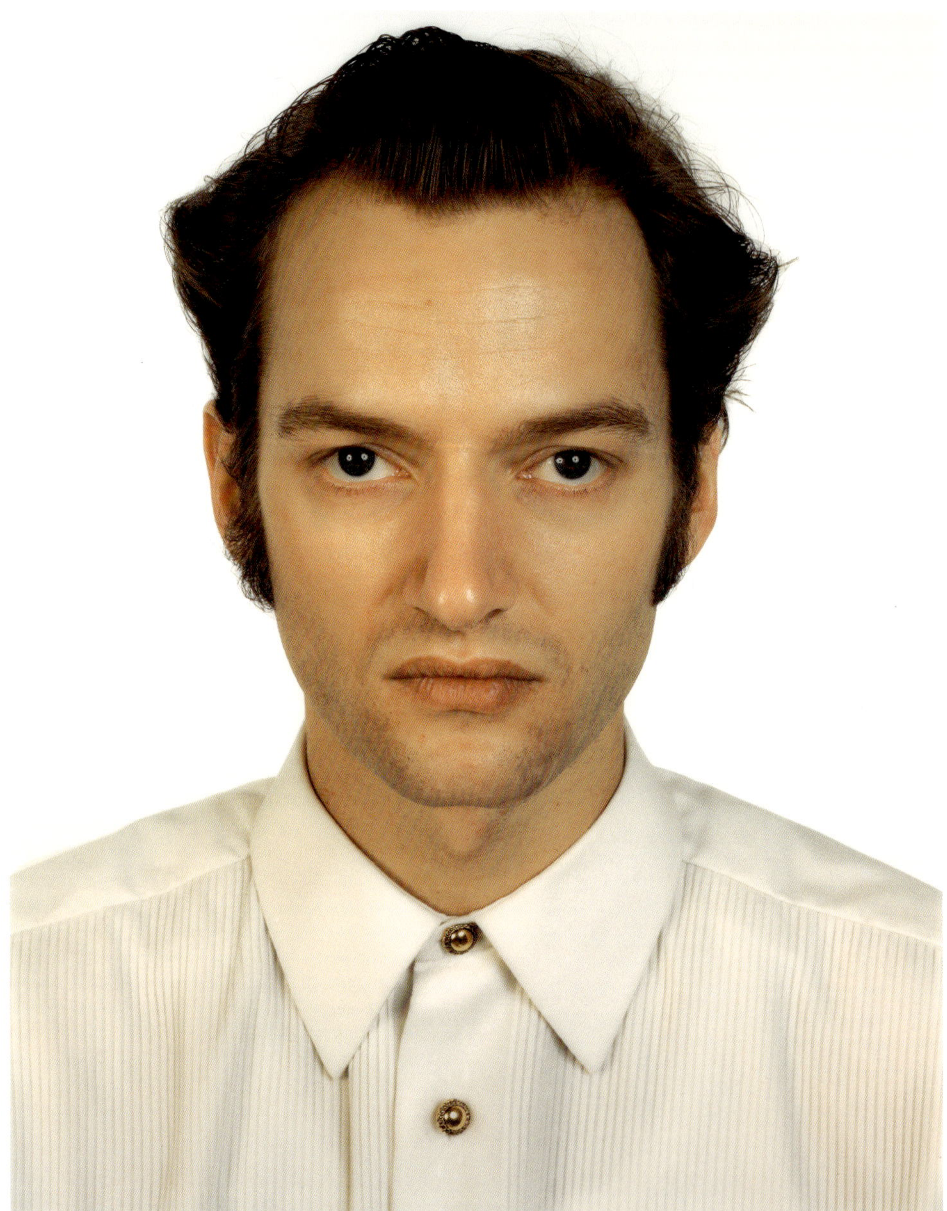

Thomas Ruff (German, born in 1958)

Portrait, 1986

Chromogenic print (Ektacolor) laminated to plexiglas

210.2 x 165.1 cm (82¾ x 65 in.)

Ernest Wadsworth Longfellow Fund 1989.51

Thomas Ruff is one of several now-famous contemporary photographers—including Andreas Gursky, Candida Höfer, and Thomas Struth—who studied under Bernd and Hilla Becher at the Düsseldorf Art Academy. This monumental image belongs to a series of distinctive color portraits of art school friends and acquaintances that he produced during the 1980s. Rather than delving into the psychology of his sitters, the artist's cool, expressionless close-ups record their features in evenly lit, minute detail against a neutral backdrop. In making these oversize photographs, which are in many ways more akin to mug shots or passport photos than artistic portraits, Ruff is interested in exploring the portrait as a photographic type and investigating the documentary role such pictures play in our already image-laden culture.

Although he too makes large-scale photographic portraits, Gary Schneider's interactive and personal approach is antithetical to Thomas Ruff's more detached style. Schneider's rather unearthly images are the result of extremely close-up, almost claustrophobic long exposures—in this case, of one of his favorite subjects, his partner John Erdman. Referred to as "durational portraits," Schneider's photographs are inspired in part by the living, breathing quality and evocative blur he admired in nineteenth-century studio portraits by artists such as Julia Margaret Cameron. To create this intimate, death mask–like portrait of Erdman, the photographer meditatively played a beam of light over his friend's face throughout a protracted sitting in the dark.

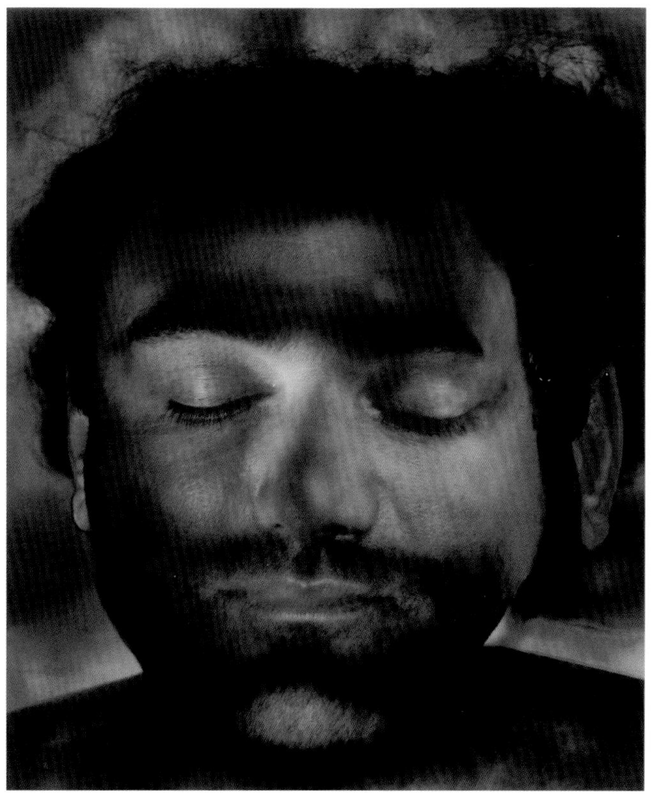

Gary Schneider (American, born in 1954)
John with His Eyes Closed, 1992
Gelatin silver print, toned
92.7 x 74.9 cm (36 ½ x 29 ½ in.)
Lee M. Friedman Fund 1996.72

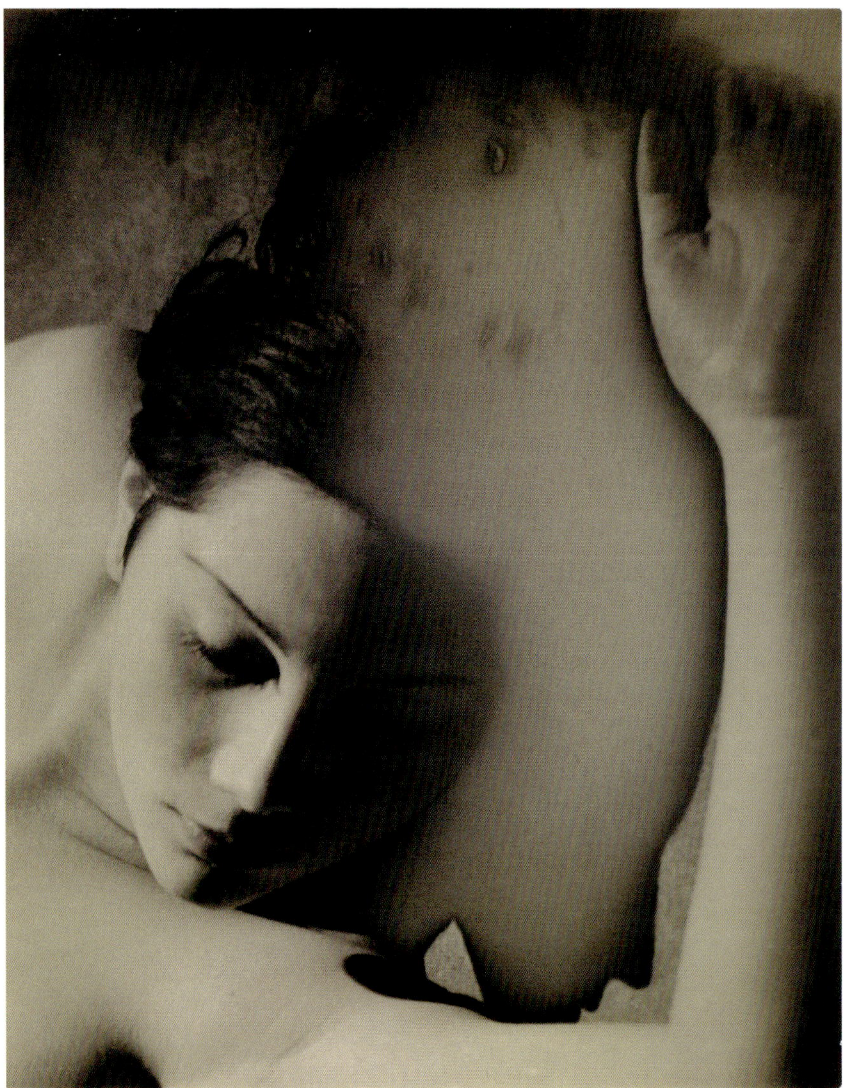

Man Ray (American, 1890–1976)

Untitled, 1932

Gelatin silver print, solarized; 29.7 x 23.1 cm (11 11/16 x 9 1/8 in.)

Graham Gund Photography Fund 1980.213

Man Ray and Ellen Auerbach, two modernist photographers who were active on both sides of the Atlantic, each created works characterized by inventive exploration of new techniques and visual effects. Born in Philadelphia and trained as a painter, Man Ray arrived in Paris in 1921 and became a member of the Surrealist circle of artists there. He took up fashion and portrait photography as a way to make a living and began to experiment with a variety of processes, including solarization—a partial reversal of tone within a print, most visible at the edges of forms, caused by momentary exposure to light during the course of normal darkroom development. Solarization was an ideal technique to capture this mysterious and hallucinatory image of the Surrealist painter and sculptor Meret Oppenheim; the glowing dark aura

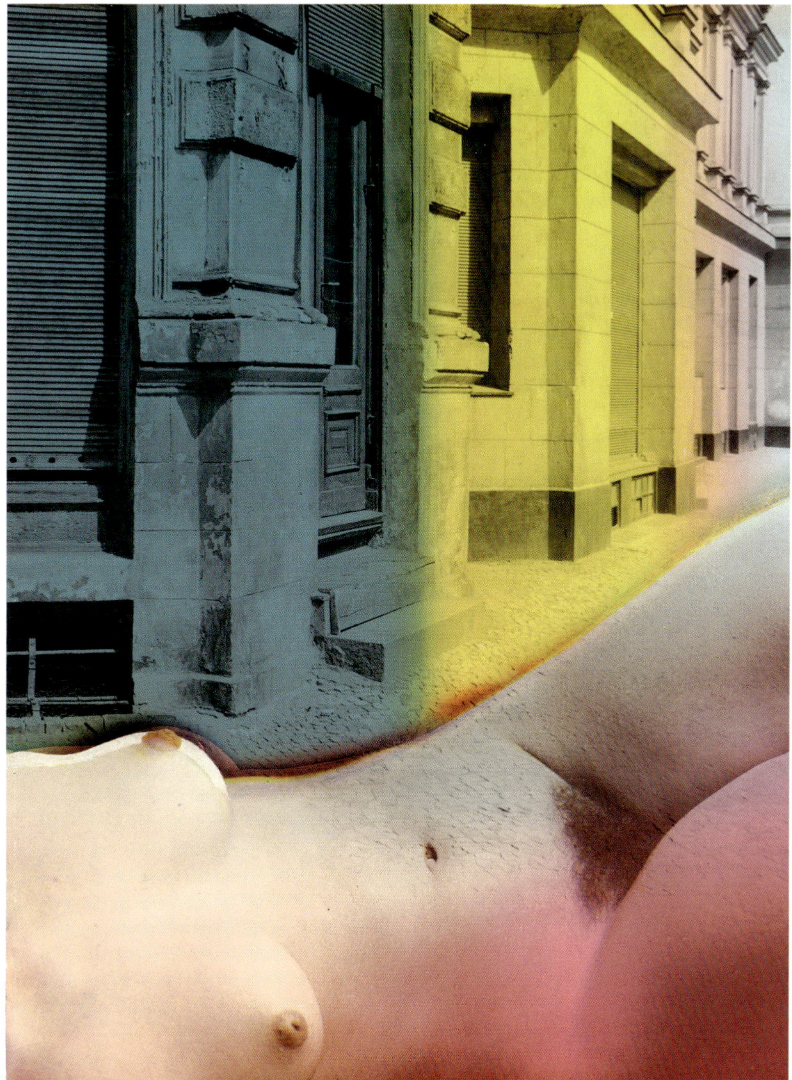

Ellen Auerbach (American, born in Germany, 1906–2004)

The Temptation of St. Anthony, about 1940

Three-color carbro print; 27.5 x 20.6 cm (10 13/16 x 8 1/8 in.)

Anonymous gift 1995.98

surrounding her head transforms her into a disembodied, dreamlike figure.

Several years later, Ellen Auerbach made this unique carbro print after fleeing Nazi Germany and eventually settling in the United States. The complex carbro process involved the meticulous layering of three different colored emulsions, which enhanced the uncanny juxtaposition of a reclining female nude and a city street in this modern interpretation of the temptation of St. Anthony. The life of the fourth-century ascetic, who was severely tested by worldly things and the weaknesses of the flesh, was a timeless subject that appealed to Auerbach and resonated with Surrealist painters, including Salvador Dalí and Max Ernst.

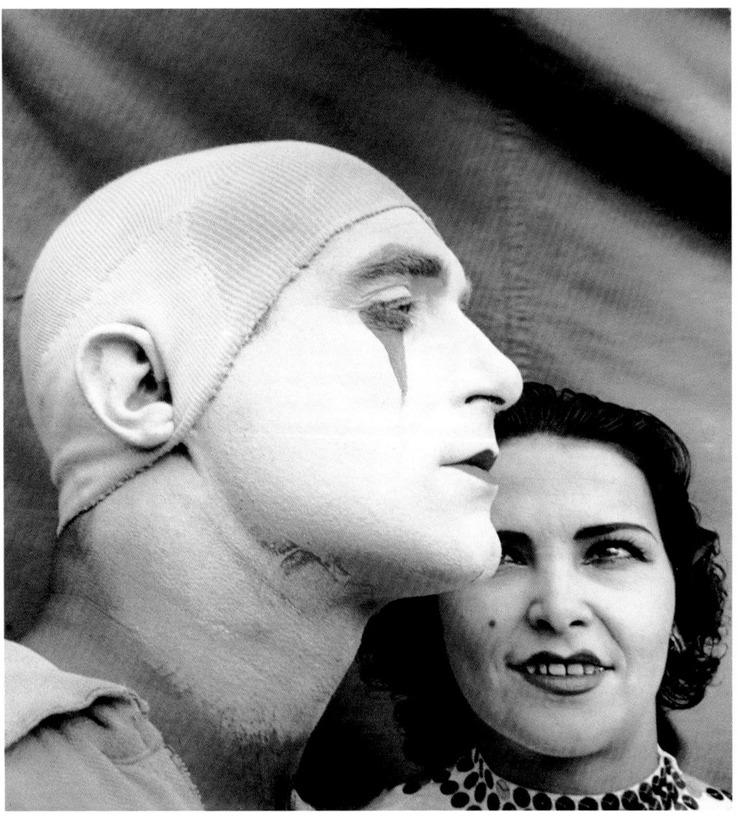

John Gutmann (American, born in Silesia, 1905–1998)

The Beautiful Clown, 1940

Gelatin silver print; 21.8 x 19.8 cm (8 ⁹⁄₁₆ x 7 ¹³⁄₁₆ in.)

Gift of Eric G. Carlson in honor of Gustav G. Carlson and Sophie M. Friedman Fund 1991.359

John Gutmann, in the United States, and August Sander, in Germany, each documented a cross-section of their respective countrymen between the wars. Born in Silesia, in what is today Poland, Gutmann immigrated to the United States in 1937, settling in San Francisco. Having worked as a photojournalist in Berlin, he was drawn to the lively social mix of his newly adopted city and was inspired to document what struck him as the exotic and unconventional aspects of American popular culture—the bustle of its street life, the ubiquitous automobile, urban graffiti, and signs. This witty pairing of a sad-eyed, painted clown and a rather predatory, heavily made-up woman is the sort of juxtaposition Gutmann particularly enjoyed, as it captured for him the "marvelous extravagance" of life in the United States.

Sander's was a much more systematic accounting of the German people that resulted in hundreds of portraits categorized by occupation and social standing. These ultimately comprised his massive book *People of the Twentieth Century*. This image of his friend Heinrich Hoerle, which emphasizes the

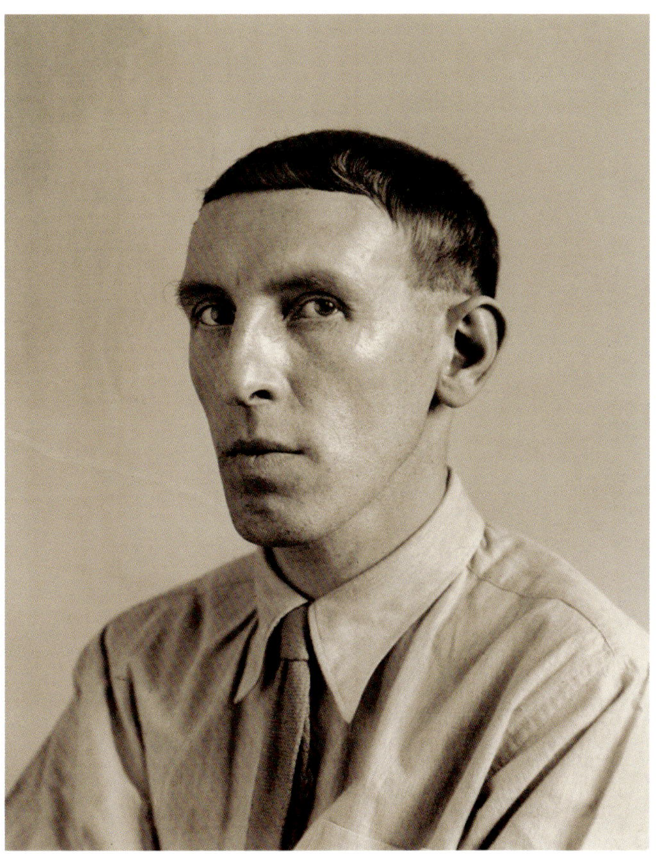

August Sander (German, 1876–1964)

Painter Heinrich Hoerle, 1928

Gelatin silver print; 29.3 x 22.4 cm (11 9/16 x 8 13/16 in.)

Sophie M. Friedman Fund 1982.151

painter's gaunt visage and wary expression, is an unusually close-up view for a photographer who favored full- or half-length poses. Produced with a large-format camera and lengthy exposures, Sander's direct, unretouched likenesses reflect a deep and nuanced understanding of Weimar culture, in contrast to Gutmann's perspective as an outsider looking in on the United States.

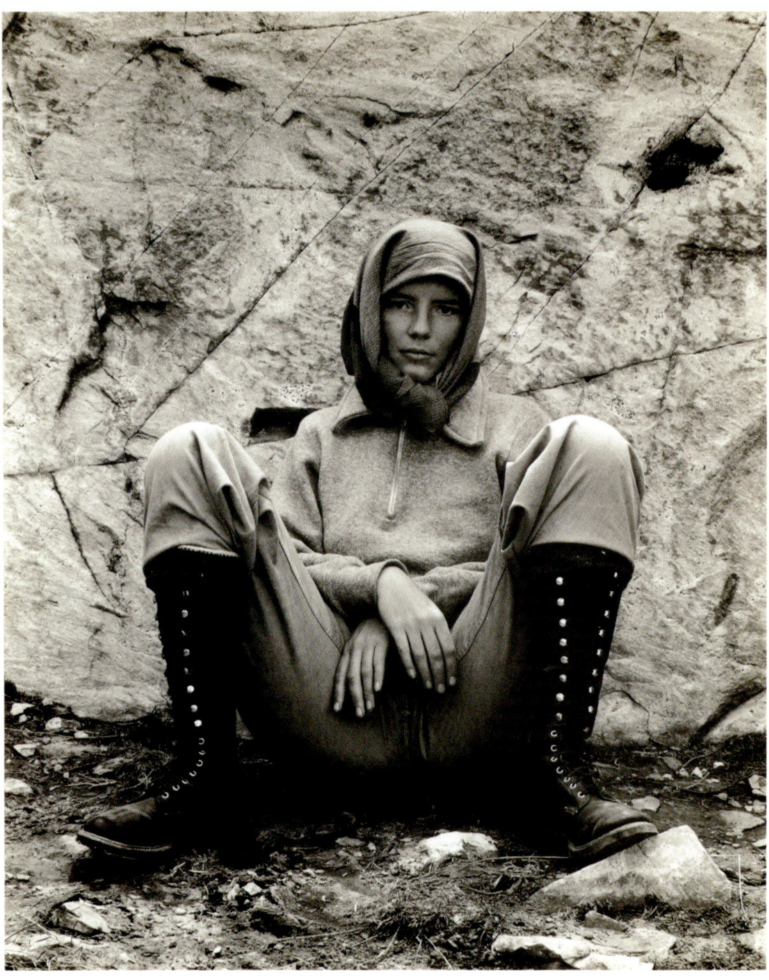

Edward Weston (American, 1886–1958)

Charis, Lake Ediza, 1937

Gelatin silver print; 24.3 x 19.3 cm (9 9/16 x 7 5/8 in.)

Gift of Saundra B. Lane in honor of Theodore E. Stebbins Jr. 2002.888

Both Edward Weston and Nicholas Nixon made revealing series of photographs of their wives that go beyond simple likeness and demonstrate the balance of power and trust inherent in human relationships. Weston's portrait of Charis Wilson at Lake Ediza, taken during a 1937 pack trip to Yosemite with Ansel Adams, is an intense and touching image of the young woman soon to become his second wife. Charis is shown seated against a vertical rock face wearing tall lace-up boots, her head swathed in a turban to ward off mosquitoes and her gaze directed at the camera with a mixture of innocence and sensuality. Weston's classic nudes of Charis from the late 1930s are some of his most highly regarded works, but this emotionally charged picture of her fully clothed is in many ways a more sensitive and moving image.

Nicholas Nixon's wife, Bebe, is similarly one of his favorite photographic subjects; he has regularly

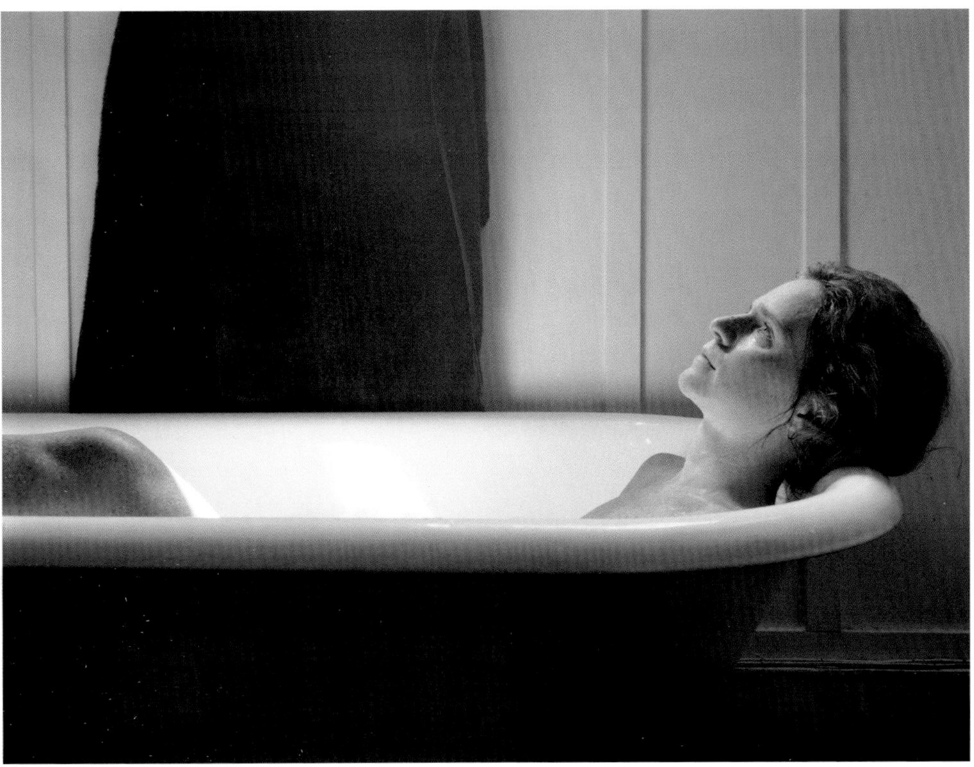

Nicholas Nixon (American, born in 1947)

Bebe, Cambridge, 1980

Gelatin silver print; 20.3 x 25.2 cm (8 x 9 15/16 in.)

Museum purchase through funds provided by the National Endowment for the Arts and Richard L. Menschel, Béla T. Kalman, Judge and Mrs. Matthew Brown, Mildred S. Lee, and Barbara M. Marshall 1990.80

focused his large 8 x 10 camera on her since 1970, a year before they were married. His portraits of her, including this one in the bathtub, are never accidental or casual, and one senses in them the depth of their long relationship and their great respect for each other. Nixon has here transformed a simple, quotidian moment into a spectacular study of glowing light on Bebe's pale, serene face as she reclines in the tub and stares up at the ceiling, seemingly lost in thought.

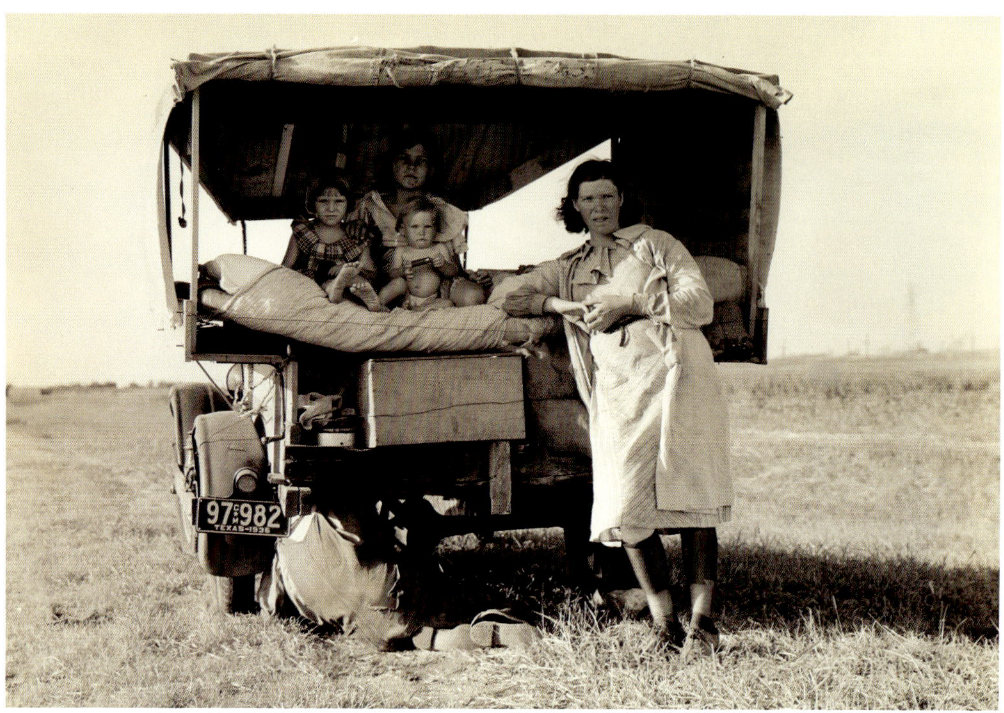

Dorothea Lange (American, 1895–1965)

Migrant Family, Texas, 1936

Gelatin silver print; 21.8 x 30.6 cm (8 9/16 x 12 1/16 in.)

Sophie M. Friedman Fund 1979.15

Dorothea Lange and Gordon Parks shared a deep-seated belief in photography as a tool for social change. Almost a generation older than Parks, Lange was hired in the mid-1930s by the Farm Security Administration (FSA) to document the plight of the poor and dispossessed during the Depression. Her empathetic response to her subjects set her work apart from many of her contemporaries. This image depicts a migrant family from Texas trying to escape the drought-stricken Dust Bowl. Telling details are captured in Lange's characteristically sensitive style, including the shotgun shell held by the solemn child, the mother's weary stance and bandaged legs, and the father's hunched form as he crawls under the broken-down truck to repair it.

Gordon Parks credited FSA artists such as Lange and Ben Shahn with inspiring him to go into the field of photography during the 1930s. Completely self-taught, Parks dedicated much of his long career to recording the lives of his fellow African Americans, discovering that the camera could be a powerful "weapon against poverty and racism." In the 1940s, Parks began working for picture magazines, including *Vogue* and *Life*, tackling such wide-ranging subjects as Harlem gangs, Paris fashion shows, the slums of Rio de Janeiro, and iconic black figures—Malcolm X, Muhammad Ali, and Eldridge Cleaver, among others. His sympathy for the backbreaking labor of menial jobs is reflected in this photograph of a young woman bent over her work in a rundown tenement, looking older than her years.

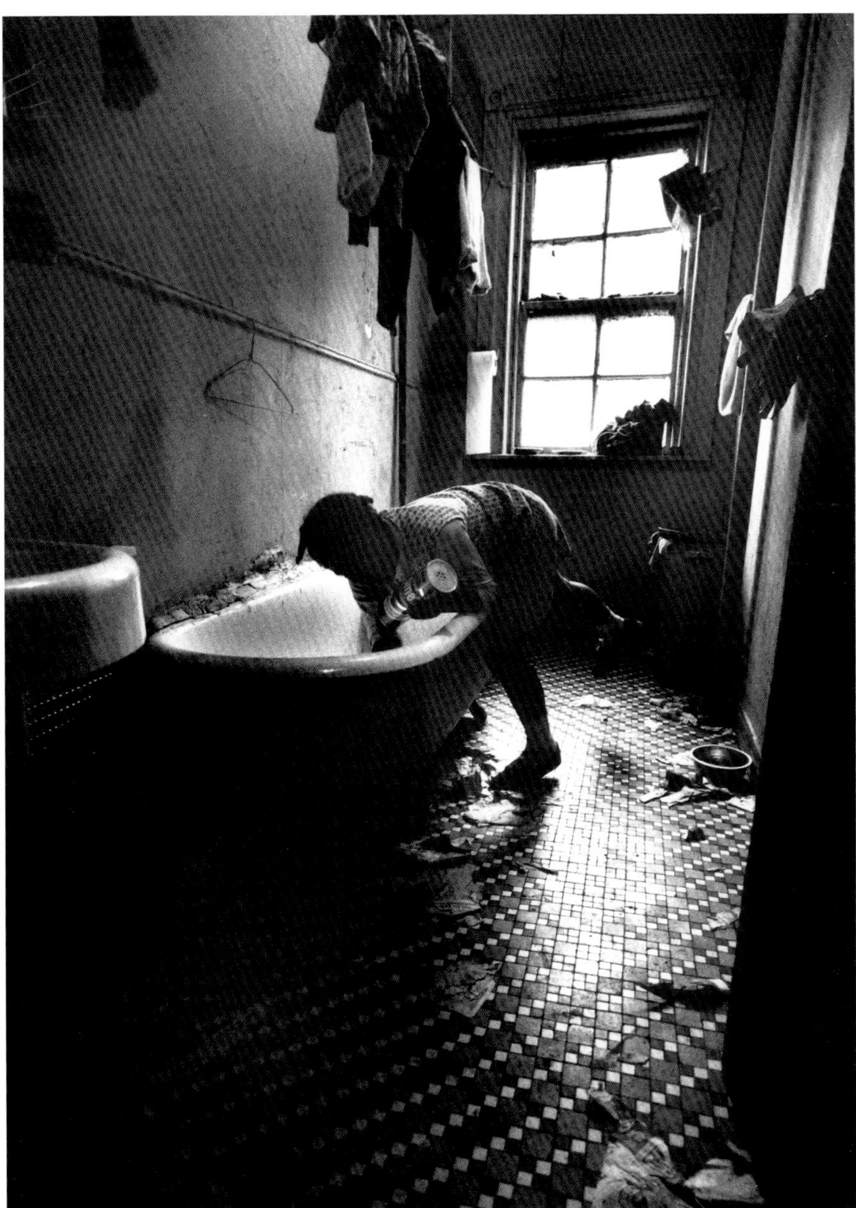

Gordon Parks (American, 1912–2006)

Rose Cleaning Bathtub, 1967

Gelatin silver print; 33.8 x 23.7 cm (13 5/16 x 9 5/16 in.)

Sophie M. Friedman Fund 2002.114

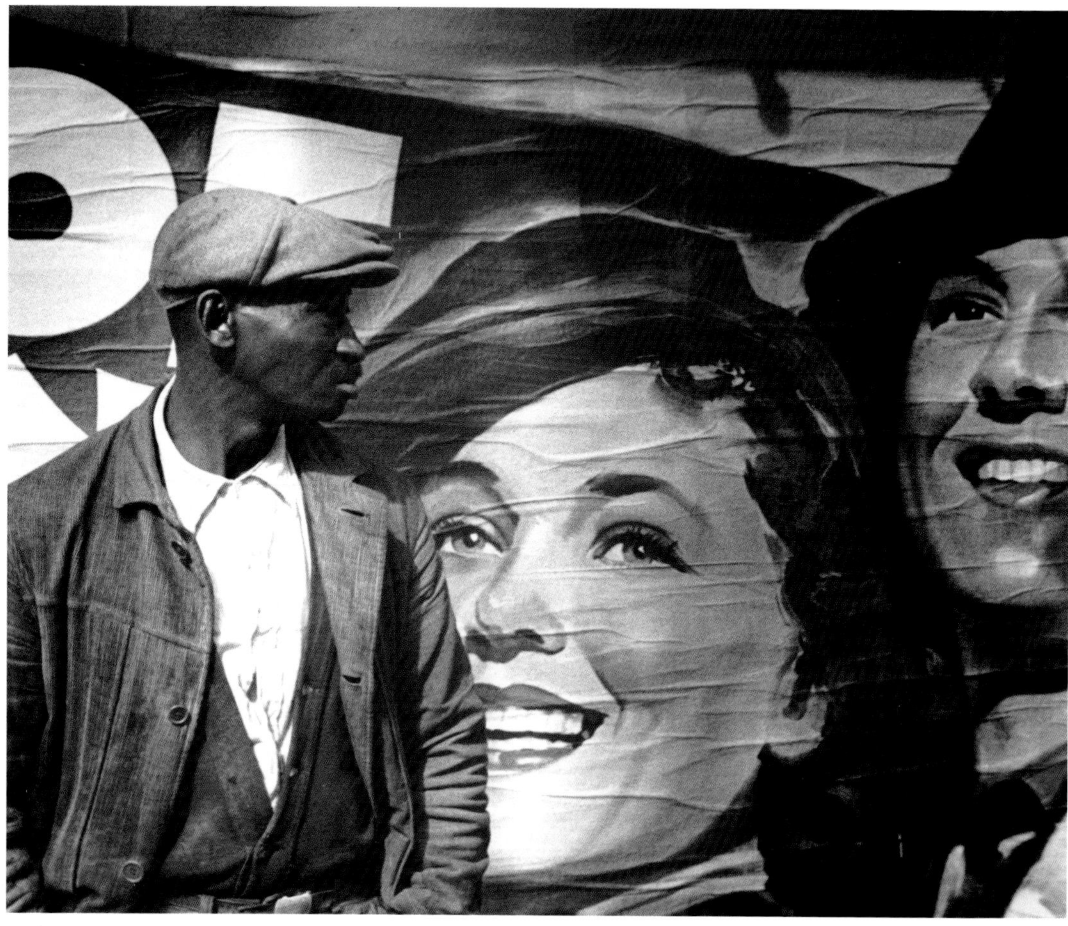

Walker Evans (American, 1903–1975)

Man and Movie Poster, New Orleans, about 1935–36

Gelatin silver print; 17.2 x 22.3 cm (6¾ x 8¾ in.)

Sophie M. Friedman Fund 1987.500

Although their goals were very different, photographers Walker Evans and Clarence John Laughlin shared a fascination with the people and culture of the American South. When Evans was hired by Roosevelt's Resettlement Administration in 1935, he embarked on one of the most productive and creative periods in his career. He made several trips to the South, where he documented the lives of the rural poor as well as residents of cities, always drawn to vernacular artifacts of American society such as urban signs and roadside billboards. This direct, uninflected image powerfully contrasts the careworn look of the black man and the cheerful smiles of the huge white faces on the weathered movie poster behind him. It was probably shot with a right-angle viewfinder, which Evans sometimes used to take

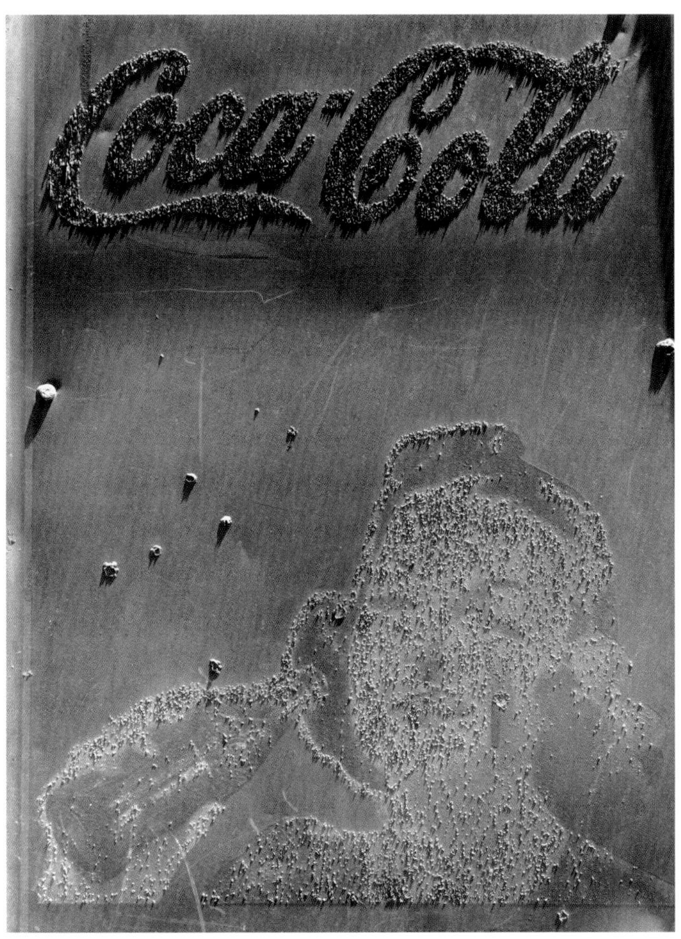

Clarence John Laughlin (American, 1905–1985)

The Spectre of Coca-Cola, 1962, printed in 1973

Gelatin silver print, ferrotyped; 34.3 x 24.8 cm (13 ½ x 9 ¾ in.)

Sophie M. Friedman Fund 1983.155

revealing pictures of people who were unaware they were being photographed.

Laughlin's career, which spanned the 1930s through the 1960s, was also inextricably entwined with the South, particularly the city of New Orleans. Like Evans, Laughlin was fascinated by the sometimes disorienting aspects of everyday things, in this case the spectral image encountered in an old Coca-Cola sign. The effect of the raking light falling across flecks of rust on the corroded tin sign conjured up for the photographer a ghostly image of a more benign past. Although Laughlin's sensibility is modernist, his work is imbued with a characteristically southern penchant for the spiritual and the poetic, the decaying and the surreal, which he shared with writers such as William Faulkner and Carson McCullers.

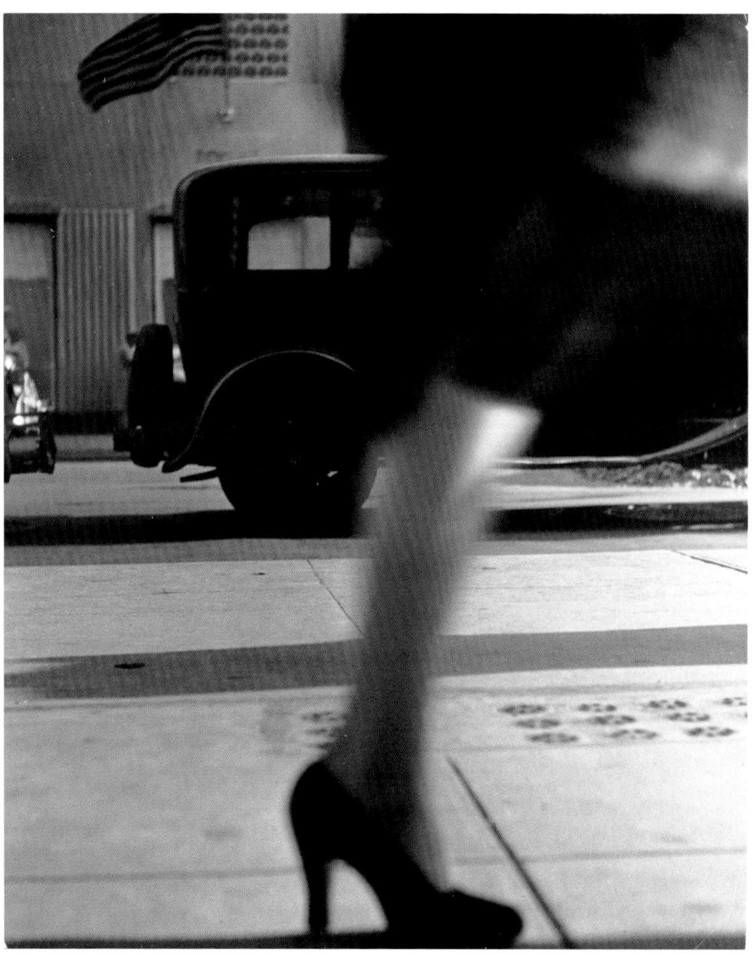

Lisette Model (American, born in Austria, 1901–1983)
Running Legs, New York, about 1941
Gelatin silver print; 34.3 x 26.9 cm (13 ½ x 10 $^{9}/_{16}$ in.)
Sophie M. Friedman Fund 1980.453

Lisette Model came to the United States in 1938, having previously studied music in her native Austria and worked as a photographer in Vienna, Paris, and Nice. She quickly fell in love with New York City and set out to capture its glamorous bustle and energy with her handheld camera. Model took hundreds of photographs of the street life and storefronts of her adopted city, reveling in its fleeting reflections and constant state of flux. Shot from a very low angle, this softly blurred image of the legs of a woman in high heels and an American flag flying across the street is a striking example of the many sidewalk pictures Model made during the early 1940s.

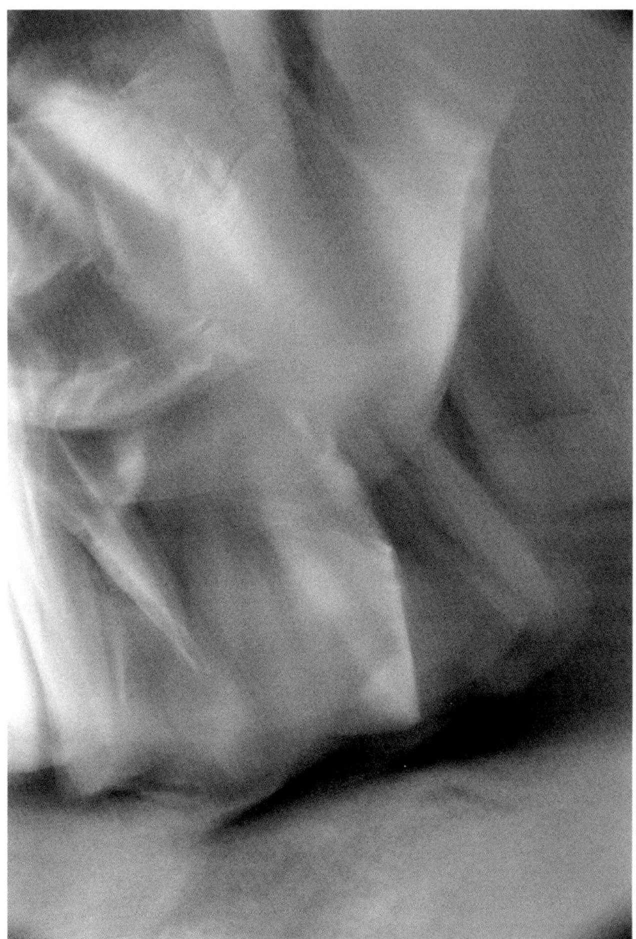

Petah Coyne (American, born in 1953)

Untitled, from the *Bridal Series*, 2001

Gelatin silver print; 101.6 x 76.2 cm (40 x 30 in.)

Horace W. Goldsmith Foundation Fund for Photography

2002.391

Like Lisette Model, contemporary artist Petah Coyne is attracted to blur. Although best known as a sculptor, in 2001 she made a series of grainy, soft-focus photographs of brides and debutantes. This large-format image of the frothy folds of a wedding gown seems an unusual choice for a feminist artist in her fifties, but Coyne's photographs have more to do with Charles Dickens's Miss Havisham left at the altar than with any youthful notions of love. She creates on the run, spinning and jumping and chasing her subjects, all the while clicking the camera shutter. Her ephemeral and fragmentary photographs are closely related to her sculptures, which are sometimes fabricated out of layer upon layer of melted white wax.

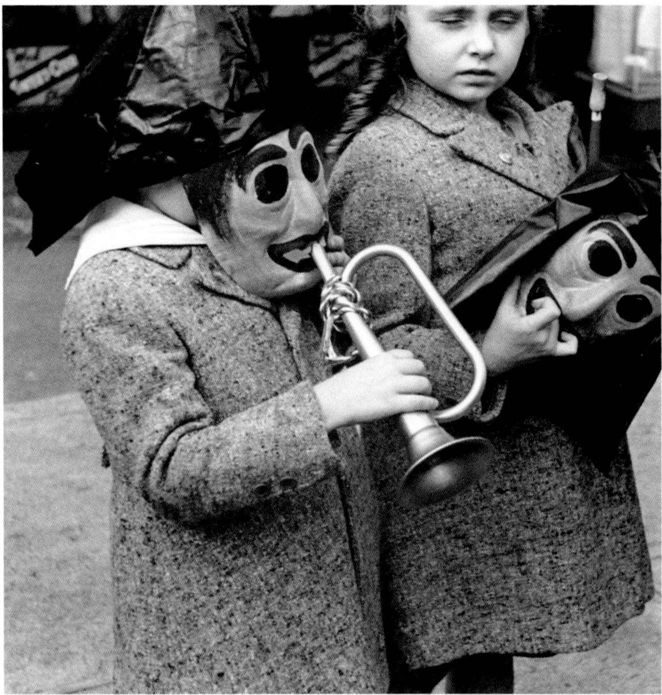

Helen Levitt (American, born in 1918)

New York, 1942

Gelatin silver print; 17.6 x 18.4 cm (6 15/16 x 7 1/4 in.)

Sophie M. Friedman Fund 1994.24

Perhaps not surprisingly, children—whether candid and unselfconscious or carefully posed in their Sunday best—have long been popular subjects, for women photographers in particular. Beginning in the 1930s, Helen Levitt wandered throughout New York City capturing the spirited play of children on the sidewalks of the poorer neighborhoods of Harlem and the Lower East Side. She worked as unobtrusively as possible with her handheld Leica, sometimes using a right-angle viewfinder to capture her subjects unawares as they took part in their imaginary games and masquerades. Shooting in both black-and-white and color, Levitt shared with her contemporaries Ben Shahn and Walker Evans a keen sense of timing and an intuitive ability to catch the telling gestures and postures of people interacting with one another in public spaces.

Children are the focus of Loretta Lux's contemporary photographs as well. Originally trained as a painter, Lux creates digitally manipulated portraits that emphasize the strange and unsettling aspects of childhood and make her sitters appear either very young or venerable and wise beyond their years. By slightly distorting the size of the children's heads and bodies, emphasizing their pale skin and pastel clothing, and focusing on their often somber expressions, the artist makes it clear that her photographs are anything but straightforward likenesses. In fact, Lux refers to them as "imaginary portraits" and claims that their disquieting appearance is meant to reflect the mysterious blend of vulnerability and self-awareness so characteristic of youth.

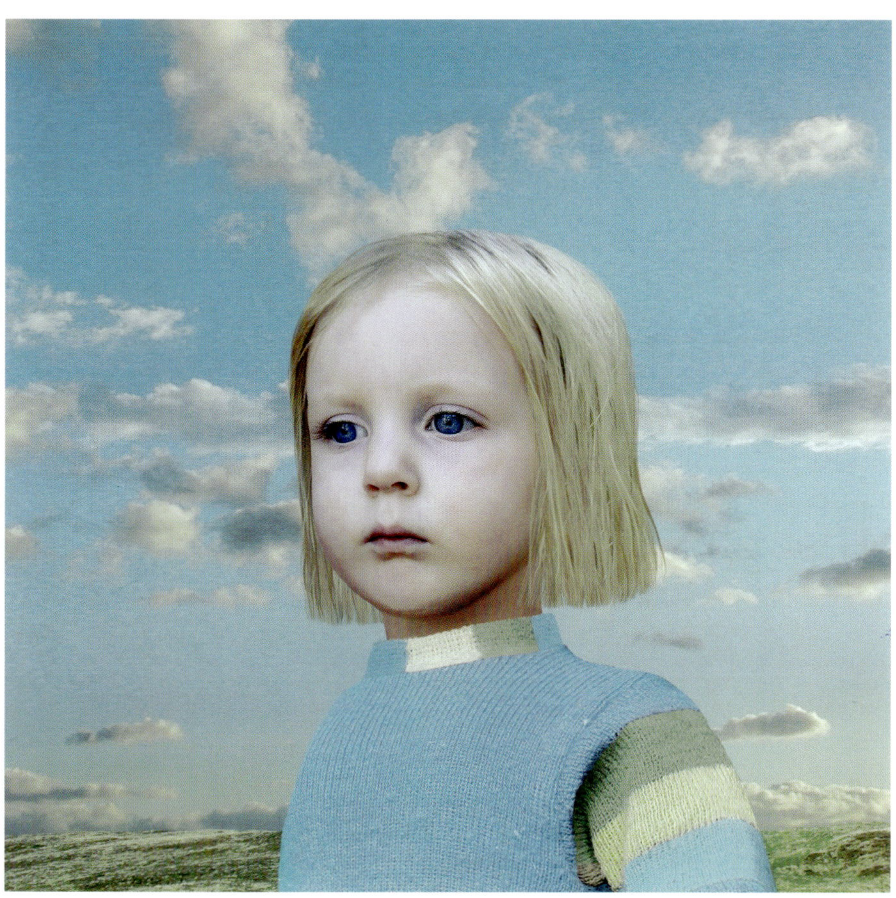

Loretta Lux (German, born in 1969)

Dorothea, 2001

Ilfochrome print; 50 x 50 cm (19 11/16 x 19 11/16 in.)

Horace W. Goldsmith Foundation Fund for Photography 2004.251

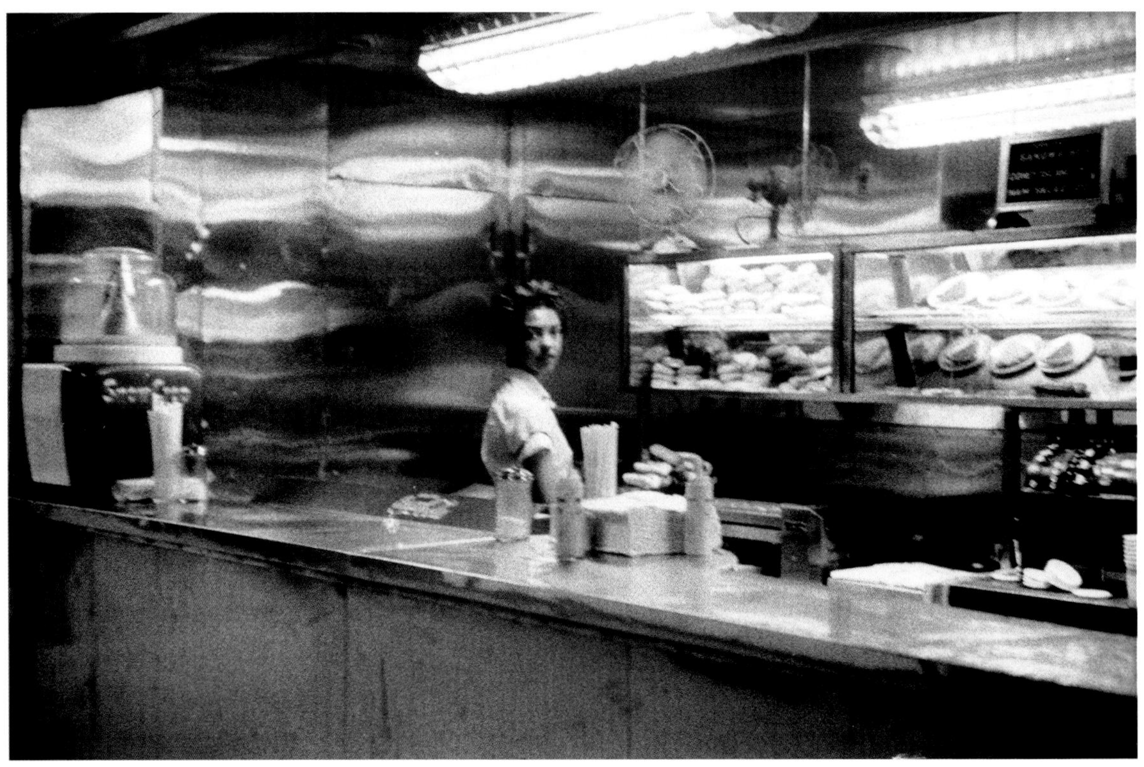

Robert Frank (American, born in Switzerland, 1924)
Coffee Shop, Railway Station, Indianapolis, 1956
Gelatin silver print; 22.3 x 33 cm (8 3/4 x 13 in.)
Sophie M. Friedman Fund 1980.225

Swiss-born photographer Robert Frank's book *The Americans* (1958) was a difficult pill for the postwar-era public to swallow. The book, which he described as a "visual study of a civilization," portrayed a society very different from the one touted in the advertisements and picture magazines of the day. As the first foreign photographer to receive a Guggenheim Fellowship, Frank crisscrossed the United States in the mid-1950s armed with a small handheld camera and high-speed film, recording his impressions in dark, grainy photographs such as this one of a railway coffee shop. The whirring fan, the glare of the fluorescent lights, and the shy glance of the young waitress suggest the pervasive loneliness and ennui that for Frank typified the United States during the cold war.

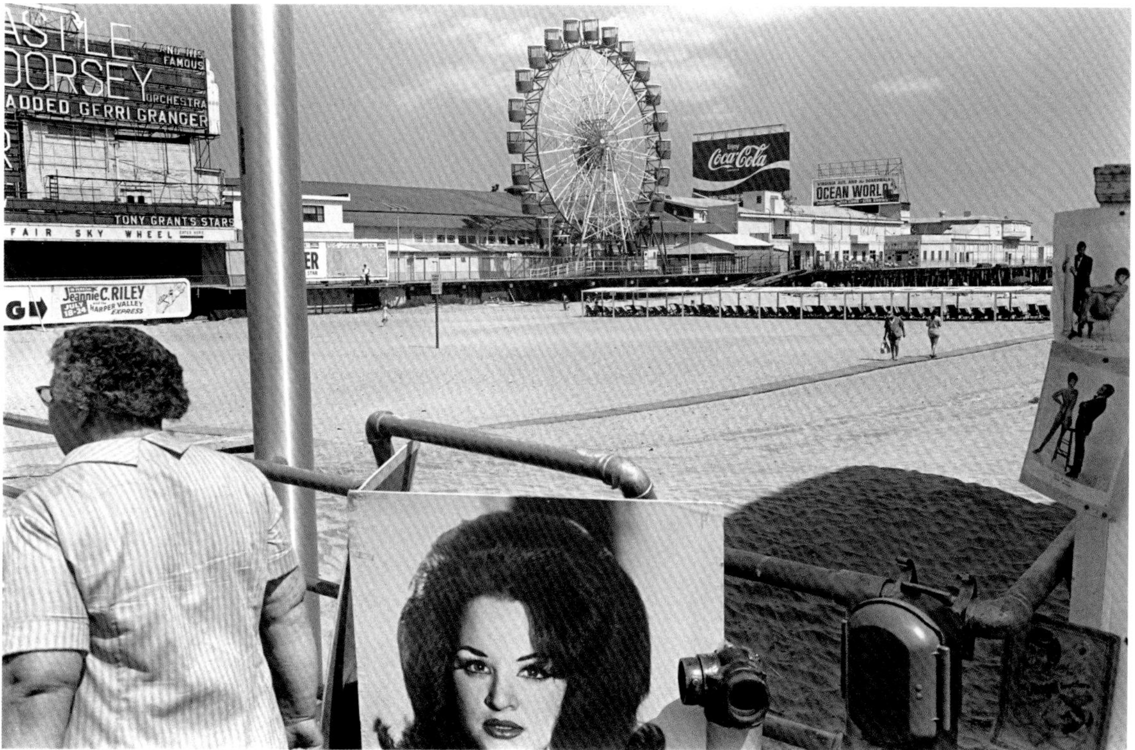

Lee Friedlander (American, born in 1934)

Atlantic City, New Jersey, 1971

Gelatin silver print; 19 x 28.4 cm (7 ½ x 11 3/16 in.)

A. Shuman Collection 1983.262

Lee Friedlander, like many who came of age in the 1950s, fell under the spell of photographers of the American social landscape who had come before him, especially Walker Evans and Robert Frank. Friedlander's dispassionate approach to his complex, yet everyday subjects is enhanced by the tendency of his wide-angle lens to compress each picture's disparate elements into an often uneasy alliance. The eccentric cropping and layering in this image of Atlantic City creates a kaleidoscopic effect in which billboards and photographs vie for our attention, including a picture of a woman whose dark bouffant hairdo perfectly echoes the shape of the Ferris wheel in the background.

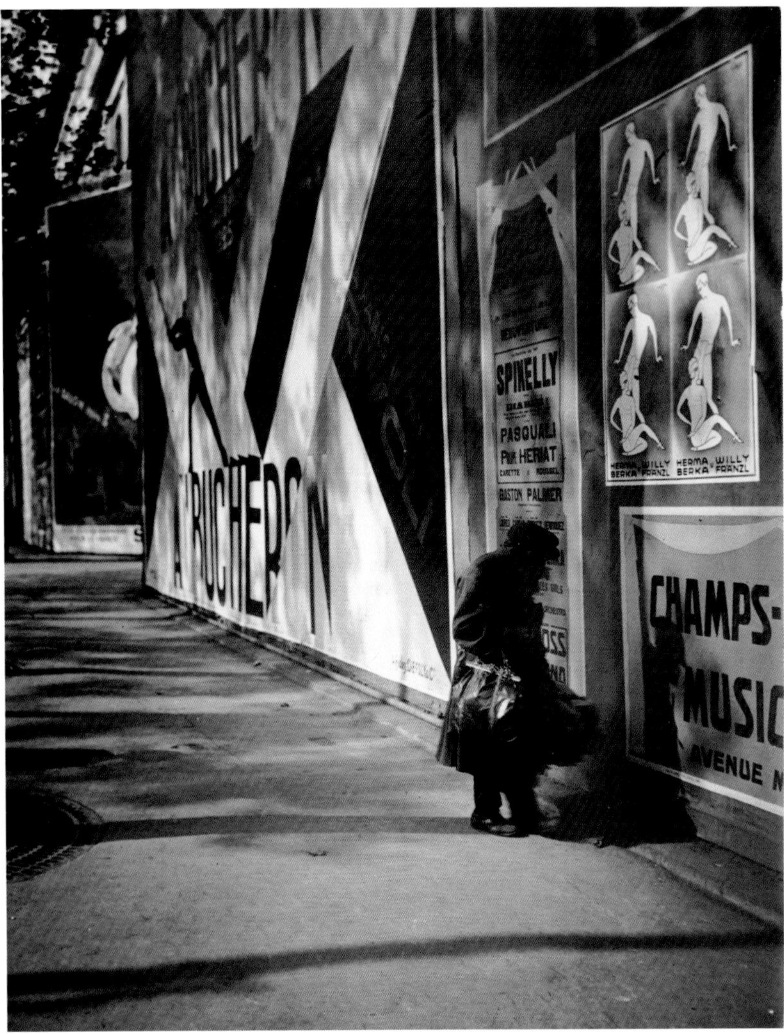

André Kertész (American, born in Hungary, 1894–1985)

Clochard and Posters, Paris, about 1926–27

Gelatin silver print; 23.6 x 17.9 cm (9 5/16 x 7 1/16 in.)

Sophie M. Friedman Fund 1981.143

Street photography is often characterized by grainy, blurred images seemingly caught on the run, but André Kertész and Michael Spano transform the flux and energy of the city into artfully composed and beautifully rendered images. Kertész arrived in Paris from Hungary in 1925, hoping to find work in an established studio or with one of the new photographically illustrated magazines. When he was not on commission, Kertész took to walking the streets of Paris, in all different seasons and at all times of day, as a way to discover the distinctive poetry of the city seen through the camera lens. Recorded as if by the glance of a casual observer, this street scene contrasts the elegant curves and repeating shapes of the

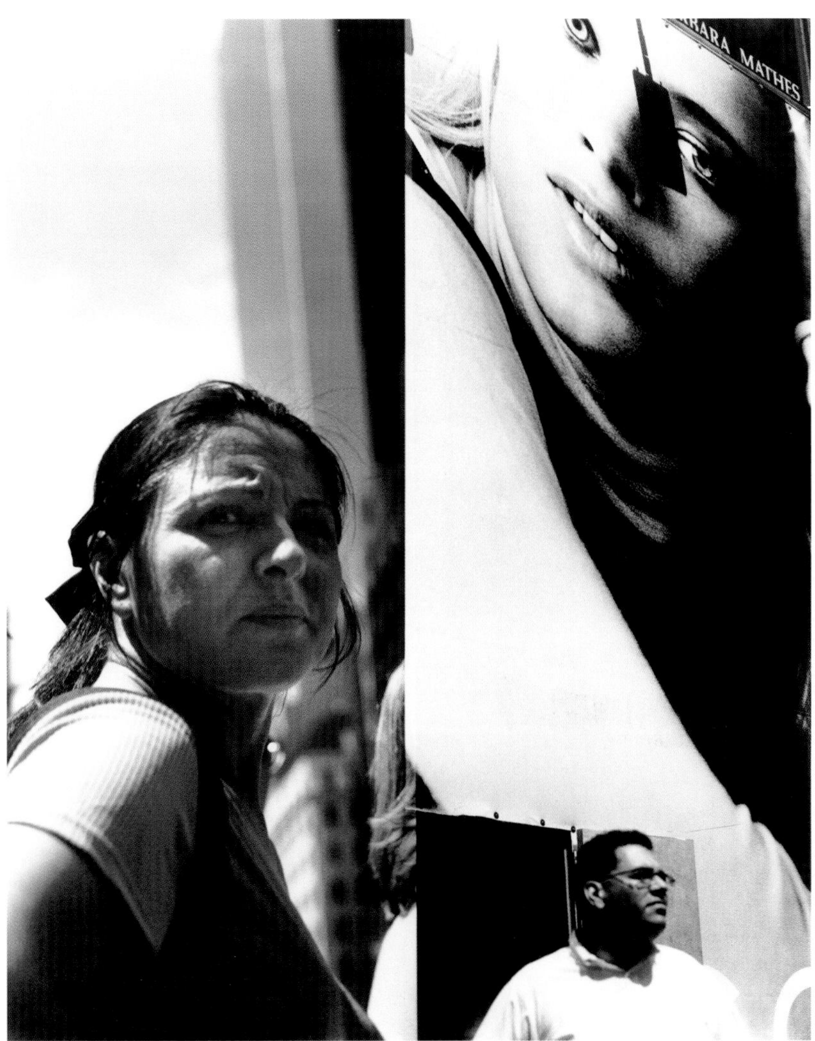

Michael Spano (American, born in 1949)

Untitled, from the *Diptych Series*, 1999

Gelatin silver print; 90 x 70.5 cm (35 3/8 x 27 13/16 in.)

Horace W. Goldsmith Foundation Fund for Photography 2000.1023

figures in the posters with the dark, hunched form of the homeless clochard standing on the sidewalk.

Michael Spano's views of contemporary New York City are created in the camera, rather than found on the street. Spano produces diptychs like this one by combining two separate exposures, taken at different times and from varying perspectives, on a single sheet of film. For this example, he juxtaposed an image of a blonde model smiling down from a billboard with another shot of a young female pedestrian squinting into the sun. Spano's technique leads the viewer to visually combine the two halves of the picture, in the process suggesting the dynamic and fragmentary encounters typical of a busy New York intersection.

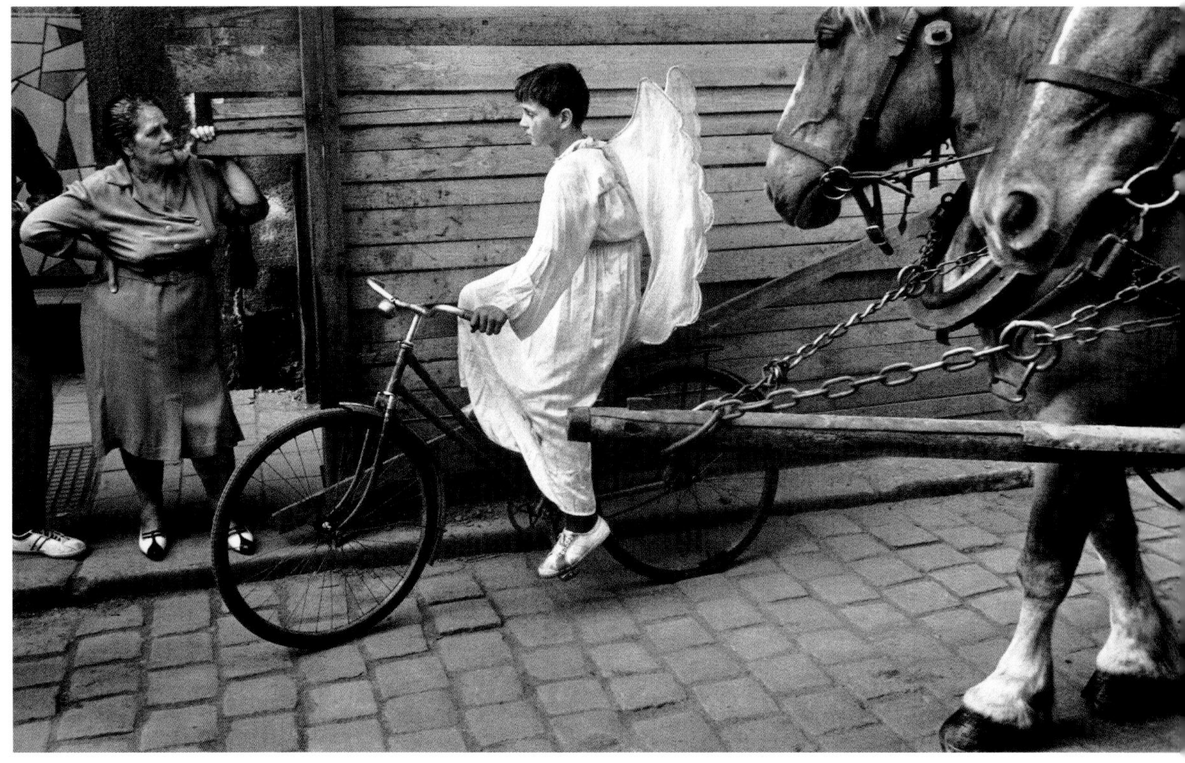

Josef Koudelka (Czechoslovakian, born in 1938)

Czechoslovakia, 1967

Gelatin silver print; 22.9 x 35.6 cm (9 x 14 in.)

Polaroid Foundation Purchase Fund 1982.160

The most intriguing photojournalists are those, like Josef Koudelka and James Nachtwey, whose work conveys deeply felt ideals and a compassion for the causes they cover. During the early 1960s, Koudelka began an extended documentary project focusing on the lives of gypsies, at first in his native Czechoslovakia and later in Romania, Ireland, Spain, and Portugal. His grainy, unsentimental black-and-white images typically portray his subjects in the context of their families and their religious faith. Koudelka sympathized with the disenfranchised state of these "outsiders" and often photographed them arrayed within shallow, stagelike spaces, as in this enigmatic image. The odd juxtaposition of an old woman, a horse-drawn cart, and a beautiful youth (presumably costumed for a church pageant) is characteristic of Koudelka's pictures, which ask more questions than they answer.

American photographer James Nachtwey, like Koudelka, was a member of the Magnum photo agency. As a young man, Nachtwey was inspired to become a photojournalist after experiencing the power of the Vietnam War and Civil Rights Movement images produced during the 1960s. His specialty became the documentation of strife and conflict all

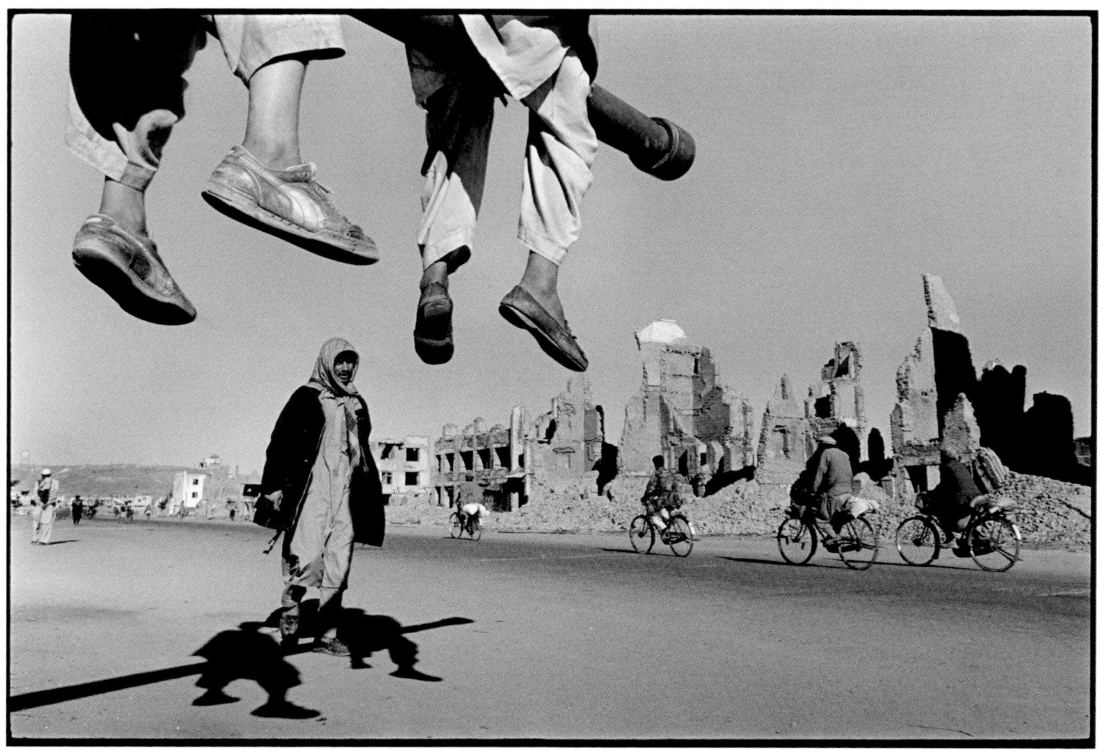

James Nachtwey (American, born in 1948)

Kabul, Afghanistan, 1996

Gelatin silver print; 32.7 x 47.9 cm (12 7/8 x 18 7/8 in.)

Horace W. Goldsmith Foundation Fund for Photography 2000.667

over the world, whether in Northern Ireland, Bosnia, the Sudan, Iraq, or Afghanistan. Nachtwey thinks of his photographs as testimonies to the horrors of war he has witnessed and is particularly drawn to record the impact of strife on children. In this beautifully composed but disturbing image, young boys' legs dangle above a bleak Kabul street from their perch atop an abandoned tank.

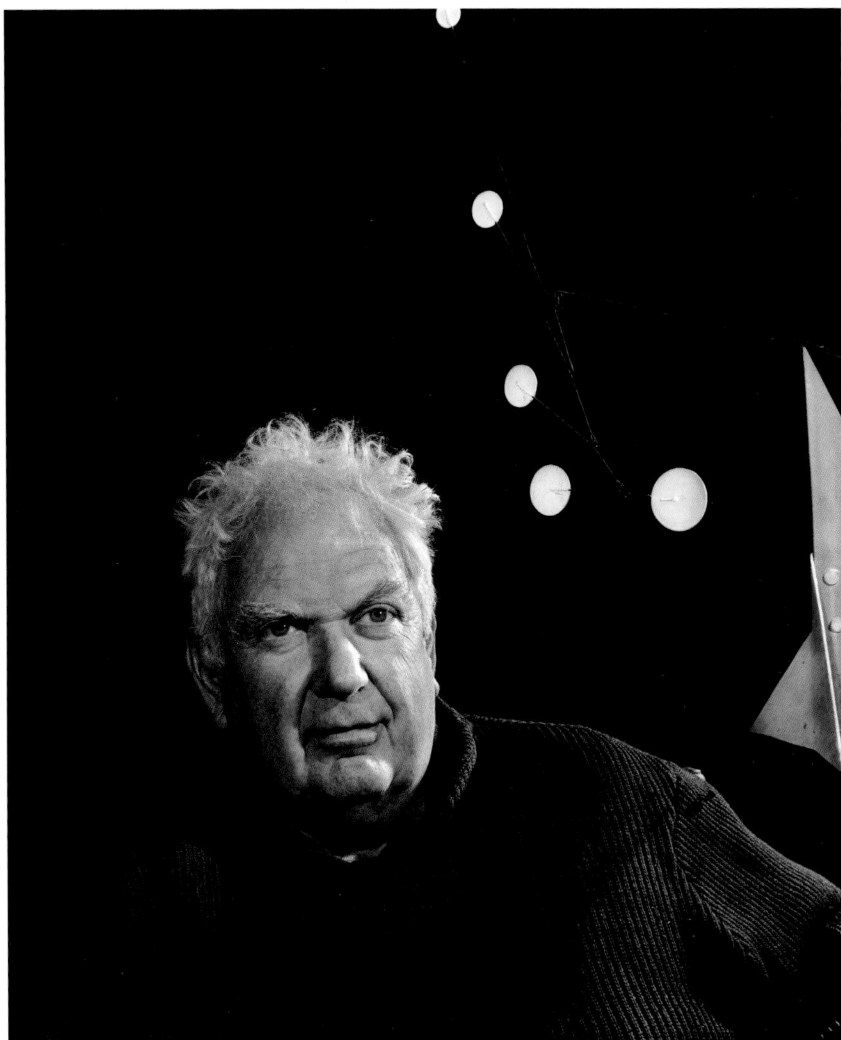

Yousuf Karsh (Canadian, born in Turkish Armenia, 1908–2002)

Alexander Calder, 1965

Gelatin silver print; 31.5 x 25.4 cm (16 ½ x 13 ¾ in.)

Gift of Estrellita and Yousuf Karsh 1998.327

Yousuf Karsh began his career in photography as an apprentice to the Boston studio photographer John Garo. Very early, he determined that his goal was to portray the famous people of his day and to transmit the idea of greatness and genius, as well as the individuality of his sitters. Bold use of light and dark contrasts augments the power of his portraits, and large negatives give them a crisp presence. His subjects typically dominate the foreground and have heroic monumentality. Here, Alexander Calder is shown with his sculpture. The metal disks and star shape stand out against the darkness like a heavenly constellation, while the artist's head seems to float in space like a rugged planet.

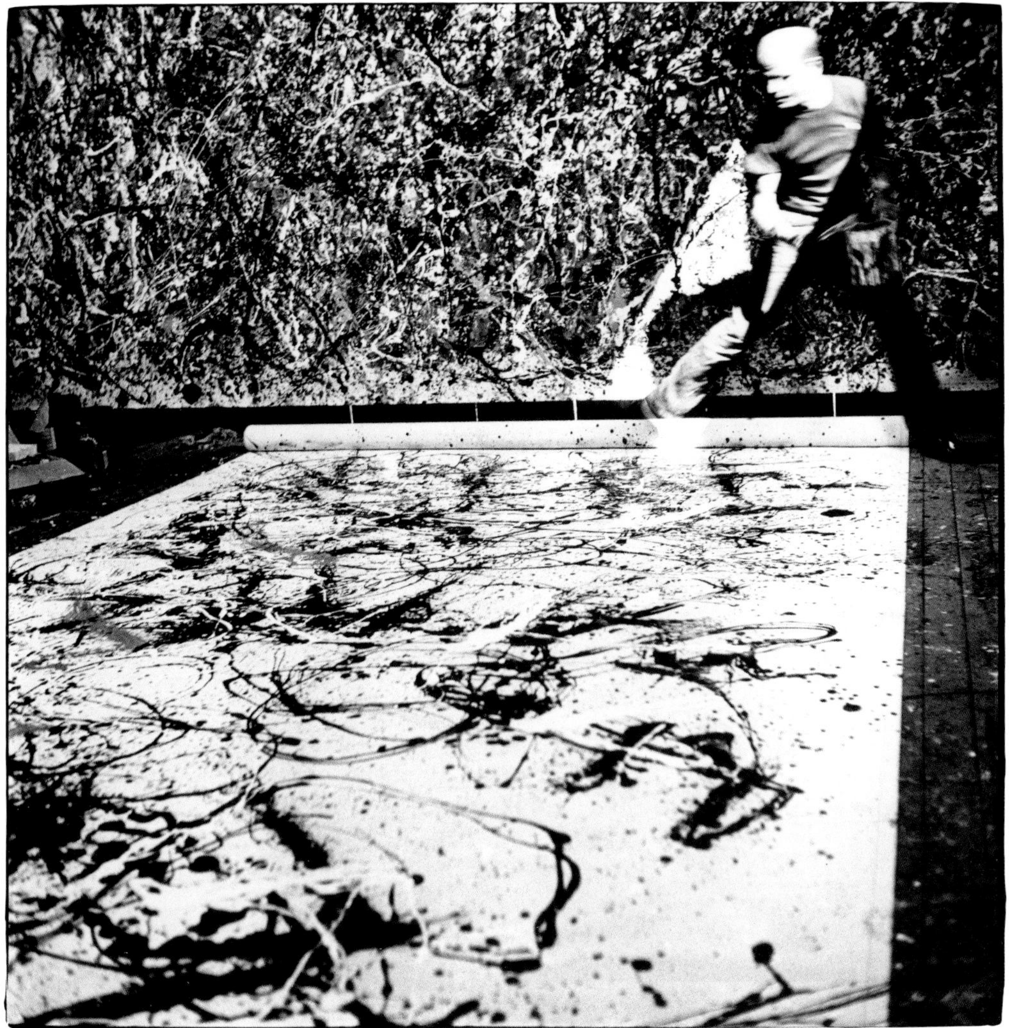

Hans Namuth (American, born in Germany, 1915–1990)

Jackson Pollock Painting, 1950

Gelatin silver print; 57 x 40.6 cm (22 7/16 x 16 in.)

Gift of Mildred and Herbert Lee 1980.258

In 1950, Hans Namuth made a series of photographs of Jackson Pollock painting that was of seminal importance in educating the public and artists alike about Pollock's revolutionary new style. Images showing Pollock stepping into, out of, and around his canvas, flinging paint with bold gestures, clarified and validated the process of "action painting" as a creative act. This example reveals Pollock's total physical and mental involvement in his art. The painter strides through a stream of sunlight as he circles his canvas, his blurred form visually confused with his work by light and dark contrasts. Unconscious of the photographer, Pollock is literally in his painting, embodying the kinetic power of his artwork.

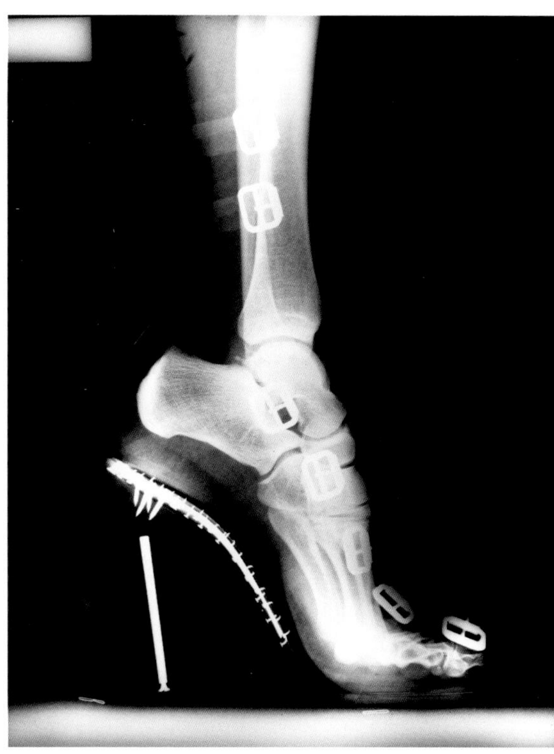

Helmut Newton (German, 1920–2004)
High-Heeled Boot by Karl Lagerfeld, Monte Carlo, 1995
Gelatin silver print from an X-ray negative
60.5 x 49.8 cm (23 13/16 x 19 5/8 in.)
John H. and Ernestine A. Payne Fund 2006.1862

The photographing of fashion for promotional purposes came into being around the turn of the twentieth century, when the printing of camera images alongside text became feasible. Since then, fashion photographers have created dazzling advertisements of seductive glamour. The most memorable contributors to this field have usually managed not only to satisfy clients' directives but also to imbue their work with a personal style.

Helmut Newton, who was born in Germany and was based for many years in Paris, became well known in the 1970s for images that convey a provocative, voyeuristic objectification of women. He used the X-ray, a tool generally associated with medical examinations, to make this rendering of a high-heeled buckled boot. Through the X-ray, the photographer created an eye-catching representation and a seemingly clinical, as well as sardonic, comment on the lengths to which women are willing to go to appear alluring.

The American photographer Herb Ritts produced a body of work in the 1980s and 1990s that seems to embody the outdoor lifestyle and glamour of the southern California beautiful set. This photograph, taken at El Mirage Dry Lake in California, appeared on the cover of Italian designer Gianni Versace's September 1990 catalogue and incorporates a formalism and contemporary sensuality characteristic of Ritts's aesthetic. Like Newton's X-ray image, Ritts's photograph appeals through its boldly contrasting lights and darks.

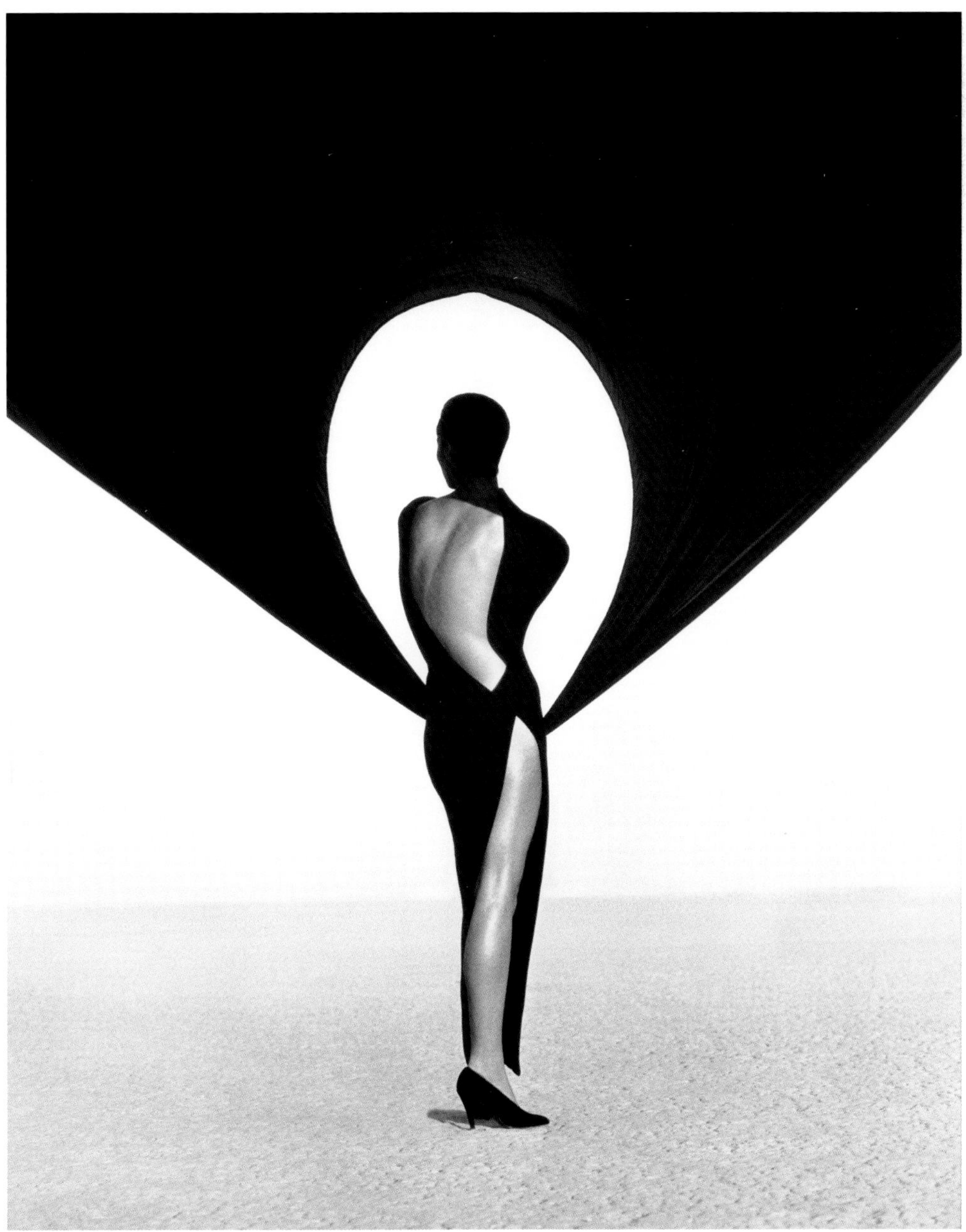

Herb Ritts (American, 1952–2002)

Versace Dress, Back View, El Mirage, 1990

Gelatin silver print

137.2 x 109.2 cm (54 x 43 in.)

Gift of Herb Ritts 2000.854

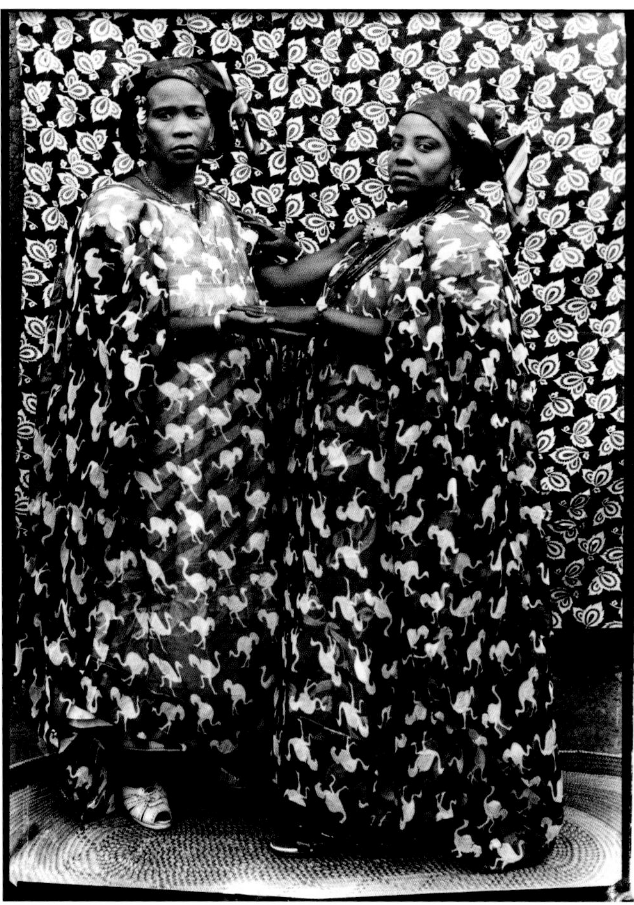

Seydou Keïta (Malian, 1923–2001)
Untitled, 1958, printed in 1997
Gelatin silver print; 60.9 x 50.8 cm (24 x 20 in.)
Horace W. Goldsmith Fund 2000.1005

This monumental pair of women was documented by Malian photographer Seydou Keïta in the late 1950s, at the height of his career. Trained as a carpenter and furniture maker, Keïta first experimented with photography while still a teenager and eventually opened a commercial portrait studio in a bustling neighborhood of Mali's capital city, Bamako. Keïta was particularly admired for the flattering poses and inventive props he gave his sitters. These two figures stand in the photographer's open-air courtyard, where their patterned dresses and headscarves create a wonderful dissonance with the graphic design of the textile backdrop. The women's serious expressions and gestures underscore their status in the community and show off their graceful hands and elegant gold jewelry.

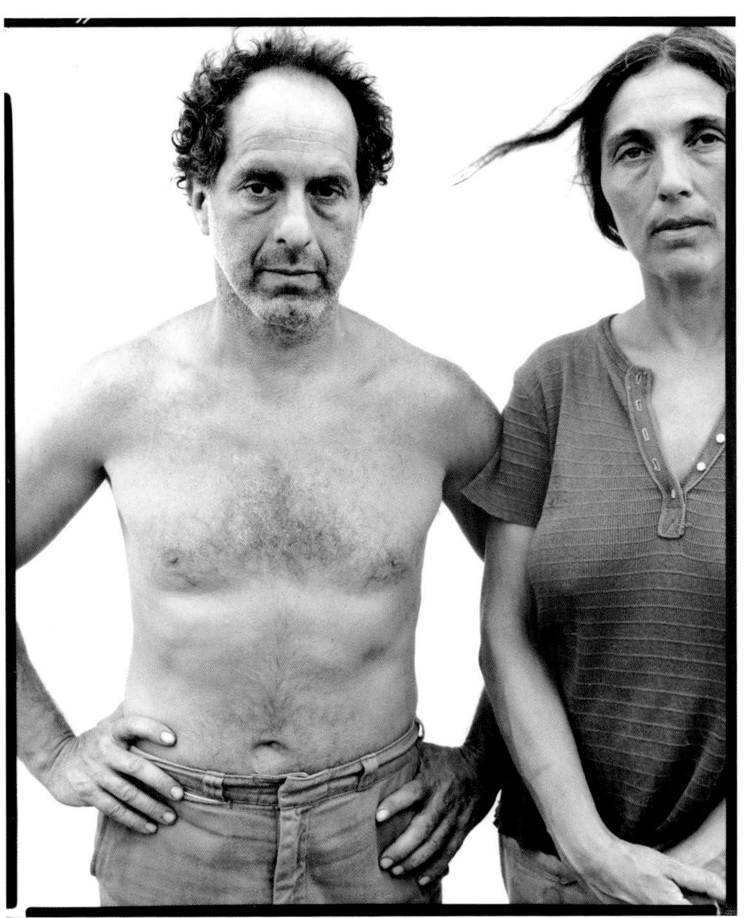

Richard Avedon (American, 1923–2004)

Robert Frank, photographer, and June Leaf, artist, Mabou Mines, Nova Scotia, July 17, 1975

Gelatin silver print, 24.8 x 20.1 cm (9 ¾ x 7 15/16 in.)

Gift of David Bakalar 1979.308

In 1944, Richard Avedon was discovered by the art director at *Harper's Bazaar*, Alexey Brodovitch, and his career as a groundbreaking fashion photographer was launched. By the 1960s, he had begun to photograph an even wider range of subjects, from Civil Rights activists and Vietnam War protestors to the political, intellectual, and artistic elite. Fascinated by the power of portraits made with a large-format view camera, Avedon soon developed a distinctive style that involved placing his sitters against a stark white background and photographing them frontally. This image of the photographer Robert Frank, whose book *The Americans* influenced a whole generation of photographers, and his wife, the artist June Leaf, has all the unflinching authenticity and intimacy of Avedon's best work.

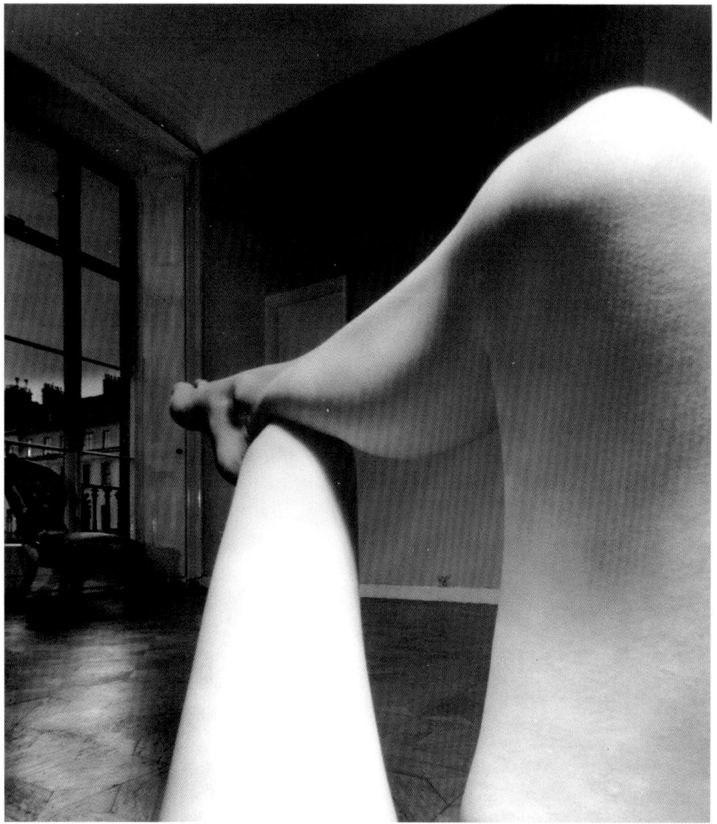

Bill Brandt (English, born in Germany, 1904–1983)

Belgravia, London, from the series *Perspectives of Nudes*, 1951

Gelatin silver print; 22.9 x 19.5 cm (9 x 7 11/16 in.)

Sophie M. Friedman Fund 1985.434

Both Bill Brandt and John Coplans often fragment and distort the human body in their work, transforming the figure into something alternately alien and abstract. Beginning in the mid-1940s, Brandt made an extensive series of nudes set in eerily dark, nearly empty interiors in London's Belgravia, St. John's Wood, and Campden Hill neighborhoods. He had worked as an assistant to Man Ray during the 1930s, and his exposure to French Surrealism gave him a taste for exploiting the camera's "vision." Shot in raking light from exaggerated perspectives with a Kodak wide-angle camera like those police use to document crime scenes, Brandt's images alter his sitters into strange, undulating shapes, converting the female nude into molded topographic forms not unlike the sculptures of his contemporaries Henry Moore and Barbara Hepworth.

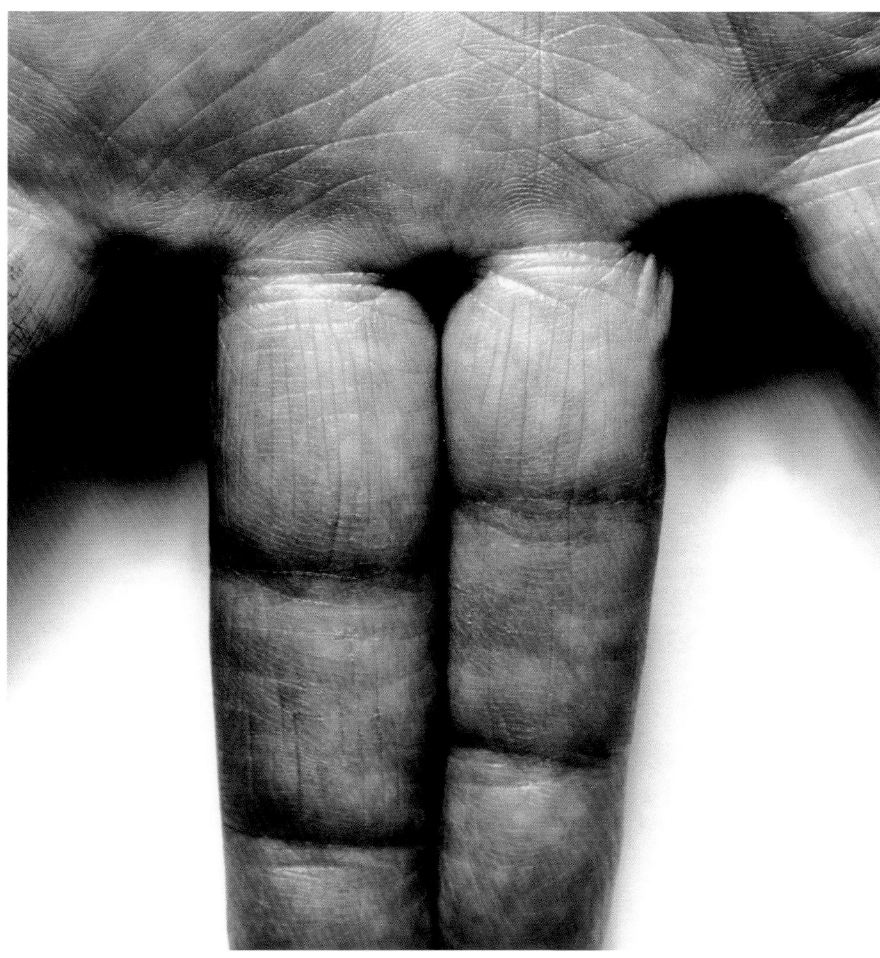

John Coplans (American, 1920–2003)

Self-Portrait, from the series *A Body of Work*, 1987

Gelatin silver print; 76.2 x 68.8 cm (30 x 27 1/16 in.)

Sophie M. Friedman Fund 1990.252

When Coplans took up photography in 1980 at the age of sixty, having already worked for many years as a painter, teacher, critic, curator, and museum director, his focus was his own aging body—posed against a neutral background and isolated and cropped so that the parts are often nearly unrecognizable. His extensive series of naked, rather than nude, studies never include his head or face, challenging our notions of self-portraiture and our celebration of the idealized human form. Here, two of Coplans's fingers, greatly enlarged and shown extremely close-up, take on the look of a torso, buttocks, and legs, with their wrinkled texture suggesting something almost more animal than human.

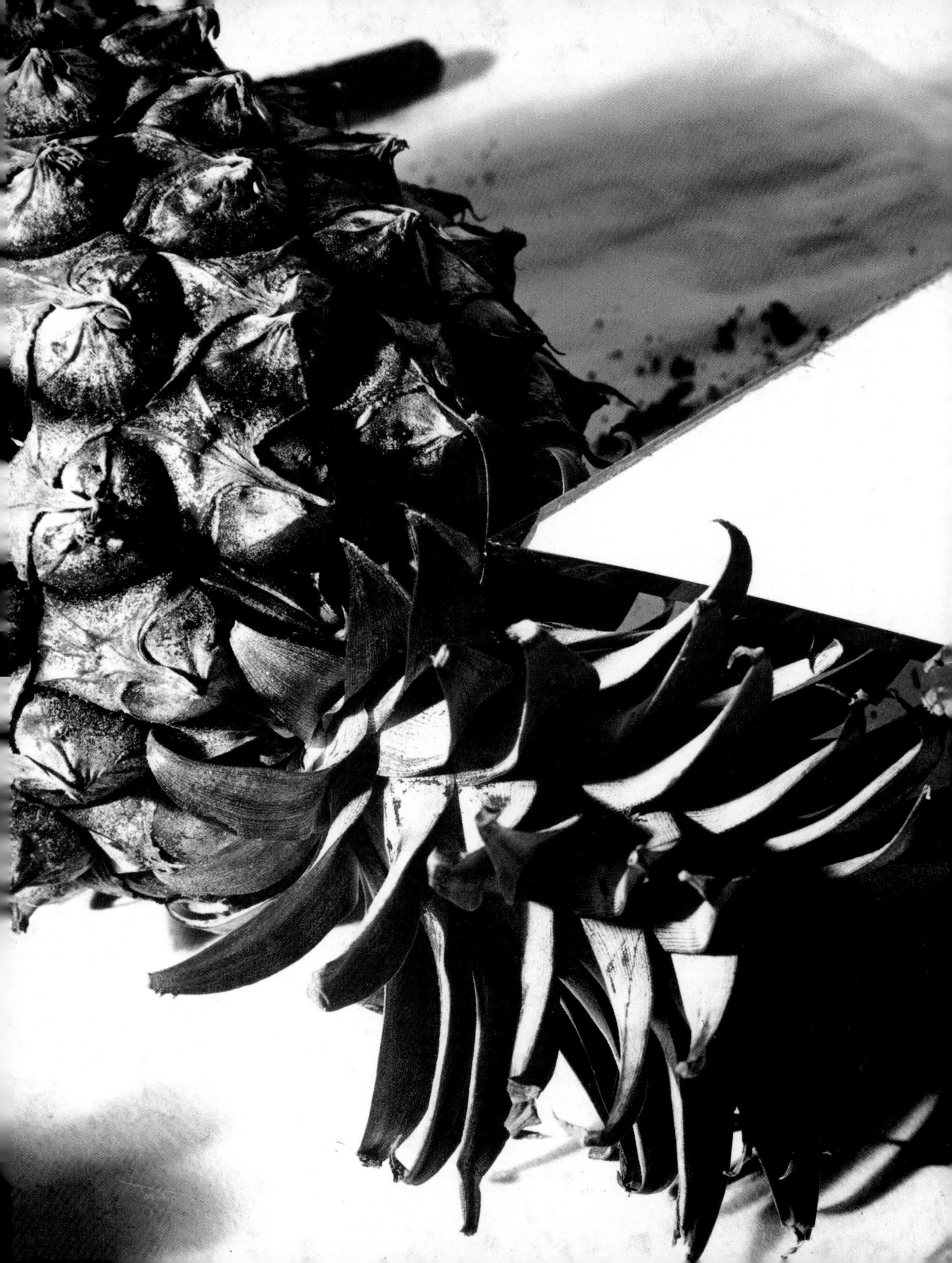

2 ARCHITECTURE, SCULPTURE, AND STILL LIFE

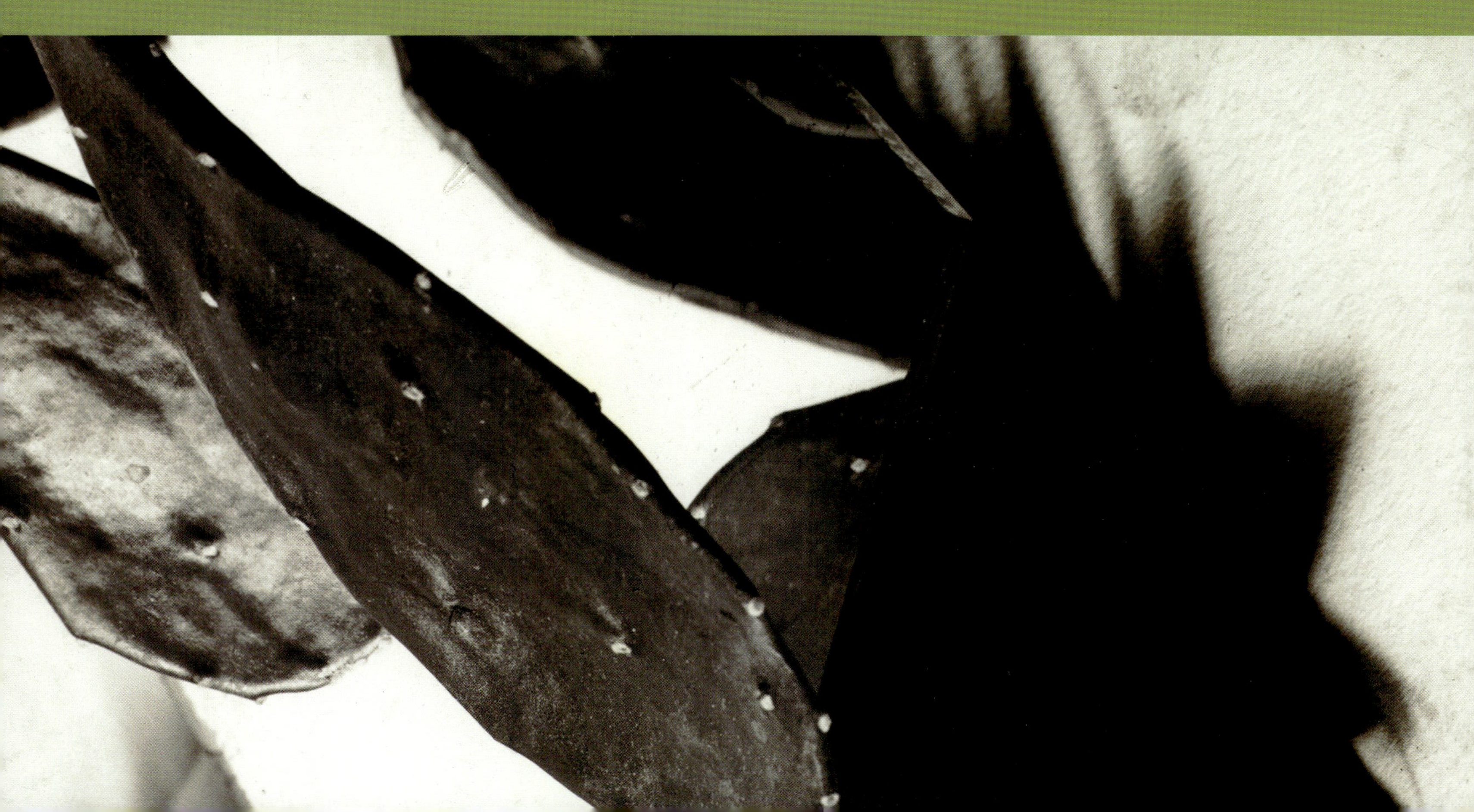

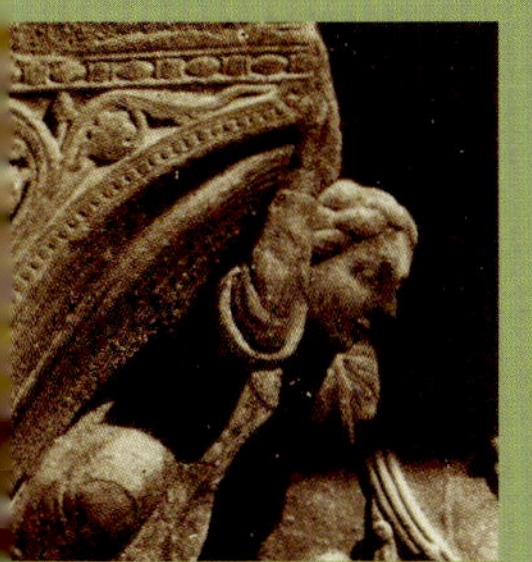

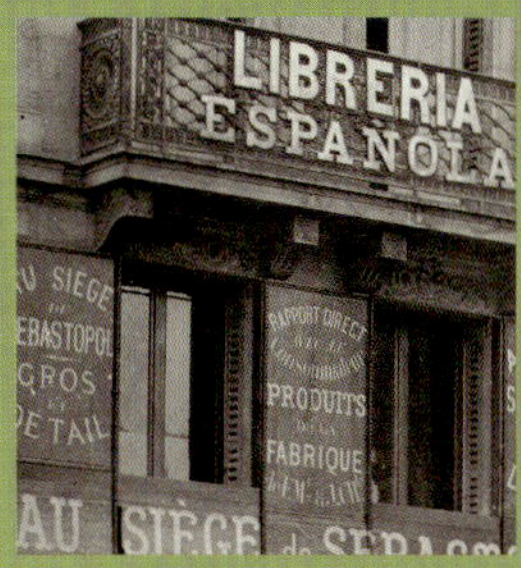
LIBRERIA
ESPAÑOLA
GROS
PRODUITS
FABRIQUE
SIEGE

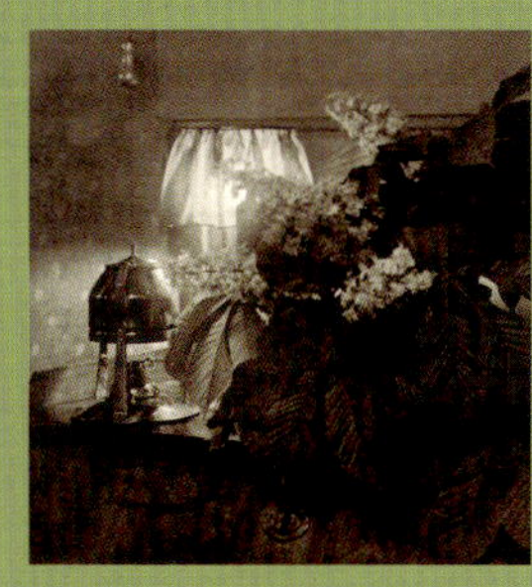

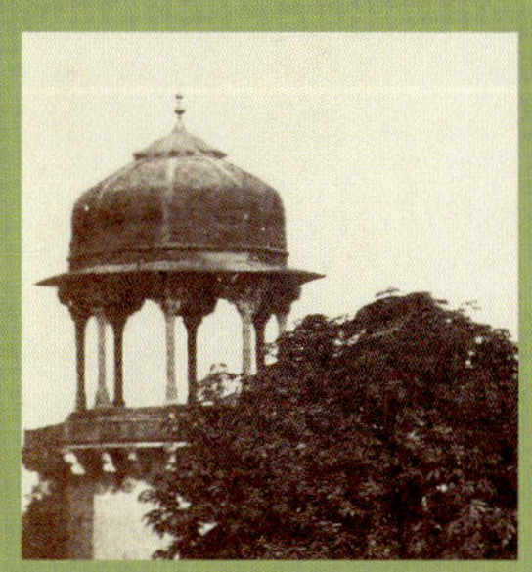

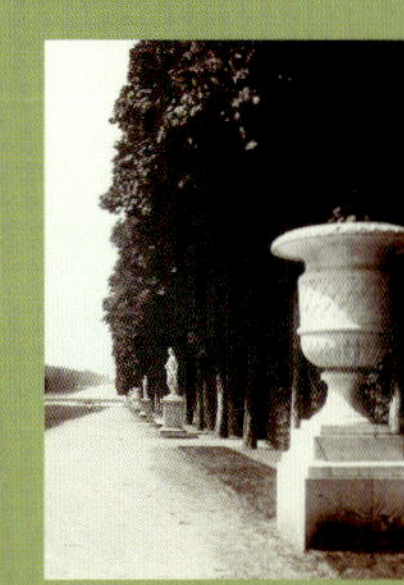

Architecture, Sculpture, and Still Life

The inanimate objects of this world have long ignited the imagination of photographers. Pioneers of the medium carried out many of their early experiments by training their lenses on things that were obligingly stationary, such as objects arranged on a ledge or rooftops seen from a window. Since then, photographers have mined the potential of the inanimate world from a multiplicity of approaches. They have recorded great monuments of architecture to preserve them for the collective memory, and they have made portraits of the humblest cabins and shacks. They have documented paintings, sculpture, and decorative objects, giving these works of art new layers of symbolic meaning, and they have recorded tangible bits and pieces of the everyday—glassware, a few pieces of fruit—on a simple table. The lively range of their expression can be seen on the pages that follow.

The photographing of inanimate objects is a dramatically different experience from that of making a portrait or photographing the natural landscape. This work offers the person behind the lens a luxury of time and more opportunity to deliberate on the composition of his or her image. Some photographers who choose the static world as their subject are captivated by the camera's ability to interpret geometric form. Many are attracted by the way in which their medium visually compresses the three-dimensional world into a flat, two-dimensional plane. The camera and its lens often reorder space and scale.

In the modernist years after 1900, photographers capitalized on such visual compression in their recording of volumetric form. They took pictures from oblique angles, from extremely close up, or from far away in order to evoke surprising abstract qualities. They depicted sharply focused detail in close-ups excerpted from a larger view. They drew attention to shapes, patterns, and textures by varying the intensity or the angle of light. For many of these men and women, this way of working was more direct, more "straight," and truer to what was unique about art made with the camera. The emphasis on formal structure that was, in effect, the primary subject of their work reset the aims of image making with the camera, and the significance of their contribution meant that photography would never be the same.

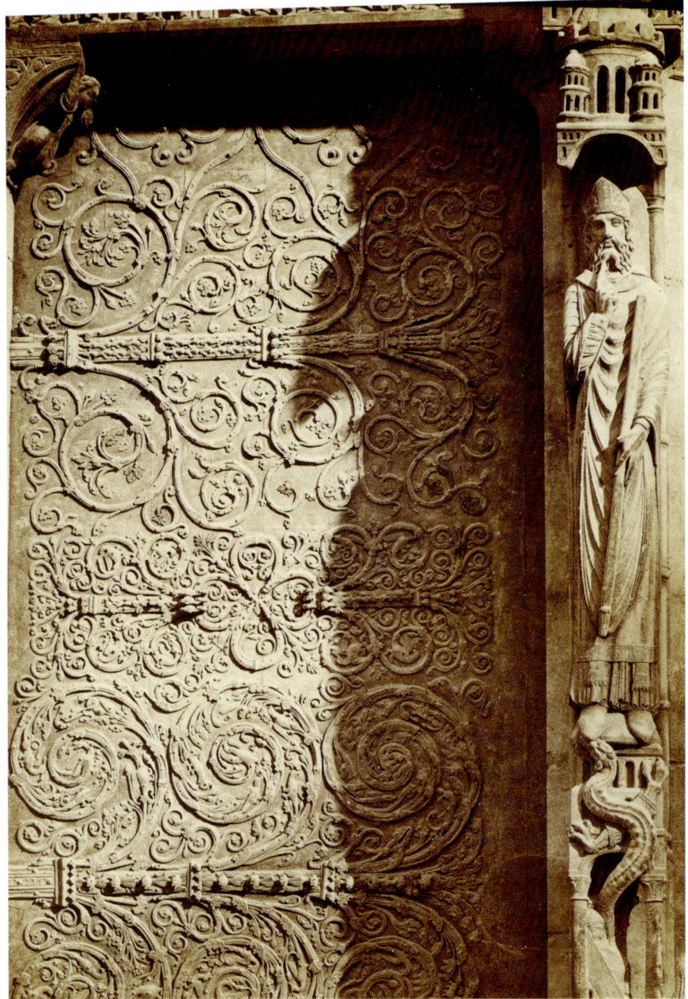

Auguste-Rosalie Bisson (French, 1826–1900)
Louis-Auguste Bisson (French, 1814–1876)
Vantail de la porte Saint Marcel, Notre Dame, Paris, about 1853–57
Albumen print; 39.2 x 25.6 cm (15 7/16 x 10 1/16 in.)
Charles Amos Cummings Fund 1990.473

The Bisson frères and Nadar were among the most prominent French photographers of their day. The Bissons, active in photography since the 1840s, excelled at large-scale photographs of architecture and sculpture, while Nadar, who began his career as a caricaturist familiar with the major figures of bohemian Paris, is best known for his penetrating portraits of Second Empire celebrities. Nadar was also an intrepid photographic experimenter, the first to attempt both aerial photography and, as early as 1858, underground photography, using reflectors and electric light generated by Bunsen batteries.

In this detail of Notre Dame cathedral in Paris, the Bissons showcase the genius of medieval ironwork and sculpture. The flat composition, reminiscent of an ornamental engraving, uses a deep zone of shadow to

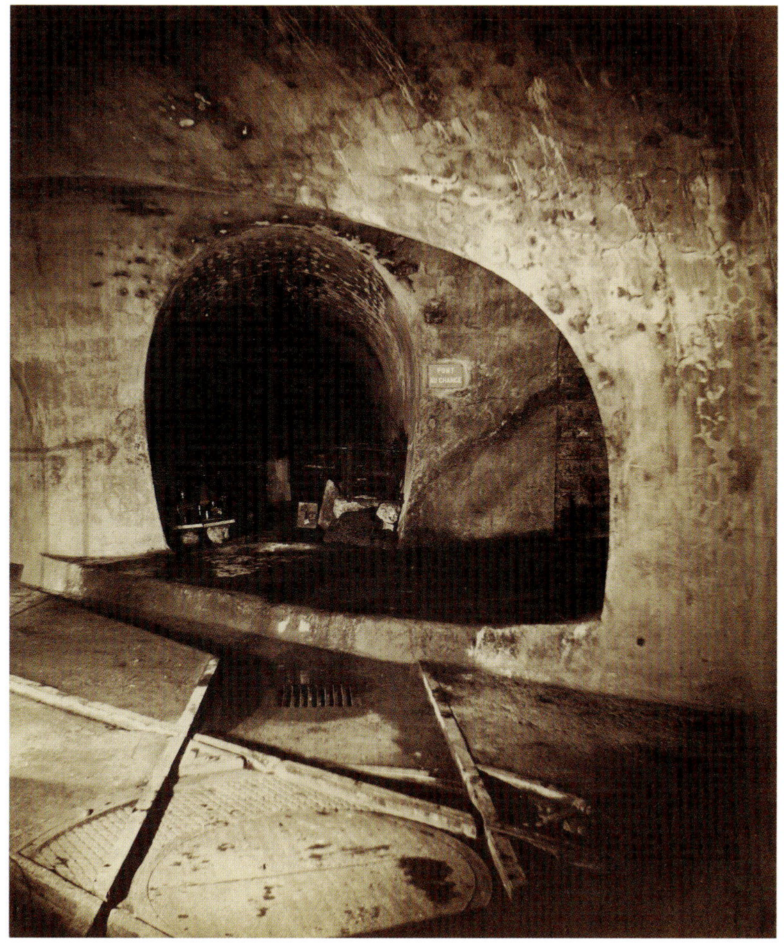

Nadar (Gaspard Félix Tournachon)

(French, 1820–1910)

Subterranean Paris (Pont au Change), 1864–65

Albumen print; 24.8 x 19.6 cm (9¾ x 7 11/16 in.)

Charles Amos Cummings Fund 1984.431

divide, and thus highlight, the intricate wrought-iron arabesques decorating the door and the elongated figure of Saint Marcel adorning the trumeau.

Nadar's 1864–65 photographs of the newly renovated sewers of Paris reveal an amazing subterranean world. This silent, vaulted city paralleled the animated new Paris rising aboveground in the urban renewal projects of Baron Georges-Eugène Haussmann, its tracks, pipes, and canals echoing the streets and intersections of the familiar sunlit world. In this image, a network of underground tracks converges at the Pont au Change. Nadar's composition plunges us deep into the silent tunnels, where his artificial light illuminates the technology of underground engineering while the mystery and drama of an older subterranean world loom beyond its reach.

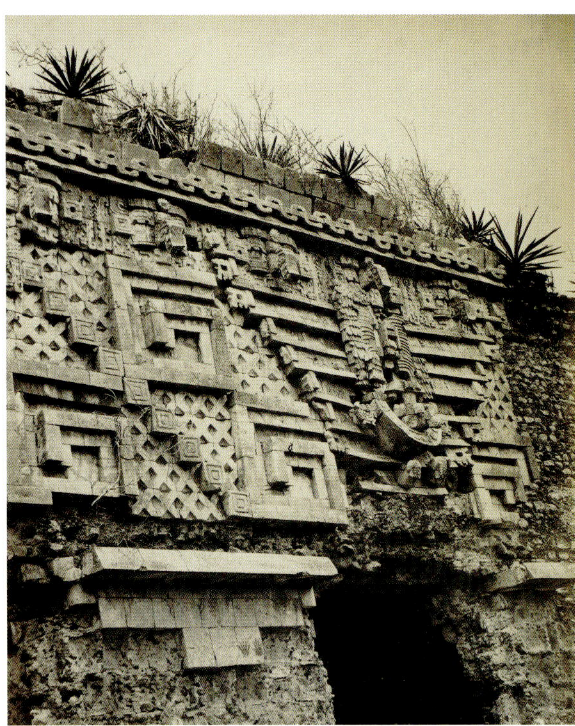

Désiré Charnay (French, 1828–1915)

Palace of the Governor, Uxmal, Mexico, 1858–61

Albumen print; 70.4 x 53.9 cm (27 11/16 x 21 1/4 in.)

Charles Amos Cummings Fund 2000.660

The invention of photography gave access to distant and ancient civilizations through images taken by intrepid explorers and agents of empire alike. Frederick Catherwood's daguerreotypes from his 1841 exploration of the Yucatán with John Lloyd Stephens inspired the adventurer Désiré Charnay to photograph Mayan ruins in Mexico. Charnay wrote of the difficulties of using the wet plate process in the intense heat at Uxmal: either the collodion dried too quickly or the chemicals decomposed. Still, he found it preferable to the paper process for achieving the sharpest possible recording of architectural detail and inscriptions. In this photograph of the governor's palace, the careful stonework that animates the building's surface is fully revealed by Charnay's skillfully modulated exposure.

John Murray learned photography in 1849 while he was stationed near the Taj Mahal with the army medical service of the East India Company, and he became an expert in the paper negative process. During his forty years in India, he traveled widely in the north to photograph the masterpieces of Mughal architecture. The waxed paper negative, which did not need immediate developing, was well suited to his project. Emperor Akbar's tomb, dating from the seventeenth century, is seen here in both a paper negative and a positive albumen print. Murray blackened the sky in the negative so that in the print it has a uniform tone that balances the spaciousness of the courtyard, allowing the architectural ensemble to dominate the composition.

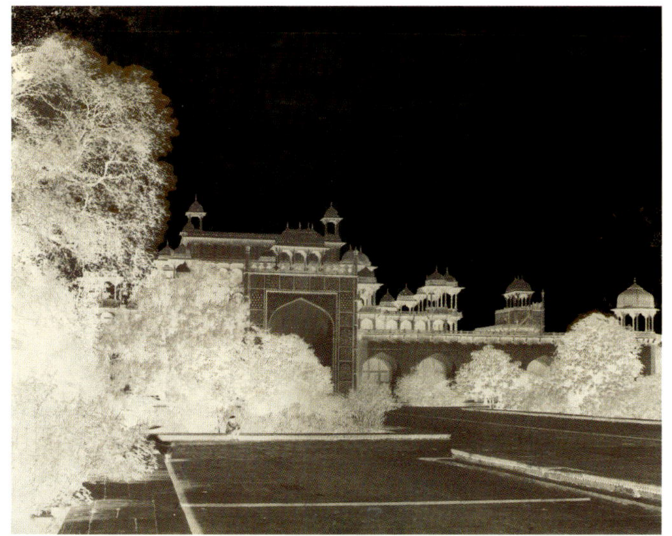

John Murray (English, 1809–1898)

Akbar's Tomb, South Front from East Side of Courtyard with Two Figures, 1858–62

Waxed paper negative; 36.7 x 47 cm (14 7/16 x 18 1/2 in.)

Sophie M. Friedman Fund 1999.529

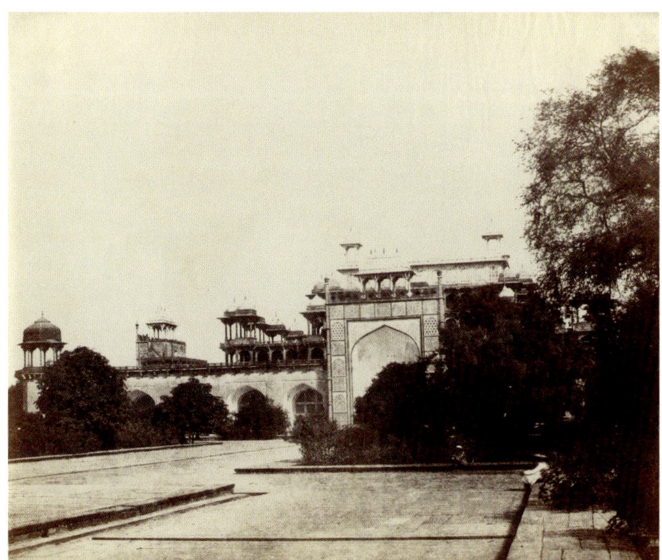

John Murray (English, 1809–1898)

Akbar's Tomb, South Front from East Side of Courtyard with Two Figures, 1858–62

Albumen print from a waxed paper negative

38.3 x 44.4 cm (15 1/16 x 17 1/2 in.)

Sophie M. Friedman Fund 1999.528

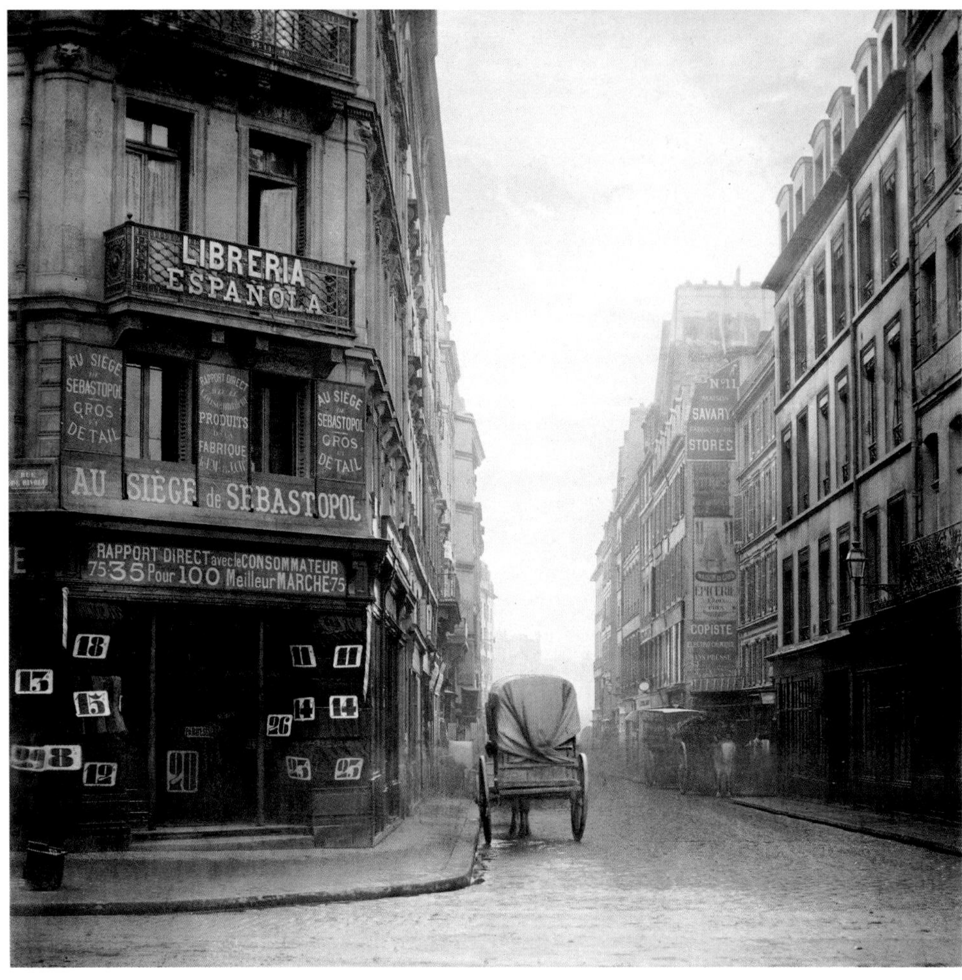

Charles Marville (French, 1816–about 1879)

"Au Siège de Sebastopol" (rue de la Monnaie from the rue de Rivoli), 1865–68

Albumen print; 27.1 x 26.8 cm (10 11/16 x 10 9/16 in.)

Charles Amos Cumming Fund 1980.217

Both Charles Marville and Eugène Atget are known for their photographs of Paris. Marville, who was named "photographer of the city of Paris" in 1862, recorded the city both before and after Baron Haussmann's massive urban renewal projects of the 1860s. Several decades later, Atget, an independent entrepreneur, created an immense archive of views of Paris and nearby palaces and parks, such as Versailles and Saint-Cloud, for a clientele of artists, libraries, and museums.

The visual drama that characterizes Marville's depiction of the rue de la Monnaie is typical of his photographs of old Paris. The converging lines of architecture, sky, and road highlight the tight narrowness of the street, an aspect of old Paris that would soon be swept away by Haussmann's wide

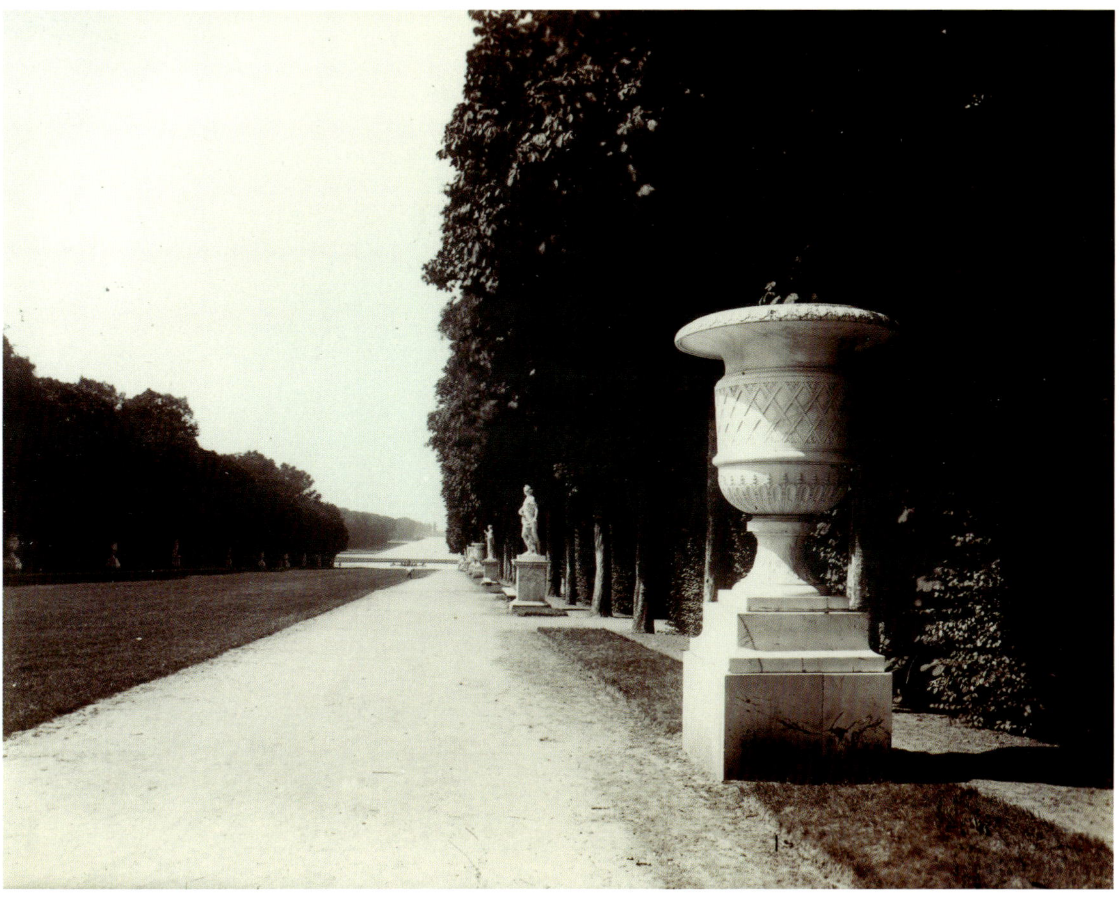

Eugène Atget (French, 1857–1927)

Versailles Park, 1902

Albumen print, gold toned; 18.1 x 21.8 cm (7 1/8 x 8 9/16 in.)

Helen B. Sweeney Fund 1989.322

boulevards. Signs and figures animate the surface of the corner building, contrasting with the empty street and the stillness of the delivery wagons waiting there.

Atget's photograph of the park at Versailles uses the same compositional device of receding lines, but in this open environment it achieves a quiet, spacious effect. Broad sweeps of pathway and sky alternate with velvety swaths of vegetation, and a rhythmic punctuation of urns, tree trunks, and sculpture marks the plunge into the distance. Atget's image is just as documentary as Marville's, yet the dreamlike quality that imbues the photograph goes beyond the factual and resonates with twentieth-century art movements such as Surrealism.

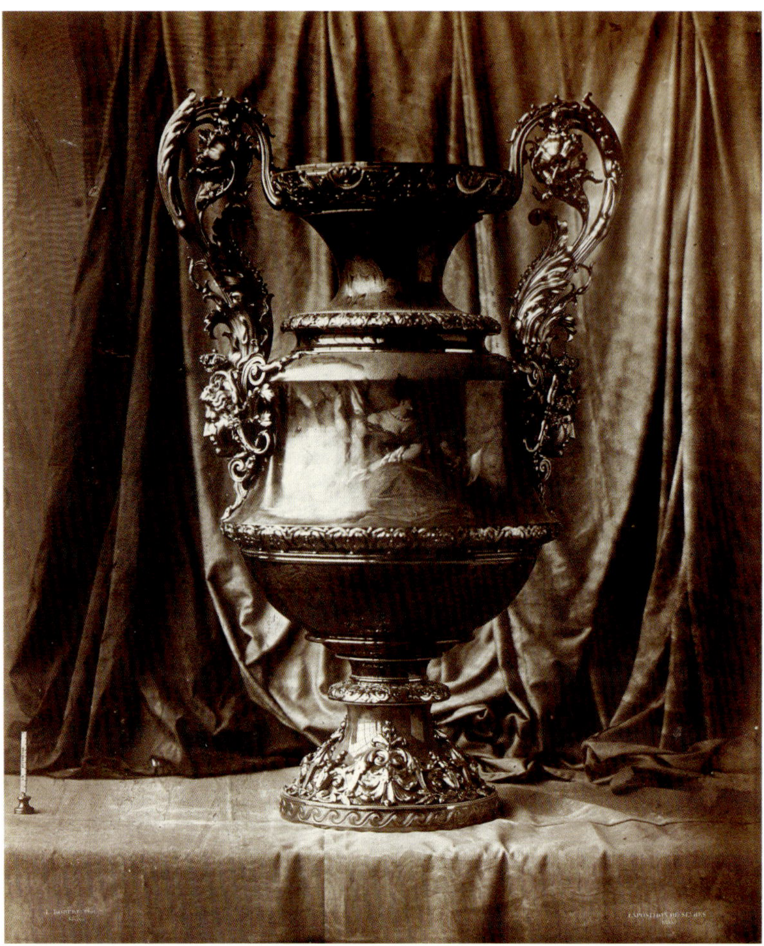

Louis-Rémy Robert (French, 1810–1882)

Sèvres Vase, 1855

Salt print from a wet collodion negative

32 x 25.7 cm (12⅝ x 10⅛ in.)

Jessie H. Wilkinson Fund 1998.72

Louis-Rémy Robert was the head of the painting and gilding studios at the Sèvres porcelain works, where a group of enthusiasts, including photographic pioneer Henri Regnault, explored the artistic possibilities of photography. This majestic depiction of a vase is part of a series of images that Robert exhibited at the Exposition Universelle of 1855, in Paris, to showcase outstanding Sèvres pieces. Robert set the vase against a display of drapery to dramatize its sculptural form and included a small measuring guide to indicate its noble scale. The vessel's gleaming surface, exquisite painting, and finely modeled detail are enhanced by the use of a glass negative yet softened by the matte surface of the salted paper print. Although made for publicity and documentation, the photograph itself achieves the status of an art object.

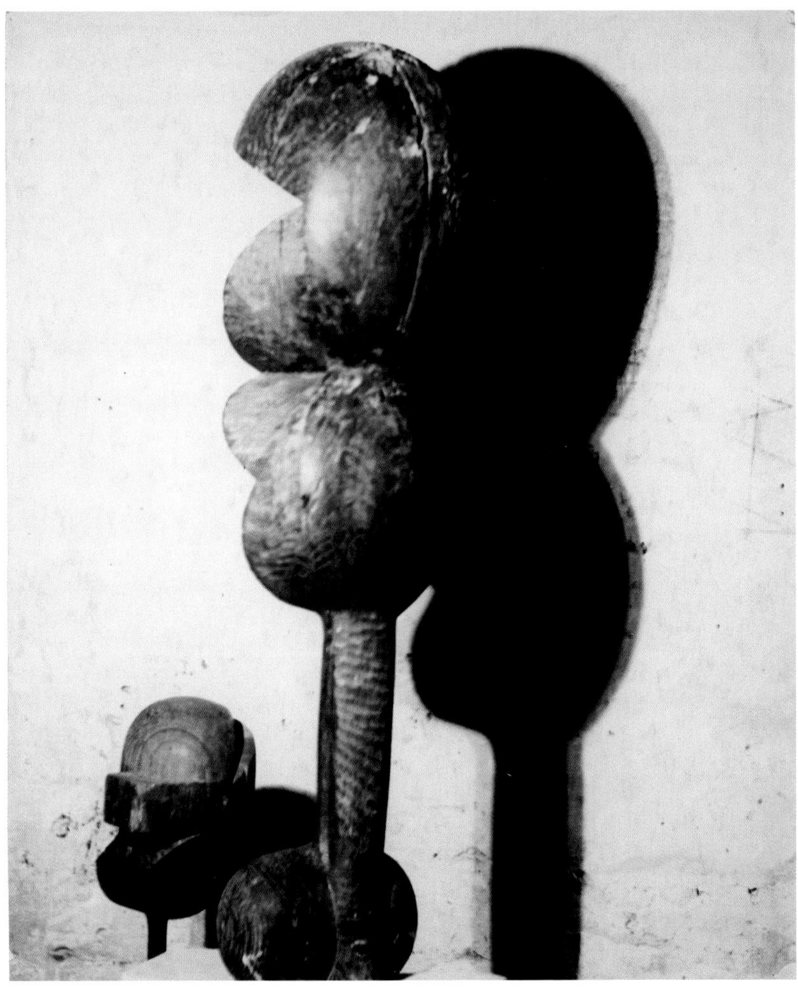

Constantin Brancusi (Romanian, 1876–1957)

Eve and Shadow, about 1922

Gelatin silver print; 30 x 24 cm (11 13/16 x 9 7/16 in.)

Sophie M. Friedman Fund 2002.150

About 1910, Constantin Brancusi started taking photographs of his sculptures to show to distant clients. He soon began using the pictures as a working aid, providing him with new ways to think about his art. In the process, he produced an important body of photographs that document individual works as well as their installation in his studio, frequently in marvelous and unexpected juxtapositions with other sculptures. The images are highly subjective. In the most expressive ones, Brancusi transforms and reinterprets his artworks, often through inventive use of light and shadow. The power of his totemic wooden sculpture *Adam and Eve* is dramatically enhanced in this photograph by his isolation of Eve and her looming black shadow. Adam is eliminated from the picture, replaced by a smaller sculpture that balances the composition.

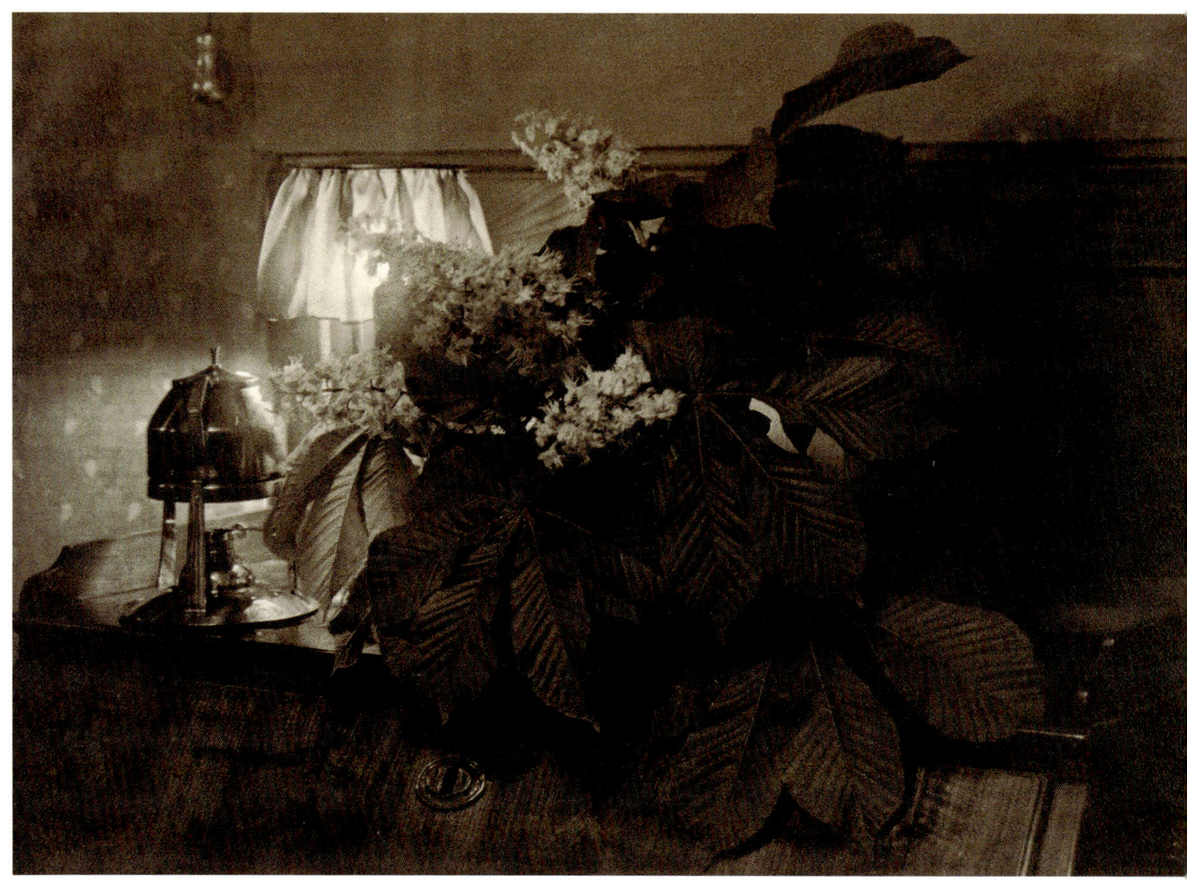

Heinrich Kühn (Austrian, 1866–1944)
Untitled (Still Life: Interior with Horse Chestnuts, Lamp, and Tea Kettle), about 1911
Platinum and gum bichromate combination print
35.9 x 48.3 cm (14 ⅛ x 19 in.)
Sophie M. Friedman Fund 1979.162

These photographs by Heinrich Kühn and Edward Steichen represent two important trends in early twentieth-century photography. Both men were major figures in Pictorialism, an international movement that conceived of photography as a fine art and emphasized broad tonal effects that minimized detail. But whereas Kühn adhered to Pictorialist principles throughout his long career, Steichen fell under the spell of European modernism and by 1920 had moved toward straight photography, characterized by strong design and simple compositions.

A warm, intimate closeness emanates from Kühn's atmospheric interior view, which features a dark mass of horse chestnuts in blossom. In counterpoint to the softly focused bough, lamplight illuminates, with varying intensity, the metal teapot, wooden desk, and ribbed leaves. A master of the gum bichromate process, Kühn made alterations in the print to achieve

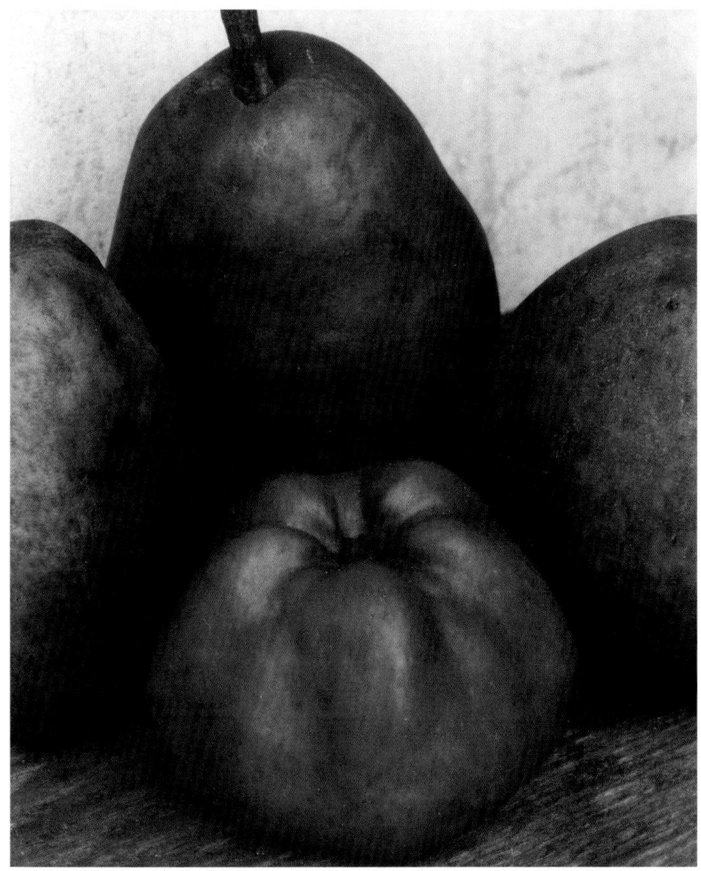

Edward Steichen (American, born in Luxembourg, 1879–1973)
Three Pears and an Apple, 1921
Gelatin silver print
24.3 x 19.2 cm (9 9/16 x 7 9/16 in.)
Sophie M. Friedman Fund 1984.584

this broad, expressive range of tones, and he used a heavy, textured paper to enhance the painterly quality.

In contrast, Steichen eschewed atmosphere to concentrate on the physical reality of his pears and apple, reflecting his new belief that photography's real strength lay in its ability to reveal essential truths through an analysis of external form. He approached his still life as an abstract problem of how to represent volume, scale, and weight. With no manipulation of the negative or print, the fruit, photographed close-up and cropped tightly in the frame, seems voluptuous, heavy, and monumental.

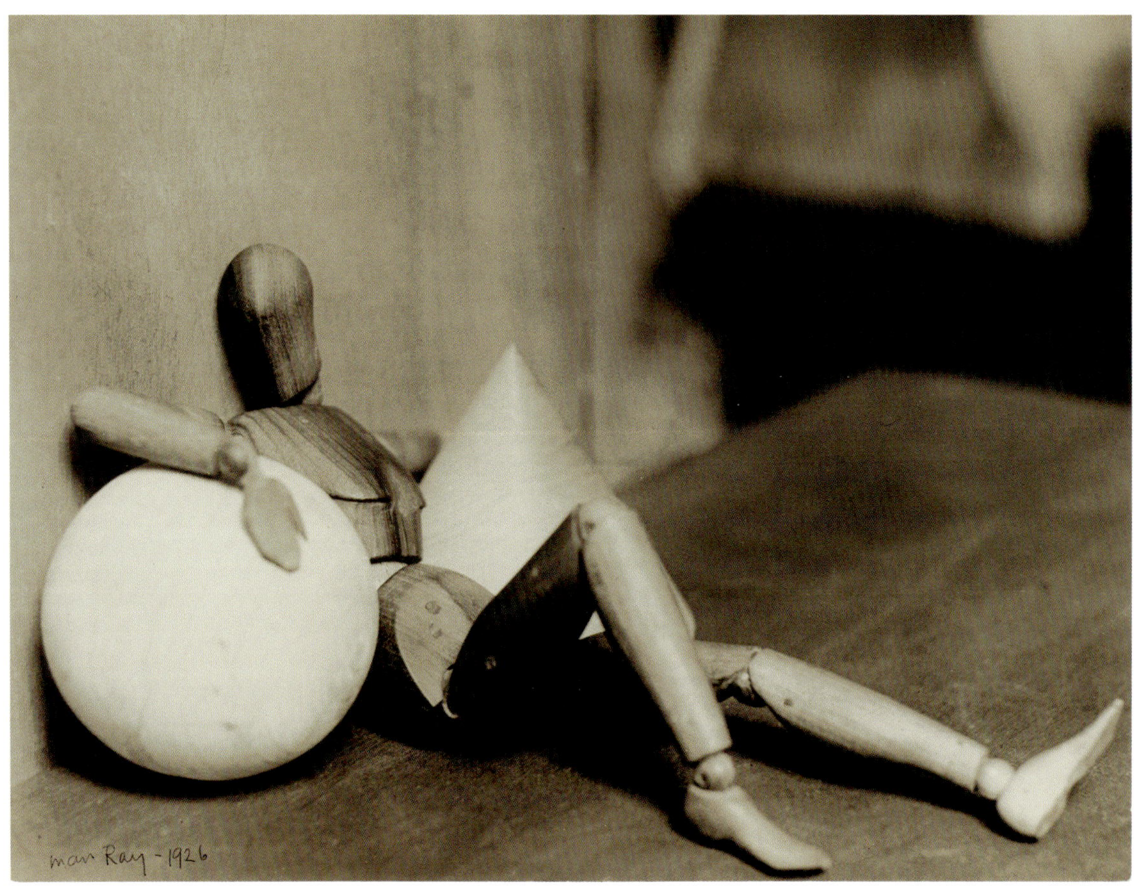

Man Ray (American, 1890–1976)

Untitled, 1926

Gelatin silver print; 28.3 x 36.2 cm (11 ⅛ x 14 ¼ in.)

Sophie M. Friedman Fund 1983.326

The tabletop still life seems an unlikely subject for modernist photographers, but during the 1920s and 1930s many artists were drawn to the enigmatic aspects of found objects and their potential as subjects for the camera. Beginning in 1926, when this photograph was taken, and continuing for more than forty years, Man Ray made a series of images based on a pair of male and female mannequins he dubbed "Mr. and Mrs. Woodman." This assemblage of an uncannily realistic figurine lounging between a large white cone and sphere would have appealed to Man Ray's interest in relating art to science and mathematics. The unlikely combination of lifelike mannequin and out-of-scale geometric forms is an ideal Surrealist juxtaposition, of the type his friend Marcel Duchamp described as "the chance meeting on a dissecting table of a sewing machine and an umbrella."

Although she initially trained as a painter, Florence Henri discovered the camera as a student at the Bauhaus, which had become a center for photographic experimentation under the influence of László Moholy-Nagy and his wife, Lucia. Like many of her

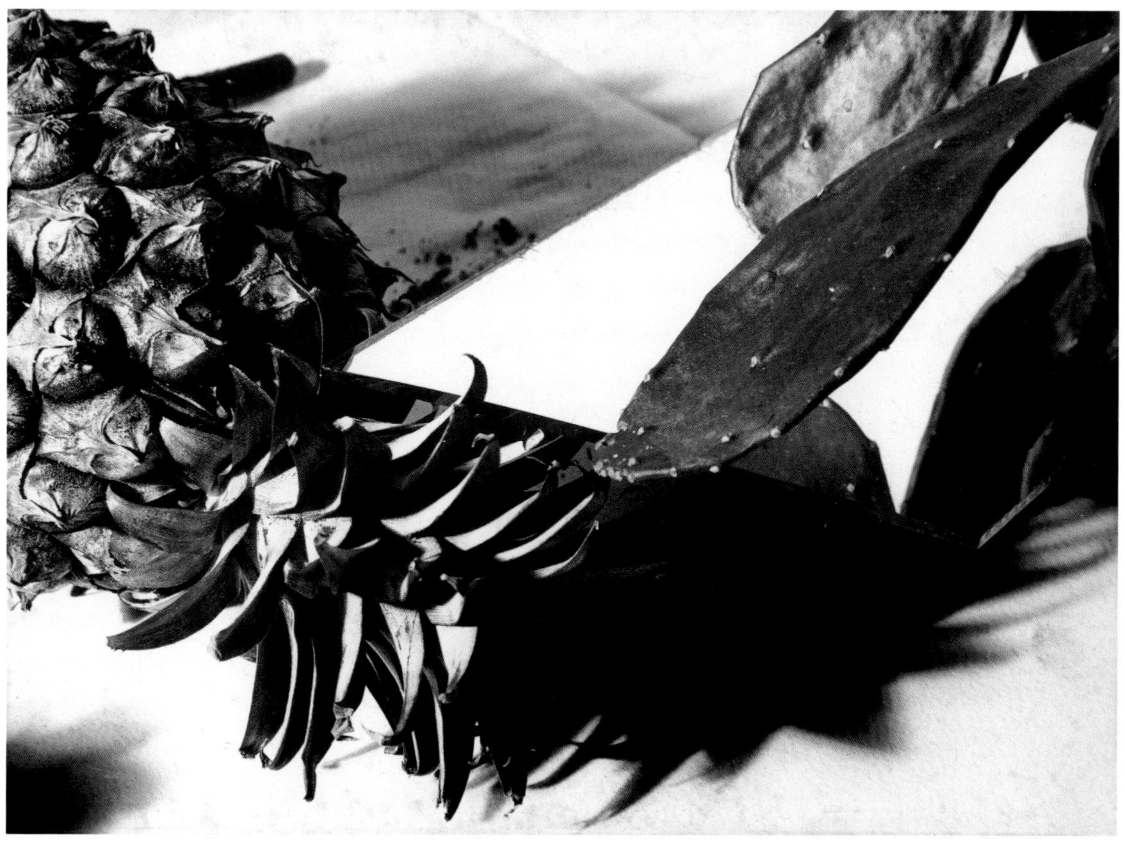

Florence Henri (American, 1893–1982)

Still Life with Pineapple and Cactus, 1931

Gelatin silver print; 22.1 x 29.1 cm (8 11/16 x 11 7/16 in.)

Sophie M. Friedman Fund 1986.25

fellow students, Henri worked in a variety of techniques, including negative prints and multiple exposures. Some of her most spatially challenging images, however, are straight photographs of everyday objects. Henri featured mirrors in a number of her still lifes, their reflective surfaces enabling her to fracture the photographic space into sharply angled shapes, such as the fragmented forms of this spiky cactus and pineapple.

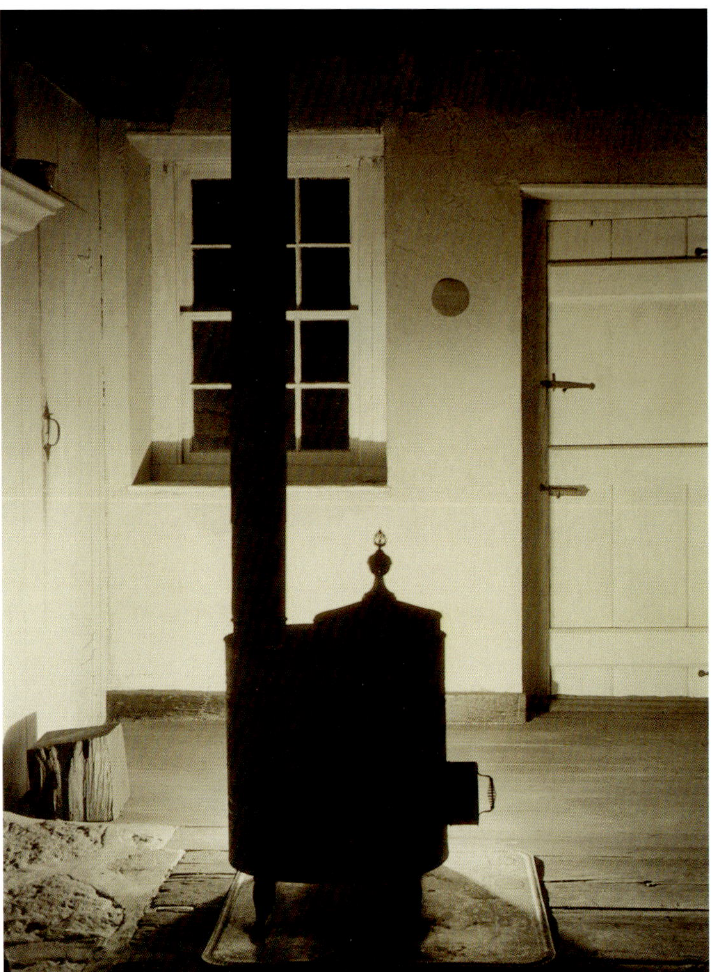

Charles Sheeler (American, 1883–1965)

Doylestown House, the Stove, about 1916–17

Gelatin silver print; 23.8 x 17.1 cm (9 3/8 x 6 3/4 in.)

Gift of Saundra B. Lane in memory of William H. Lane 2002.886

Beginning about 1910, Charles Sheeler rented a small eighteenth-century fieldstone house in Doylestown, Pennsylvania, as a weekend retreat. The simple house's unadorned whitewashed walls, cast-iron stove, and narrow wooden staircase appealed to the aspiring modernist, and the images he made of it constitute his first series of "artistic" photographs. In this example, the dark silhouette of the stove is lit from behind and set off against the stark rectilinear forms of a window and door, resulting in a surprisingly avant-garde image of an American vernacular subject. One critic, writing about these Doylestown pictures, saw the influence of Cubism in their stark compositions and sharply focused forms, claiming that Sheeler's camera had "registered certain effects and qualities hitherto seen only in the works of Pablo Picasso and his ablest followers."

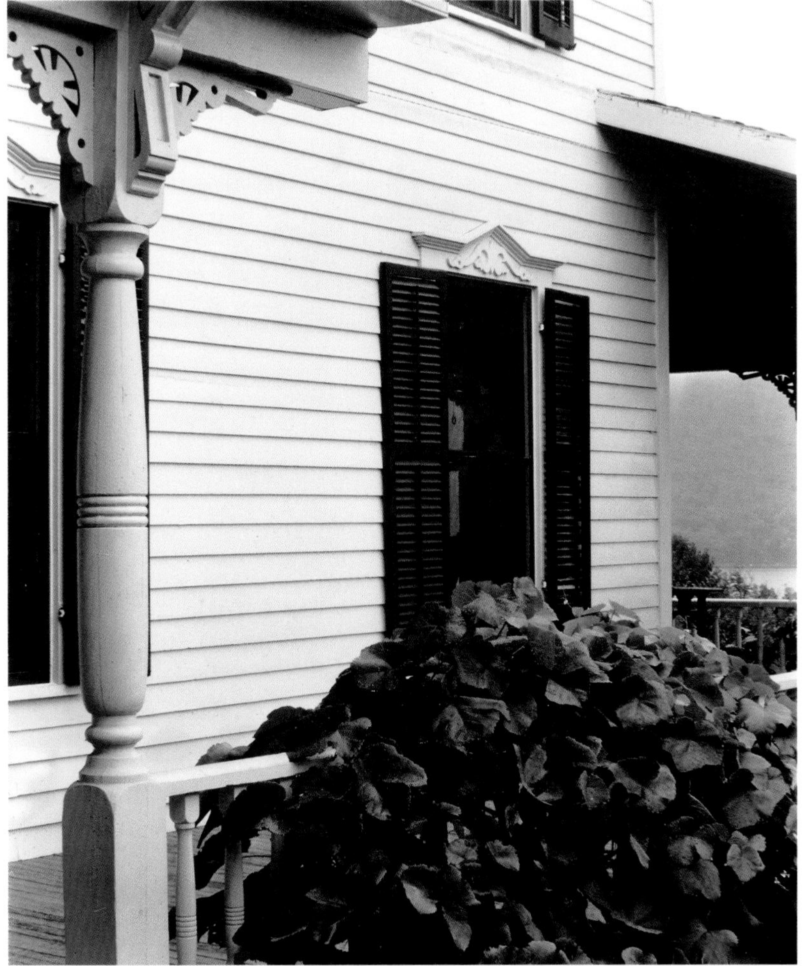

Alfred Stieglitz (American, 1864–1946)

House and Grape Leaves, 1934

Gelatin silver print; 24.1 x 19.4 cm (9 ½ x 7 ⅝ in.)

Gift of Miss Georgia O'Keeffe 50.839

Alfred Stieglitz made his earliest photographs of Lake George in the late 1910s. Just as Sheeler did in his pictures of his Doylestown house, Stieglitz focused his camera on elements of his family's summer home, a white-shingled farmhouse on the shores of the lake, several hours north of New York City. In this image from the 1930s, he was clearly drawn to the Victorian details of the house's porch and windows, simplifying their forms into abstract cutouts that echo the heart-shaped foliage of the grapevine on the railing. For Stieglitz, Lake George was both a retreat from the noise and bustle of the city and the site of some of his most influential nature studies of poplar trees, lilac bushes, grasses, and clouds.

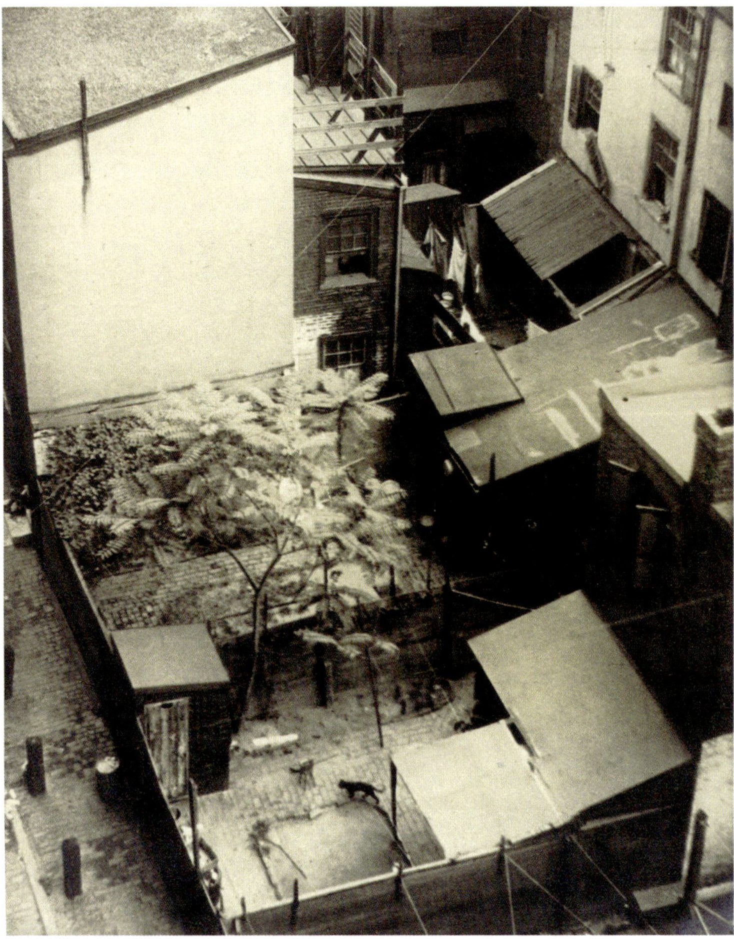

Morton Schamberg (American, 1881–1918)

Rooftops, about 1915–16

Gelatin silver print; 17.9 x 14 cm (7 1/16 x 5 1/2 in.)

Gift of Saundra B. Lane in honor of Karen E. Haas 2002.887

Morton Schamberg first studied art at the Pennsylvania Academy in Philadelphia, where he was a friend and studio-mate of Charles Sheeler. Both young men took up photography about 1910 as a way to earn a living, firmly believing that it would not distract them from their aspirations as modernist painters. They soon discovered, however, that photography was an ideal tool for rendering the geometry in their everyday surroundings, and Schamberg, in particular, began making a radical series of Cubist-inspired architectural views, including this one. Schamberg's steep camera angle, looking down onto rooftops and back alleys, causes these urban spaces to dramatically telescope from three dimensions into two and to break down into a seemingly abstract cascade of interlocking forms.

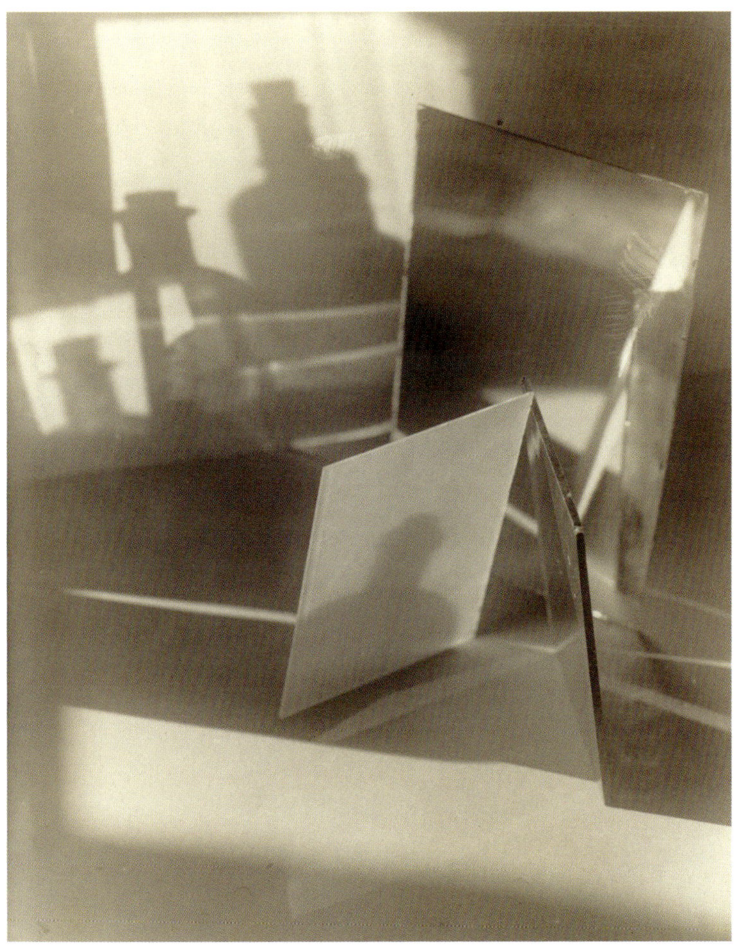

Jaromir Funke (Czechoslovakian, 1896–1945)

Still Life, about 1927–29

Gelatin silver print; 29.1 x 21.8 cm (11 7/16 x 8 9/16 in.)

Sophie M. Friedman Fund 1978.471

During the early 1920s, Jaromir Funke was taking soft-focus Pictorialist photographs on the streets of his native Prague, but he soon developed into one of the leading figures in Czech avant-garde photography with constructed still lifes such as this one. Like his American contemporary Schamberg, Funke was fascinated by the transformation and decontextualization of familiar subjects during the photographic process. By grouping and regrouping bottles and glass plates in his studio and lighting them with strong, raking light, Funke created a number of arrangements of shifting forms and shadows that verge on the completely nonrepresentational. Still, this modernist composition, with its witty play of shapes and angled tabletop, retains a lyricism and softness that is characteristic of Funke and his fellow Czech photographers.

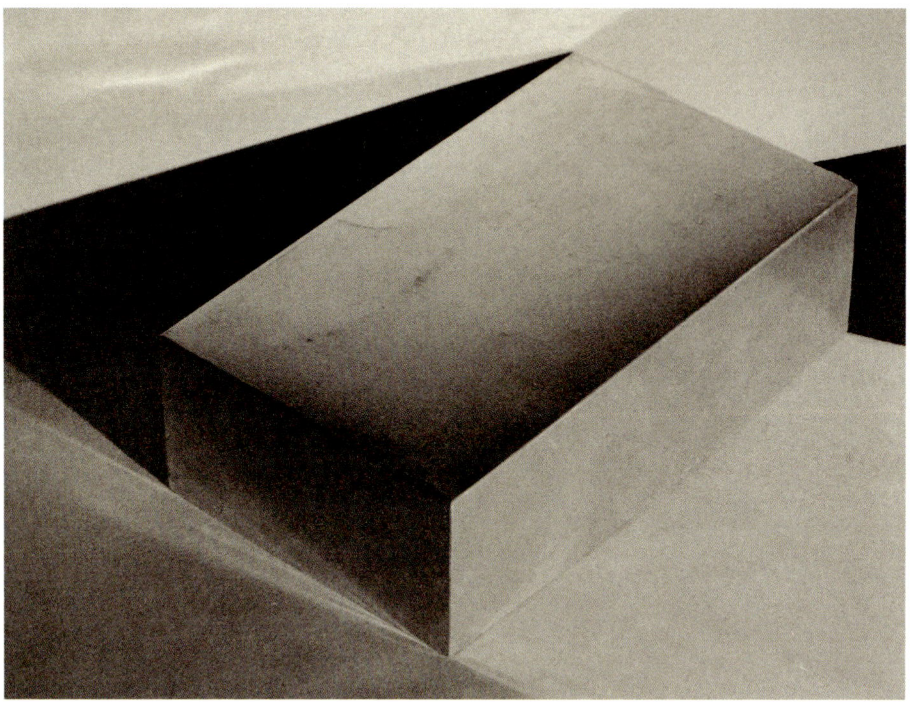

Paul Outerbridge, Jr. (American, 1896–1958)

Saltine Box, 1922

Platinum print; 8.9 x 11.5 cm (3 ½ x 4 ½ in.)

Gift of Miss Thea Cottone 32.521

Paul Outerbridge's early work, considered by some to be his best, was shaped by his studies at the Clarence H. White School of Photography in New York. His still-life abstractions of ordinary objects reflect the school's modernist emphasis on composition and design, while his devotion to the platinum printing process represents a lingering Pictorialist aesthetic of refinement and perfectionism. A contact print from a small negative, *Saltine Box* is an exquisite study of the delicate, warm tonalities characteristic of the platinum print, from the dense black of the shadows through the infinitesimal modulations of gray that describe the block. Graphically simple, the image nonetheless conveys a disturbing visual uncertainty, seeming simultaneously three-dimensional and flat.

After an early career as a street photographer in the tradition of Robert Frank and Henri Cartier-Bresson, Abelardo Morell changed direction in 1986 with the birth of his son. He began to photograph his domestic environment from new and surprising perspectives. Toys and household objects, photographed from a child's eye level, take on new meanings as the distorted sense of scale transforms a familiar reality. From a floor-level viewpoint, this tower of nesting blocks looms as large as a skyscraper, and its illustrated surfaces seem to represent an intimidating mountain of knowledge to be absorbed. The shadow cast by the blocks, the glaring light, and the large size of the print itself contribute to the idea of a daunting task ahead.

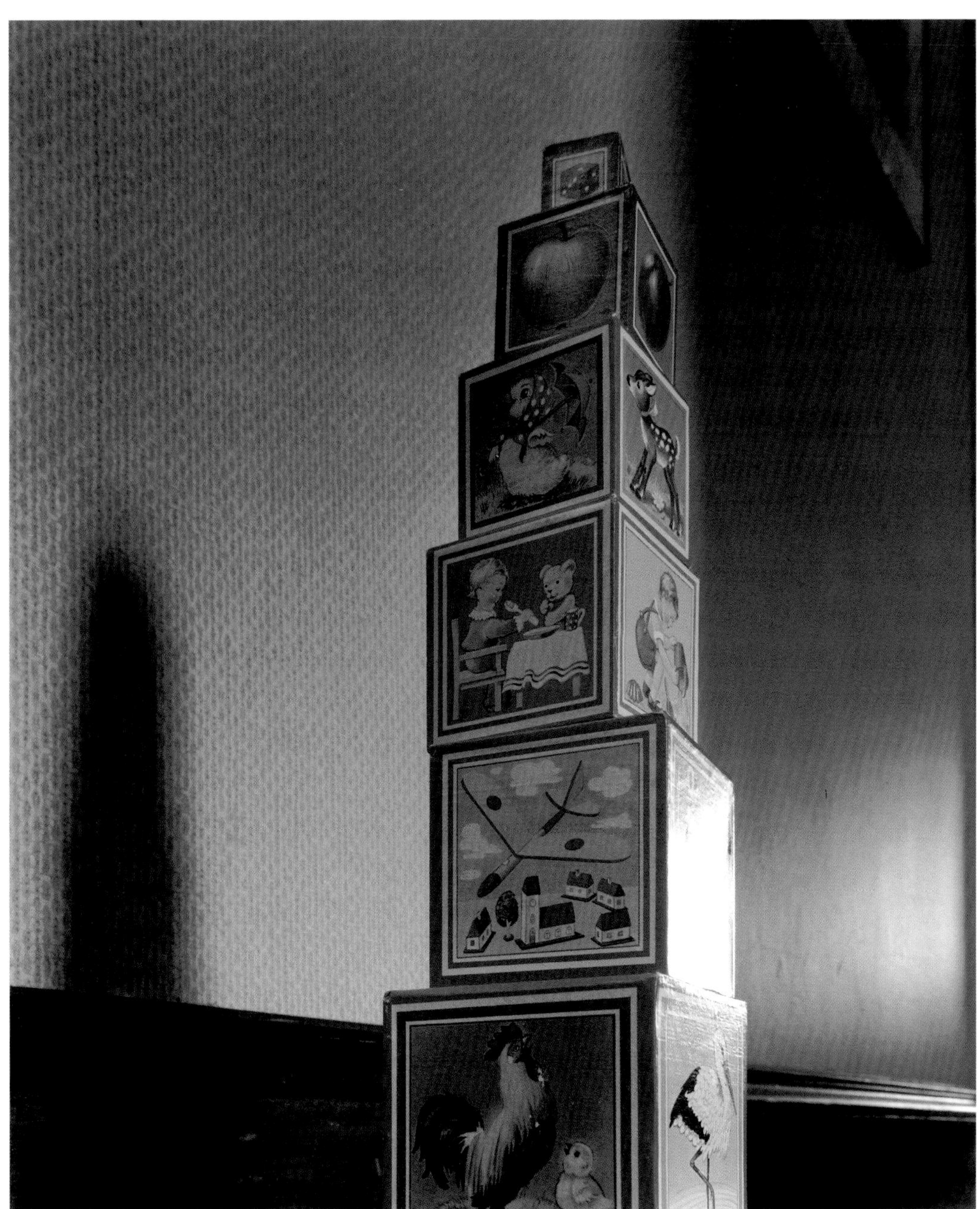

Abelardo Morell (American, born in Cuba, 1948)

Toy Blocks, 1987, printed in 1992

Gelatin silver print; 60.7 x 50.4 cm (23 7/8 x 19 3/4 in.)

Abbott Lawrence Fund 1993.17

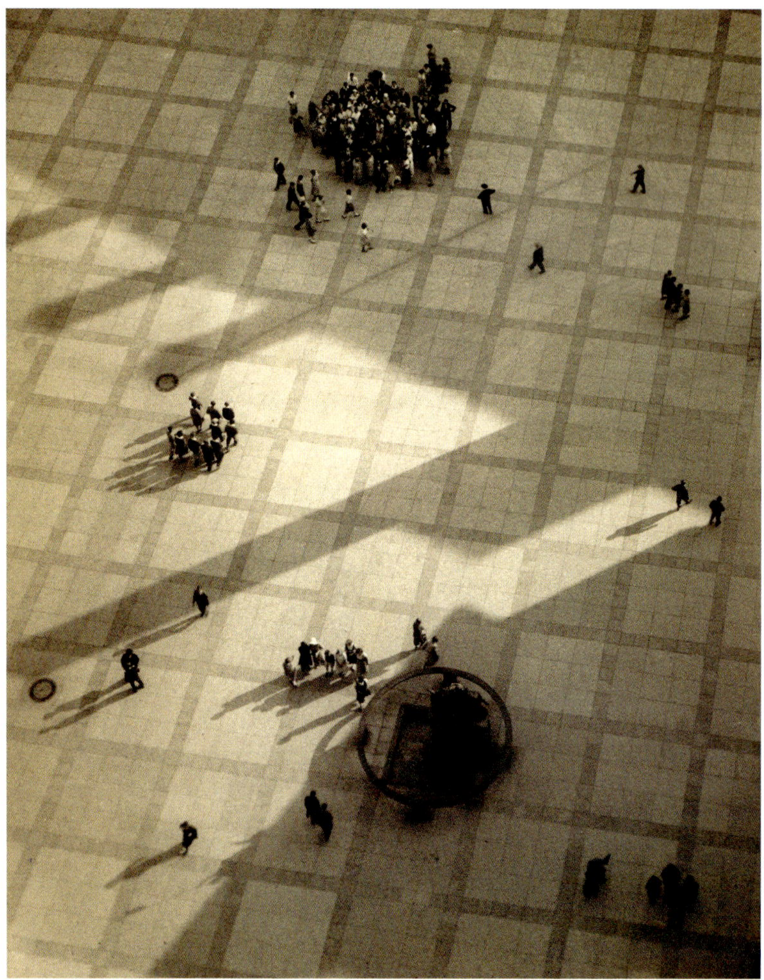

Josef Sudek (Czechoslovakian, 1896–1976)

Third Courtyard of the Castle, Prague, about 1948

Gelatin silver print; 38.6 x 29.7 cm (15 13/16 x 11 11/16 in.)

Sophie M. Friedman Fund 1984.90

Photographers caught in the wave of modernism sought fresh ways to translate the three-dimensional world into the two-dimensional photographic space. Josef Sudek lugged a large-format camera and tripod (despite having lost an arm in the First World War) around Prague to make hundreds of views of his beloved city. His cityscapes—like his still lifes, portraits, and nature views—have a quiet lyricism that led to his reputation as the "poet of Prague." To make this image of the third courtyard of the city's colossal castle complex, he climbed to the top of the nearby St. Vitus Cathedral. From that perspective, Sudek capitalized on the patterns of the people, light, and shadows across the tiled courtyard floor.

Margaret Bourke-White established her career with the photographic recording of the American

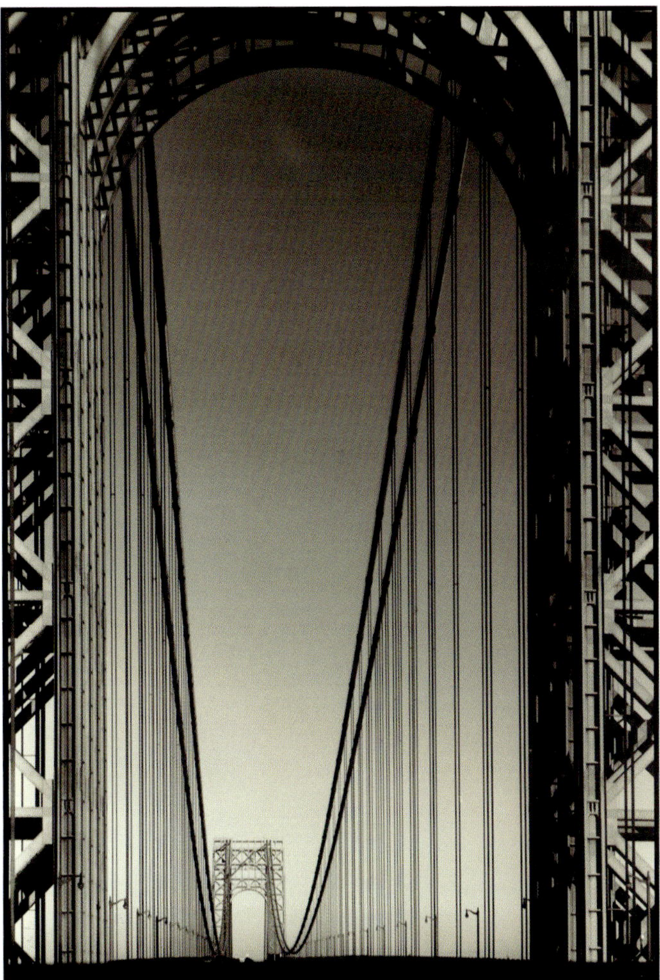

Margaret Bourke-White (American, 1904–1971)

The George Washington Bridge, 1933

Gelatin silver print; 34 x 22.2 cm (13 ⅜ x 8 ¾ in.)

Charles Amos Cummings Fund 1988.2

Machine Age. The images she made in the late 1920s and early 1930s for corporate reports and for *Fortune* and *Life* magazines are irrefutable symbols of modern industrialization. By tilting the front and back ends of a large-format camera like the one Sudek used, Bourke-White could align elements of her composition with the edges of the negative, as she did in this image of New York's George Washington Bridge. She also placed the camera at a low vantage point to better convey the majesty of the structure, which was completed in 1931 and at that time was the largest suspension bridge in the world. Bourke-White's photograph was published in *Fortune* in September 1933.

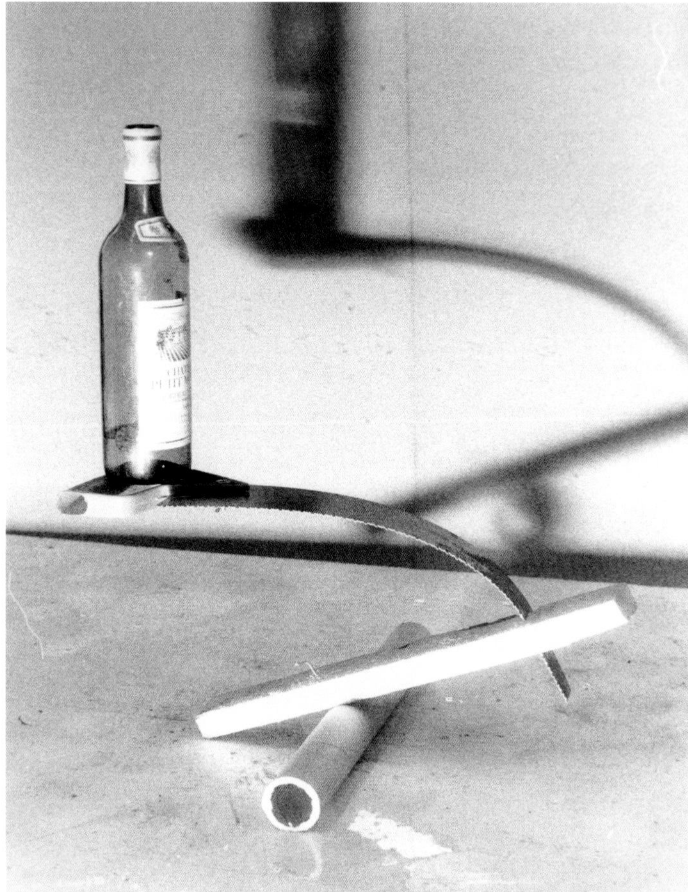

Peter Fischli (Swiss, born in 1952)
David Weiss (Swiss, born in 1946)
Ehre, Mut, und Zuversicht (Honor, Courage, and Confidence), from the series *Stiller Nachmittag* (Quiet Afternoon), 1985
Gelatin silver print; 40.6 x 30.5 cm (16 x 12 in.)
Sophie M. Friedman Fund 1989.119

Peter Fischli and David Weiss are Swiss artists who have collaborated on a variety of sculpture, film, and photography projects since 1979. Their *Stiller Nachmittag* (Quiet Afternoon) series consists of groupings of precariously balanced objects that the two men carefully arranged and then photographed in an intentionally deadpan style. The unlikely combination of unrelated everyday items in this image—a metal pipe, a piece of wood, a saw, and a bottle of wine—appear to be in a strange state of disequilibrium, brightly lit and teetering on the verge of collapse. Their artificial juxtaposition seems alternately unsettling and funny, calling into question our faith in the documentary "truth" of photography.

Like Fischli and Weiss, William Wegman has worked in many different media and enjoys poking fun at the weightiness of high art. During the late 1970s, Wegman began photographing his Weimaraner dogs with a large 20 x 24 Polaroid camera. His wonderfully humorous portraits of them are carefully orchestrated and often involve the use of props, as in this image of one of the dogs, Fay Ray, posed within a bicycle tire. The pictures have a playful spirit that is underscored by Wegman's sometimes purposely misspelled titles and not-so-subtle art historical references. In *Intirely*, for example, his canine model looks like a cross between Leonardo's *Vitruvian Man* and photographer Lewis Hine's famous *Powerhouse Mechanic*.

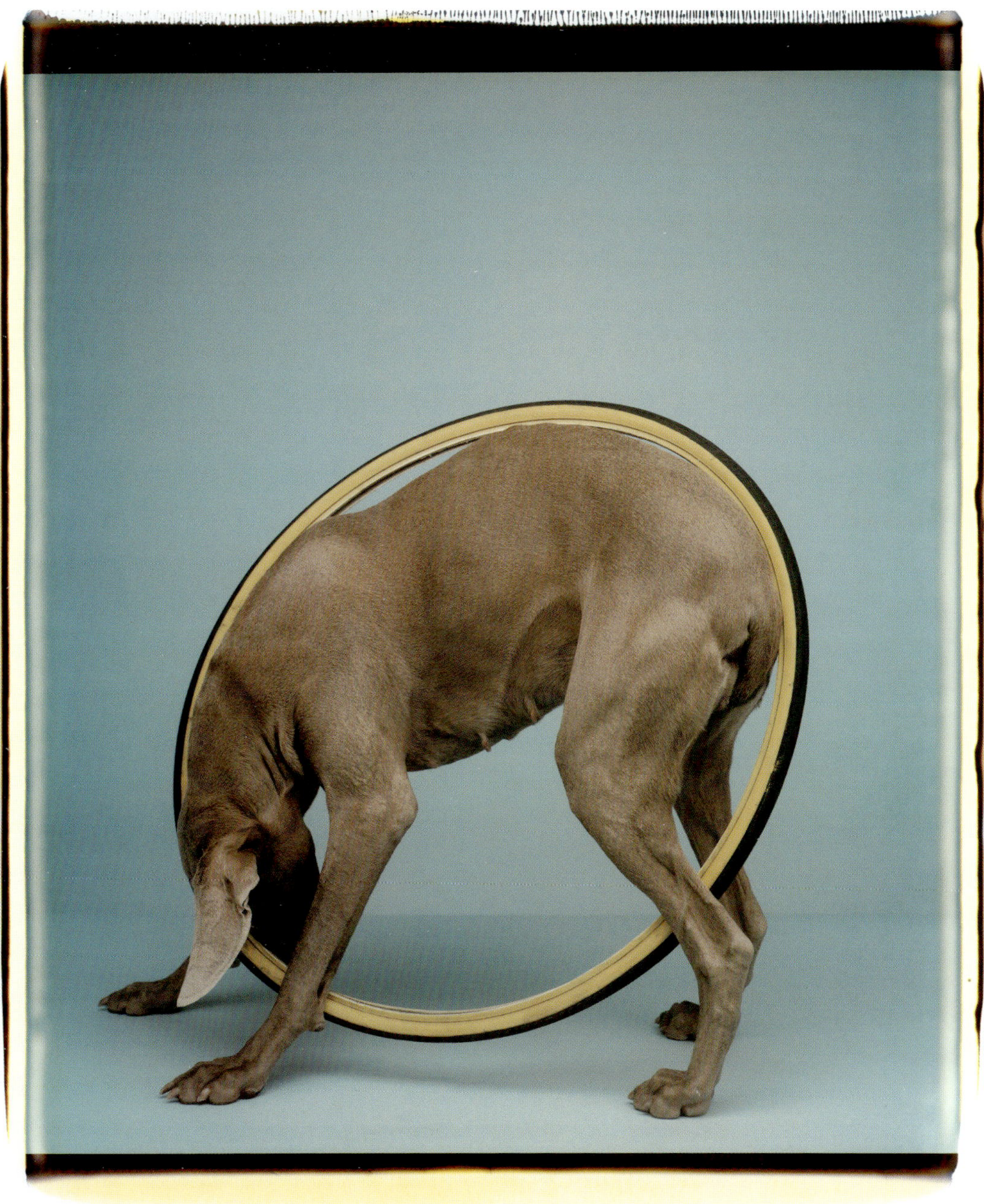

William Wegman (American, born in 1943)

Intirely, 1990

Dye-diffusion transfer print (Polaroid); 61 x 50.8 cm (24 x 20 in.)

Ernest Wadsworth Longfellow Fund 1992.155

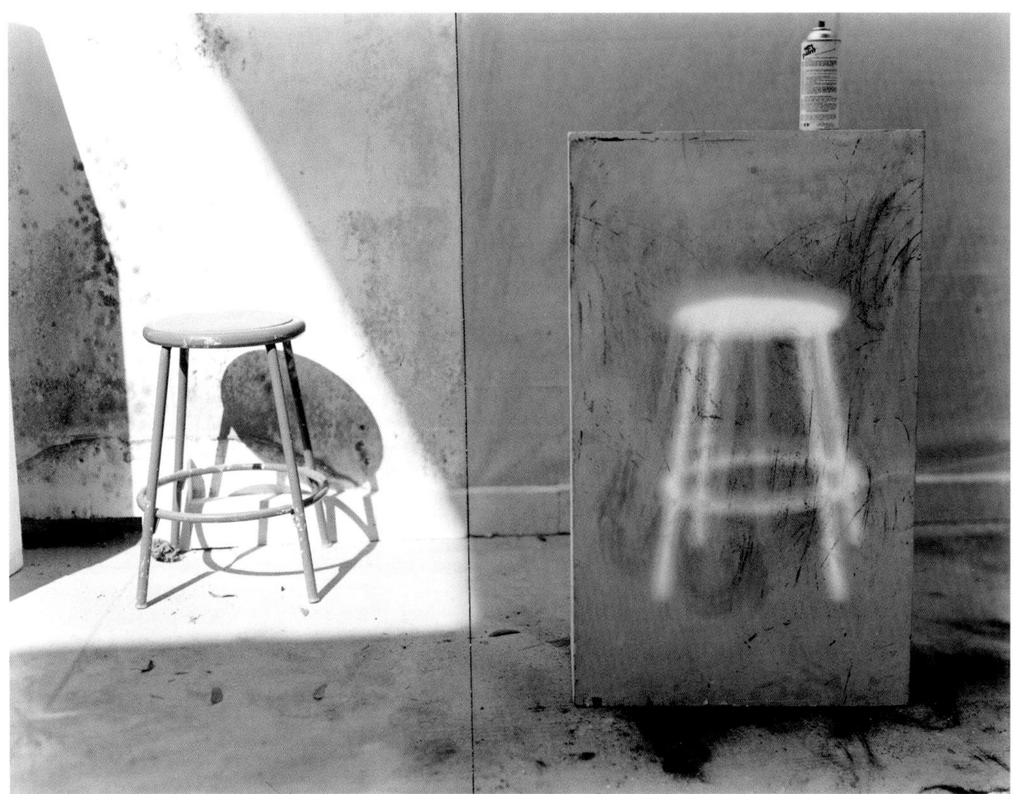

Robert Cumming (American, born in 1943)
Quick Shift of the Head Leaves Glowing Stool Afterimage Posited on Pedestal, 1978
Gelatin silver print; 19.7 x 24.9 cm (7 3/4 x 9 13/16 in.)
Museum purchase with funds donated by the National Endowment for the Arts, and Richard L. Menschel, Béla T. Kalman, Judge and Mrs. Matthew Brown, Mildred S. Lee, and Barbara M. Marshall 1990.55

The works of contemporary photographers Robert Cumming and Olivia Parker question the supposed objectivity of the medium. Both construct their photographs in the studio. Cumming's conceptual images of the 1970s often take shape as pseudo-scientific presentations, witty jokes with deeply layered meanings that address our notions of perception and illusion. This example is a false diptych that purports to be a demonstration of the scientific phenomenon described in its title. In the picture, a real stool, in bright sunlight, is shown next to its image, which seems to vibrate optically beside it. But the "afterimage" (in reality, an evanescent phenomenon) is here a spray-painted illusion, falsified "proof" that contrasts with the truthfulness of the photograph. Cumming willingly revealed his joke by including the aerosol paint can in the picture.

Parker, meanwhile, organizes juxtapositions of the

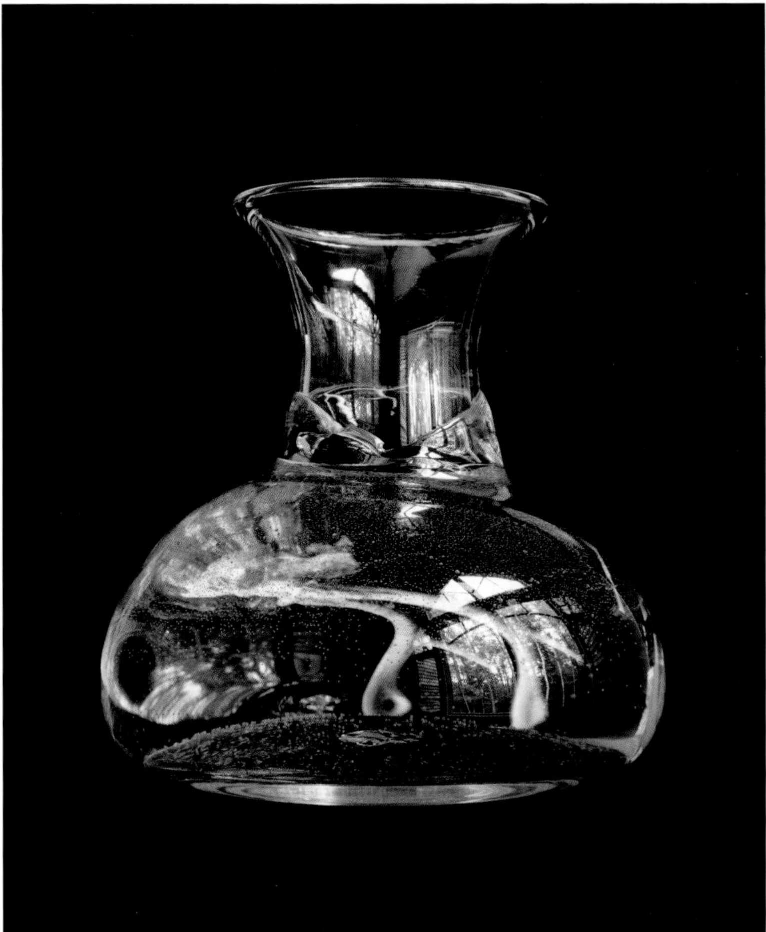

Olivia Parker (American, born in 1941)

Vessel, 1993

Gelatin silver print; 50.5 x 43.2 cm (19 7/8 x 17 in.)

Gift of Mrs. George R. Rowland, Sr. 1993.714

real that lead us into fantasy worlds. *Vessel* is the simplest of constructions: a beautiful bottle filled with water and photographed in strong, natural light. The large scale of the print reveals a world within the bottle, both real and illusory. Tiny air bubbles punctuate the watery atmosphere, and shadows cast by the decorative bottleneck swirl about like lissome fish. But equally present is the reflection of a vaulted room whose windows look out onto surrounding trees. The bottle itself has no context. Floating against a black background, it is removed from reality, and its contents become an otherworldly message within a crystal ball.

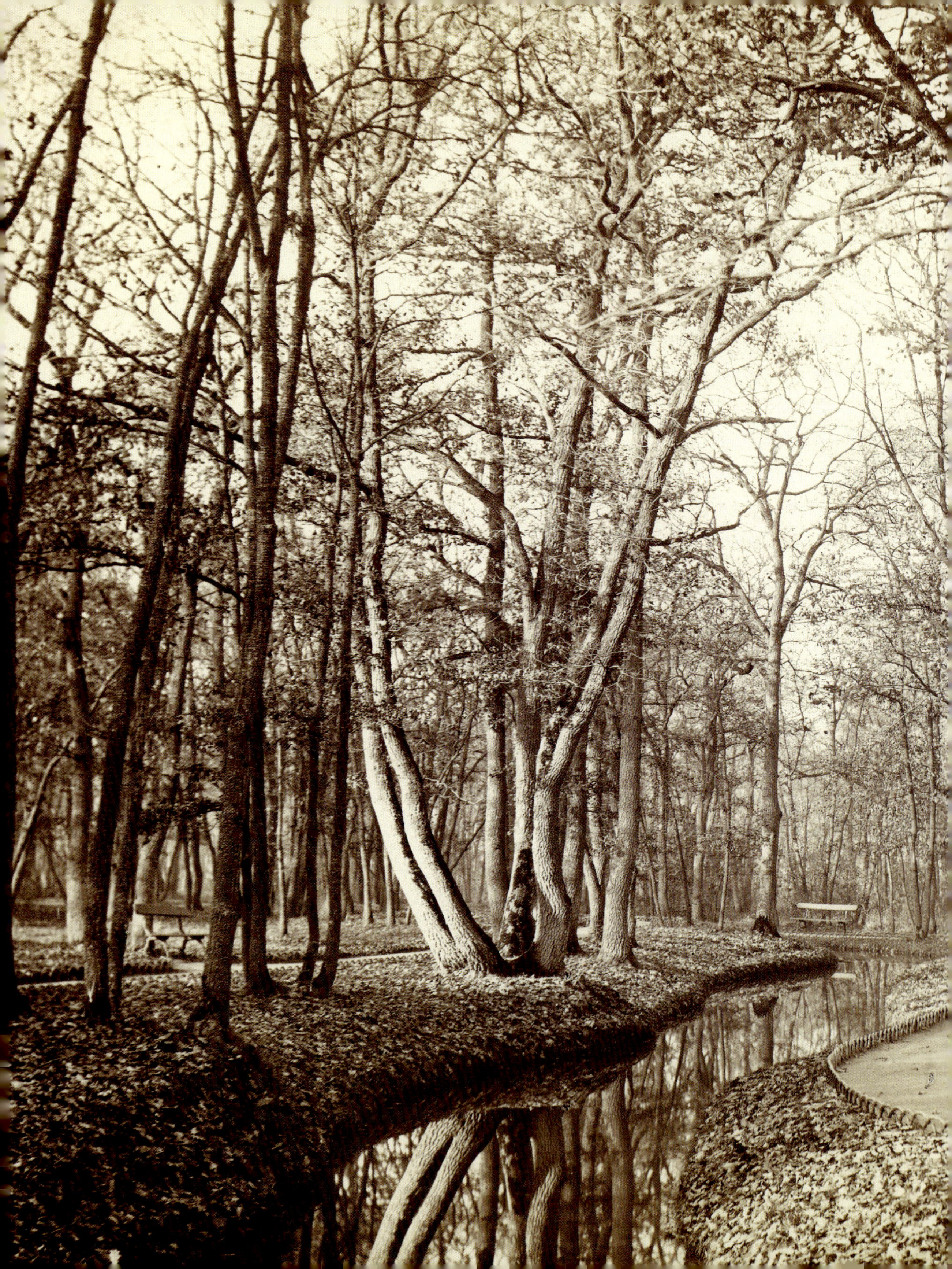

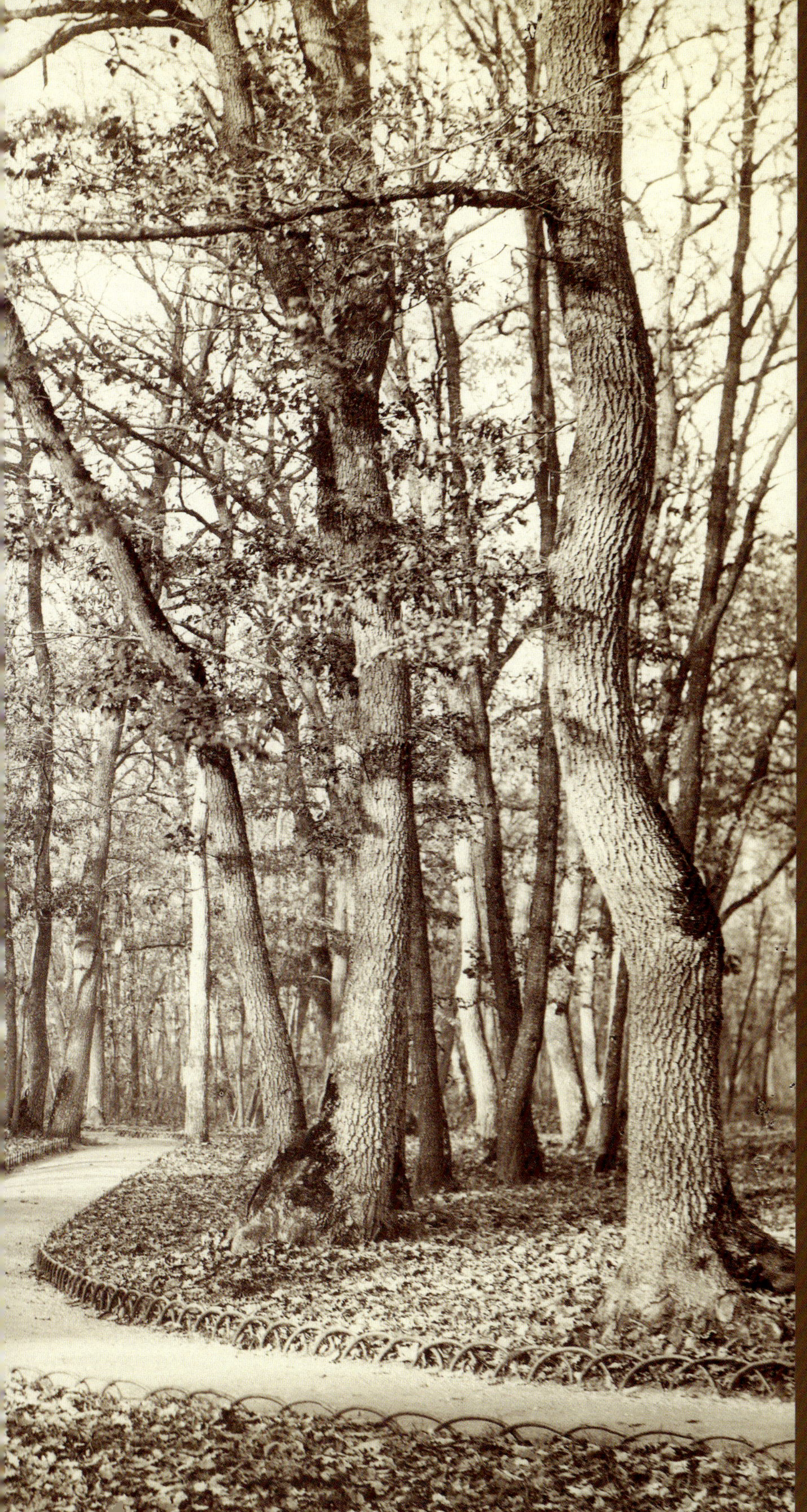

3

LANDSCAPES FROM NATURE, LANDSCAPES OF THE MIND

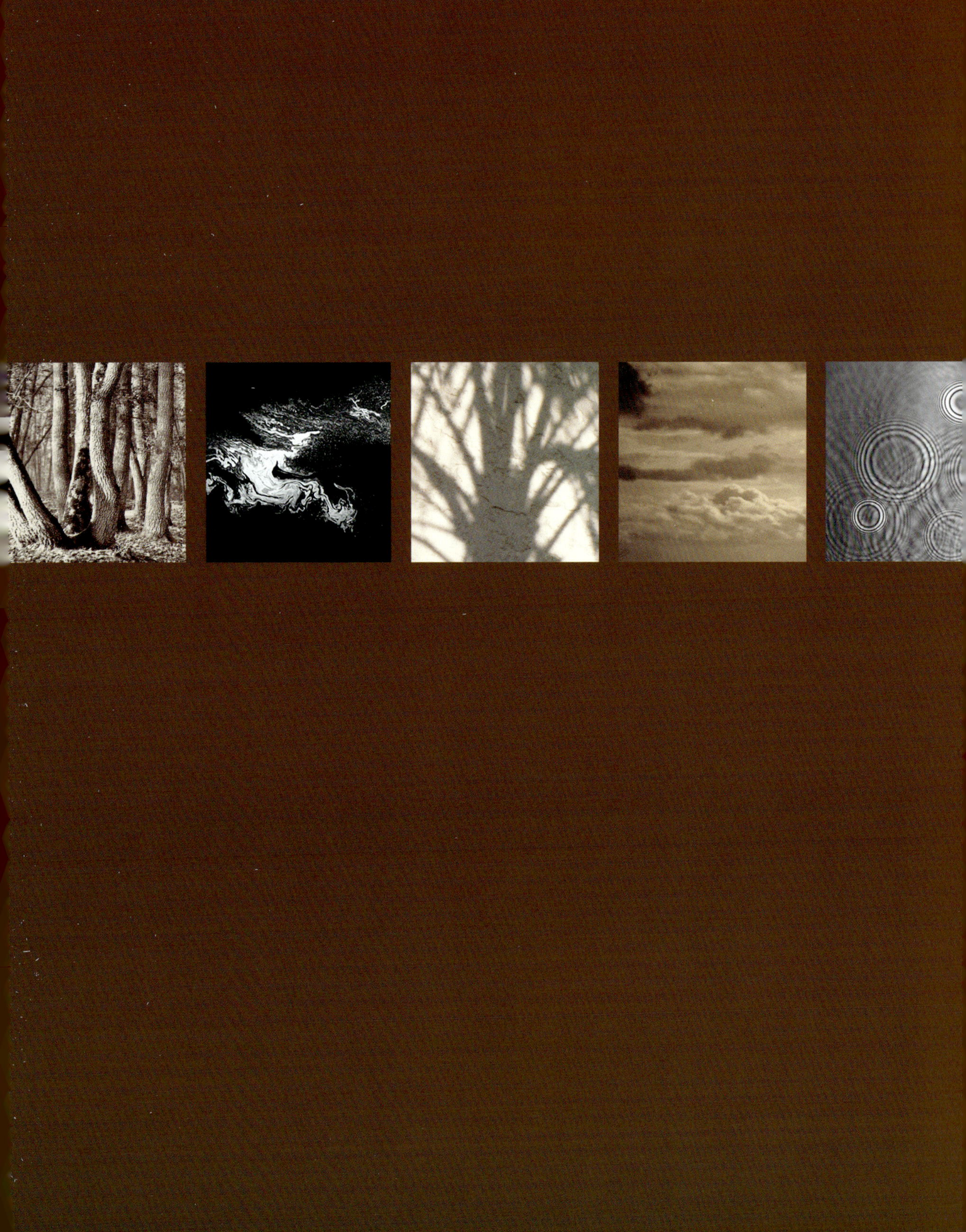

Landscapes from Nature, Landscapes of the Mind

The natural world was not easily recorded in the first few decades of photography, as varying exposure times were required for the different densities of light and tone in foliage, land, sky, and sea. Early practitioners nevertheless came to terms with the limitations of their medium and capitalized upon them, making images that suggested new interpretations of the landscape. As industrialization increased and more people moved to cities, country life and depictions of rural scenery came to be identified with ideals of simplicity and order, and were seen as sources of refuge for the weary spirit. As the business of tourism grew, so the format of landscape photographs became larger, expanding from images that could be held in the palm of a hand to "mammoth" views measuring as much as 18 x 22 inches.

At the close of the nineteenth century, the Pictorialists redefined photography's aesthetic, creating impressionistic transcriptions of the world that aimed for a metaphorical realism and the evocation of essential truths. Their ideas initiated a novel way of thinking about the possibilities for photographic expression. Camera operators became increasingly transfixed by their instrument's ability to suggest symbolic meaning, and they deliberately produced images intended for contemplation. Alfred Stieglitz advanced these ideas in his *Equivalents*, depictions of the clouds and sky taken at his family's summer home at Lake George. A looking inward to discover abstract interior landscapes was fostered through the experimental darkroom abstractions of Man Ray and László Moholy-Nagy.

By the end of the twentieth century, the philosophical approach to photographic image making had grown in strength, so that an artist such as Hiroshi Sugimoto was free to create his broadly conceptual, minimalist marine views that suggest the passage of time and the very nature of existence itself. The images illustrated here convey the multitude of outer and inner worlds that artists have captured or invented. Whereas photography was once viewed as the most literal of mediums, one that recorded the precise appearance of surfaces of this world at a particular moment, it has also become the means to evoke the most private of thoughts.

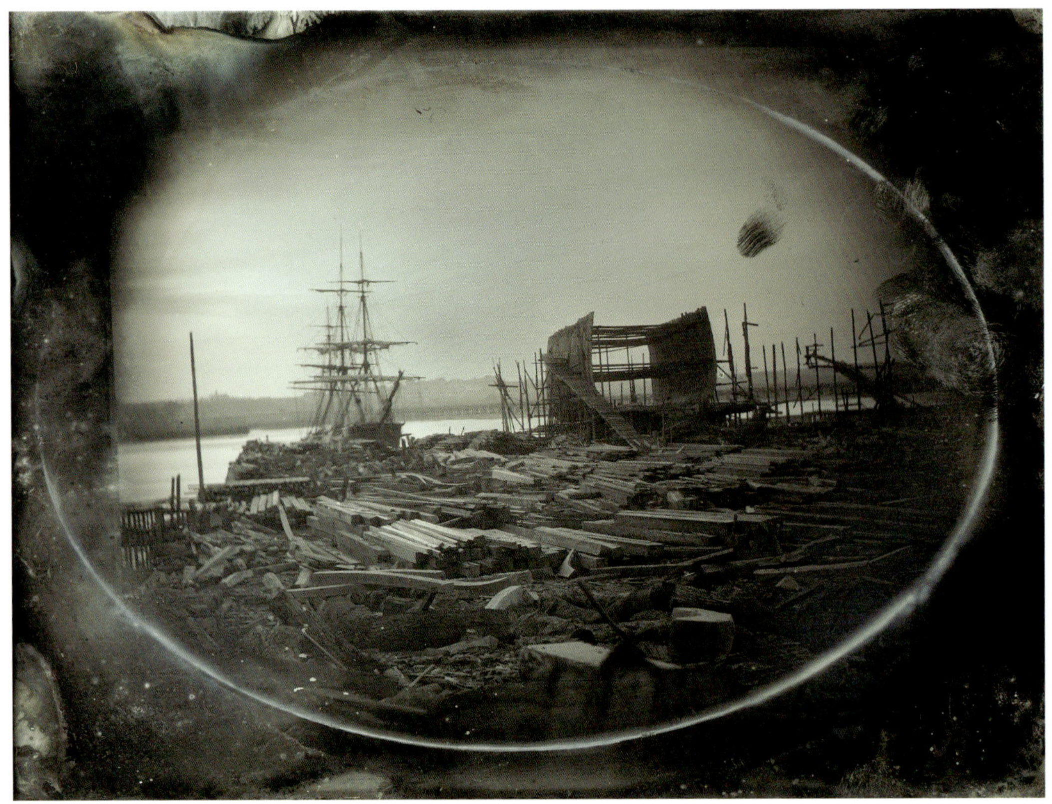

Albert Sands Southworth (American, 1811–1894)
Josiah Johnson Hawes (American, 1808–1901)
McKay's Shipyard, East Boston, about 1855
Daguerreotype; 16.7 x 21.7 cm (6 9/16 x 8 9/16 in.)
Gift of Richard Parker in memory of Herman Parker 1994.124

During the mid-nineteenth century, Boston was an important center for photography in the United States. The daguerreotype firm of Southworth and Hawes excelled at creating incisive character portraits of the era's most prominent citizens. Along with their views of well-known buildings, familiar locales, and noteworthy events, the studio's work amounted to a kind of collective portrait of the country at mid-century. Oliver Wendell Holmes, a noted author, physician, and member of New England's intellectual aristocracy, praised the importance of photography in the history of human progress in articles for the *Atlantic Monthly*. Holmes also invented a new type of stereoscopic viewer and practiced photography as a gifted amateur.

In an exceptional series of views taken at the shipyard of Daniel McKay, Southworth and Hawes presented a portrait of American enterprise. McKay's technologically advanced operation in East Boston used steam-powered sawmills and derricks to streamline construction of his legendary clipper ships. This daguerreotype, originally vignetted by an oval mat, brings us into the heart of the business. Stacks of timber fill the foreground, while a construc-

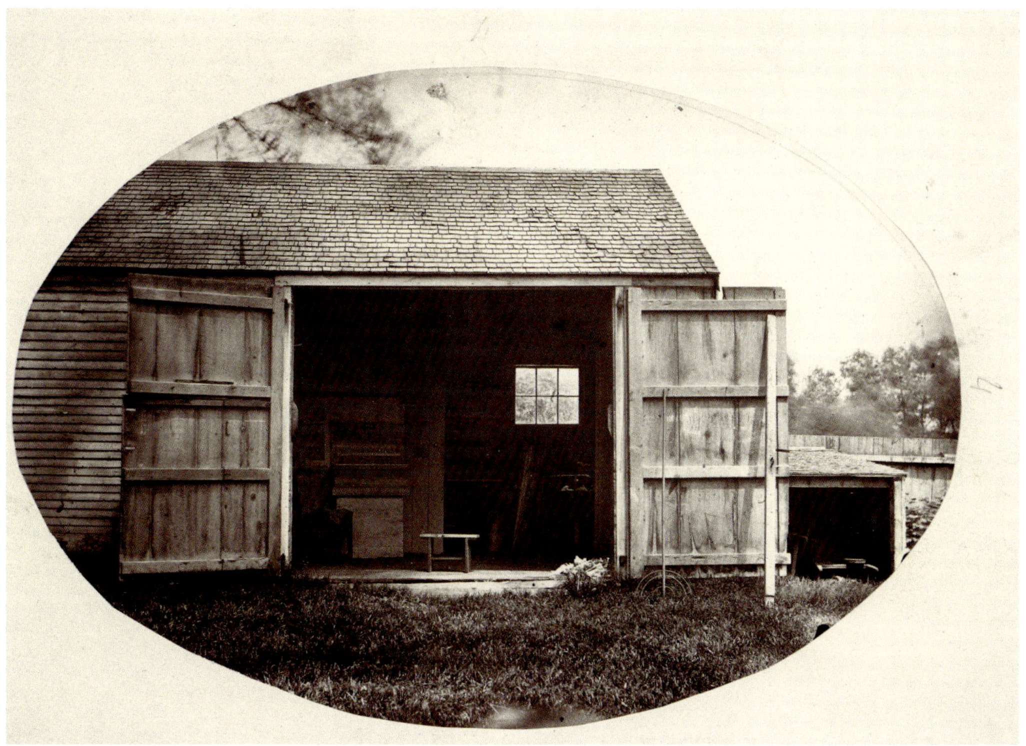

Oliver Wendell Holmes, Sr. (American, 1809–1894)

The Shed, 1864–65

Albumen print; 13 x 18.5 cm (5 1/8 x 7 5/16 in.)

Bequest of Mrs. Edward Jackson Holmes,

Edward Jackson Holmes Collection 65.606

tion bay and a clipper ship in the middle distance complete a story of American mercantile and maritime success.

Holmes's image of a shed on his Cambridge property emphasizes its clean, geometric lines. The oval format tightens the composition and concentrates our attention on the alternation of sunlit surfaces and dark voids that defines the structure. A bright interior window shines near the center of the picture, suggesting a view beyond the surface toward the inner reality of honest simplicity that underlies the New England spirit.

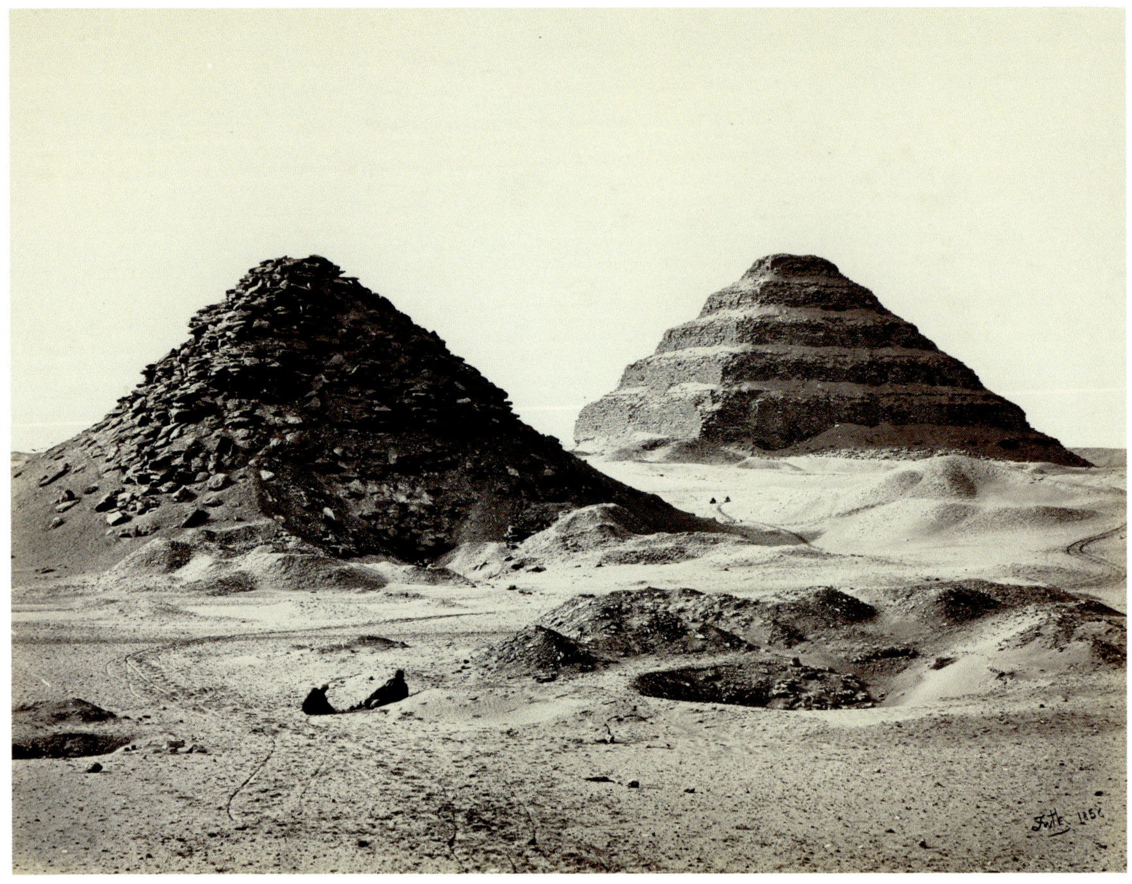

Francis Frith (English, 1822–1898)

The Pyramids of Sakkarah, 1858

Albumen print; 38.1 x 49.2 cm (15 x 19⅜ in.)

William E. Nickerson Fund 2002.622

These two views represent a mature phase in the history of photography when both the technique of the large glass-plate negative and the mass production of the albumen print had been mastered. Francis Frith undertook three photographic expeditions to Egypt and Palestine between 1856 and 1860, with the aim of creating a stock of images to be used for book illustration and stereo views. In 1859, he founded one of the most successful photographic printing works of the nineteenth century. The visual records he brought back from his travels were of such technical excellence that they not only documented the ancient civilizations but also evoked their power and majesty. In his large view of the great necropolis at Sakkarah, a small pillaged pyramid serves as a dark sentinel for the structure crowning the horizon, the fabulous step pyramid of the pharaoh Zoser, considered the most ancient building in the world.

Pompeo Molins produced photographs for the tourist trade at a time when the "Grand Tour" of

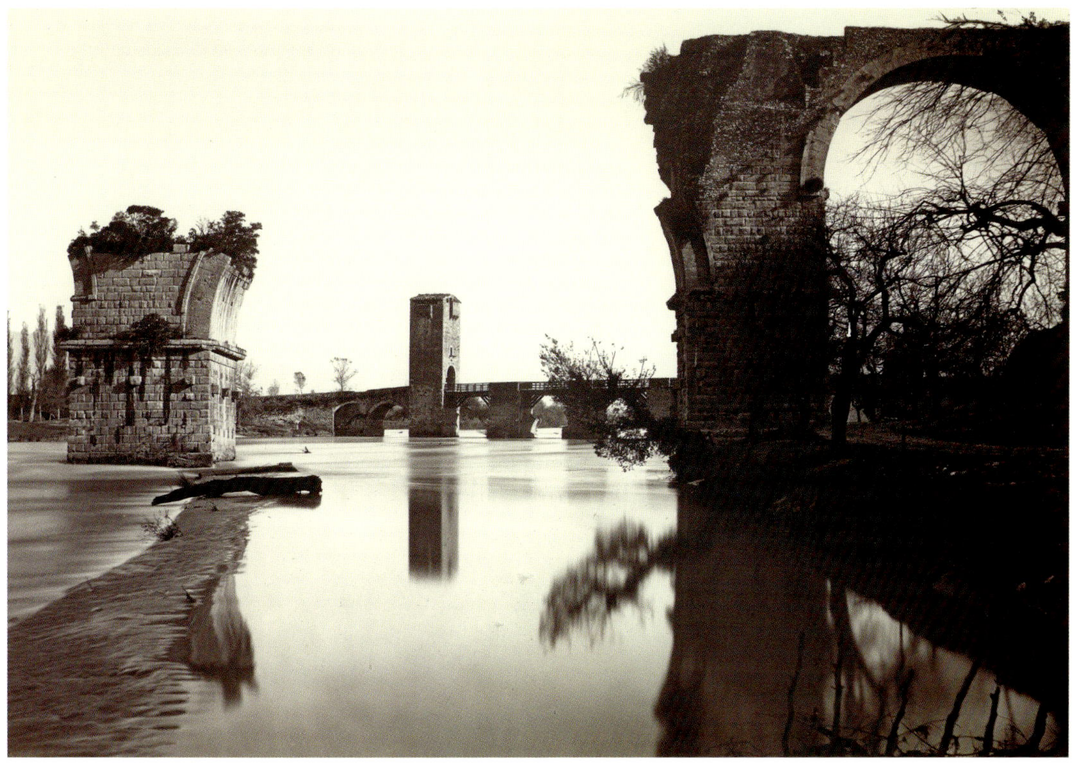

Pompeo Molins (Italian, 1827–about 1893)

Augustan Bridge at Narni, after 1865

Albumen print; 26.3 x 37 cm (10 3/8 x 14 9/16 in.)

Gift of the Classical Department (photo-library), Museum of Fine Arts, Boston 1980.26

Europe, with Italy as the centerpiece, was more popular than ever. In his *Augustan Bridge at Narni*, the massive ruins of the Roman monument combine with their reflection and a tangle of vegetation to form an impressive gateway through which an expanse of tranquil river leads to the tower of a medieval bridge. The flow of time and persistence of culture through the centuries is captured as a photographic souvenir for the nineteenth-century tourist.

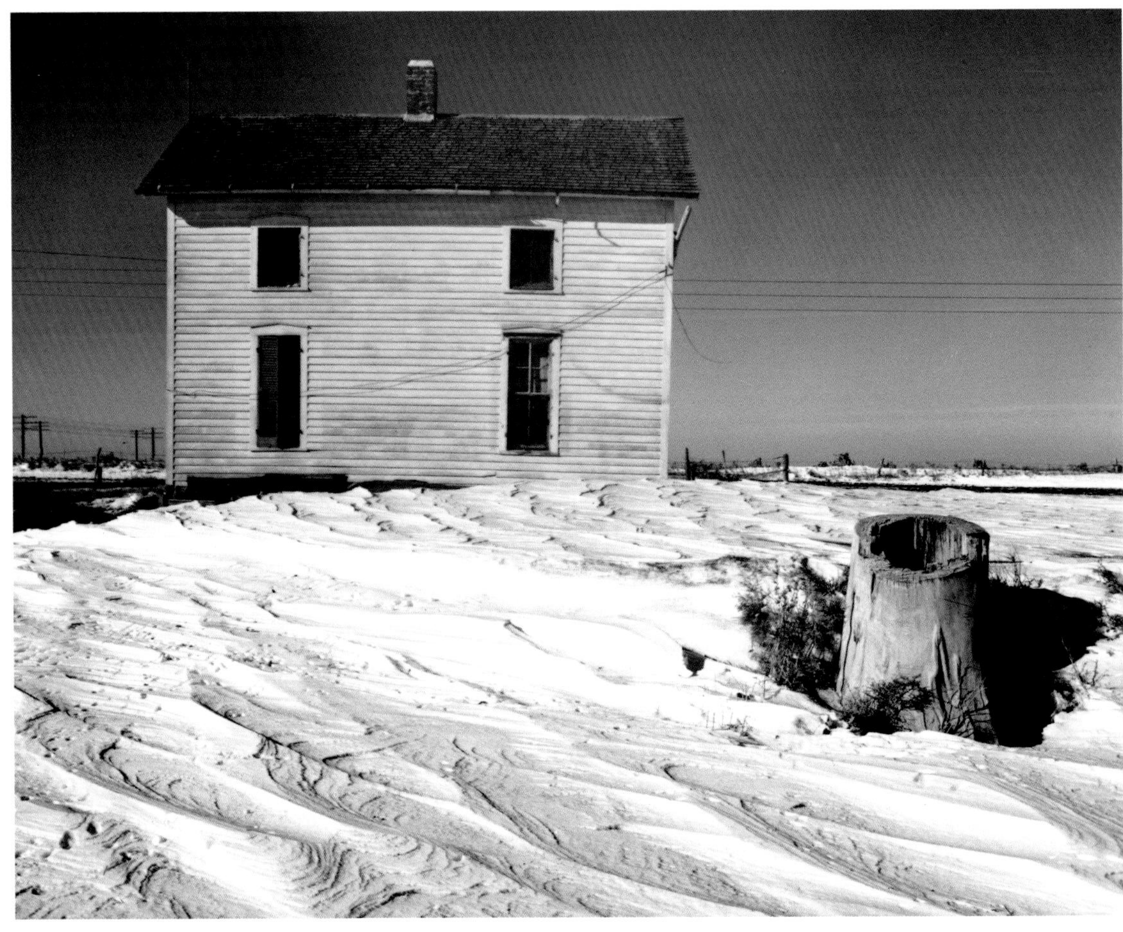

Wright Morris (American, 1910–1998)

Abandoned House, from the series *The Inhabitants*, 1941

Gelatin silver print, ferrotyped; 19.9 x 24.1 cm (7 13/16 x 9 1/2 in.)

Charles Amos Cummings Fund 1994.243

During the 1930s and 1940s, both Ansel Adams and Wright Morris made photographs of simple buildings such as farmhouses, barns, and small-town businesses set in their surrounding landscapes—in Adams's case, his native California, and in Morris's, rural Nebraska, where he grew up. Unlike many of their contemporaries, however, they did not choose these subjects for social-documentary ends. The Farm Security Administration encouraged its government-funded photographers to take pictures that reflected the hardship and suffering of the Depression, but neither Adams nor Morris saw this as their role as

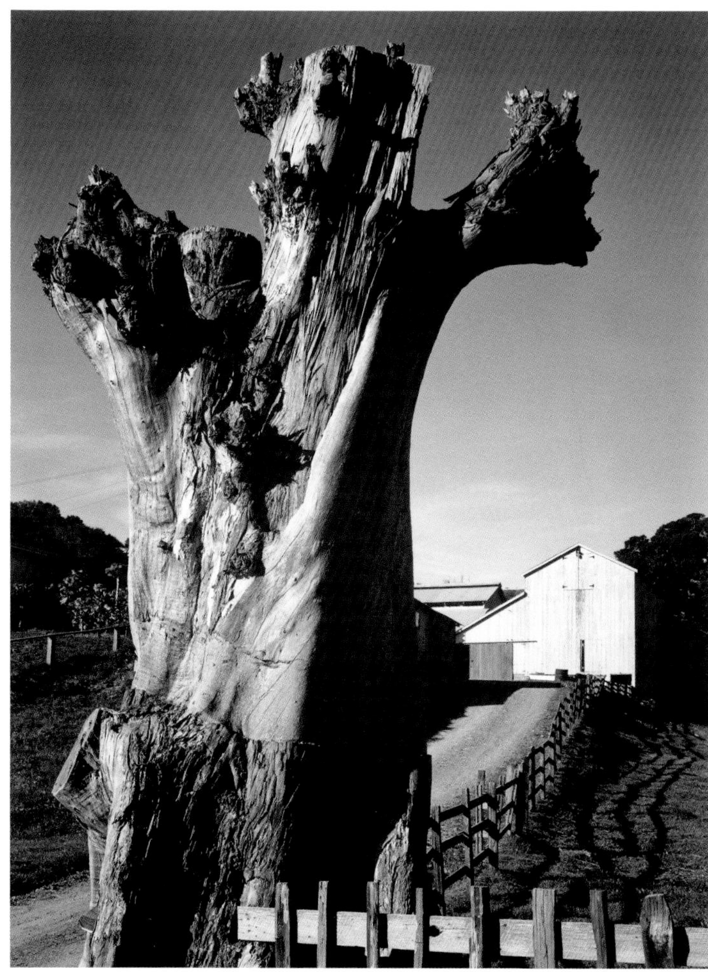

Ansel Adams (American, 1902–1984)
Near Bolinas, California, about 1938
Gelatin silver print; 24.1 x 17.5 cm (9 ½ x 6 ⅞ in.)
Gift of Mrs. George R. Rowland, Sr. 1992.325

photographers. For them, the capacity of their large-format view cameras to record the stark functional forms, eroded surfaces, and patina of age was much more important; Adams, in particular, believed that people needed beautiful images to inspire them during difficult times.

Morris, who was a writer as well as a photographer, paired pictures like *Abandoned House* with narrative texts in his book *The Inhabitants* (1946). He obviously felt affection for the austere house and bleak landscape of the midwestern plains and admired the ability of the photograph to describe the quotidian details of the setting in the same way that his writings gave voice to the people who lived there. In contrast, Adams's Marin County barn is strangely dwarfed by the anthropomorphic stump in the foreground. His focus is on the graphic shape of the white building and the network of dark shadows running along the fence, rather than on the individuals who worked the land.

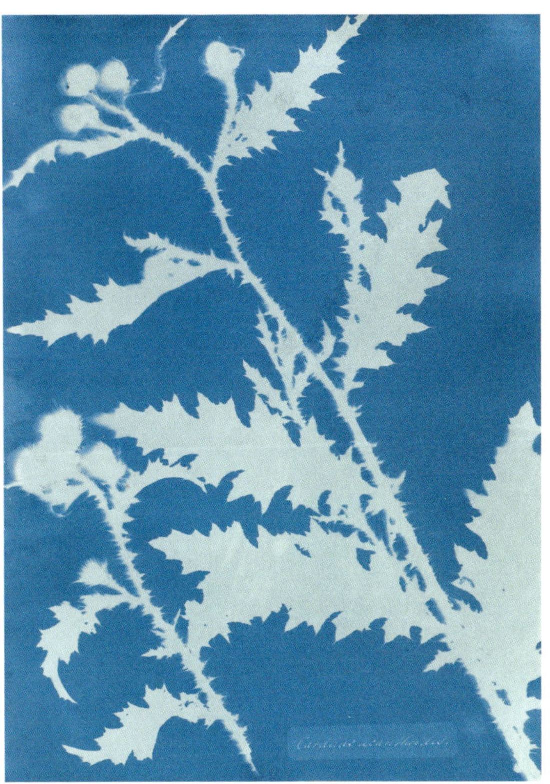

Anna Atkins (English, 1799–1871)

Thistle (Carduus acanthoides), about 1854

Cyanotype; 34.9 x 24.8 cm (13¾ x 9¾ in.)

Sophie M. Friedman Fund 1986.593

Anna Atkins and Imogen Cunningham were pioneer photographers at very different moments in the history of the medium. Atkins, a trained botanist with a background in scientific book illustration, became interested in the new invention of photography as a means of recording her botanical specimens. Using the cyanotype, a highly stable chemical variant of Talbot's photogenic drawing technique that Sir John Herschel had recently invented, Atkins published the first photographically illustrated book, *Photographs of British Algae: Cyanotype Impressions*, in installments between 1843 and 1853. Cunningham, who was a leading West Coast Pictorialist in her early career, created a series of plant studies during the 1920s that were landmarks in the development of a modernist, sharp-focus aesthetic in photography.

Atkins's *Thistle (Carduus acanthoides)*, from her later publication *British and Foreign Flowering Plants and Ferns*, is an artful presentation of a scientific subject. The featured plant spreads its bold form diagonally across the paper, overarching a smaller specimen. Its rough leaves and stems are sharply delineated against the characteristic Prussian blue background of the cyanotype, the accuracy of the representation confirming the value of the technique for scientific illustration.

Cunningham's *Exploding Bud (Billbergia)* exemplifies the technique she used for her plant studies, making close-up details even more abstract through dramatic contrasts in lighting. Here, the highlighted bud seems to emerge as we watch, its intense energy bursting through the velvety blackness of the surrounding shadows. A metaphor for the reproductive force of nature, the bud nonetheless documents aspects of its species with the sharp-focus clarity of the best scientific illustration.

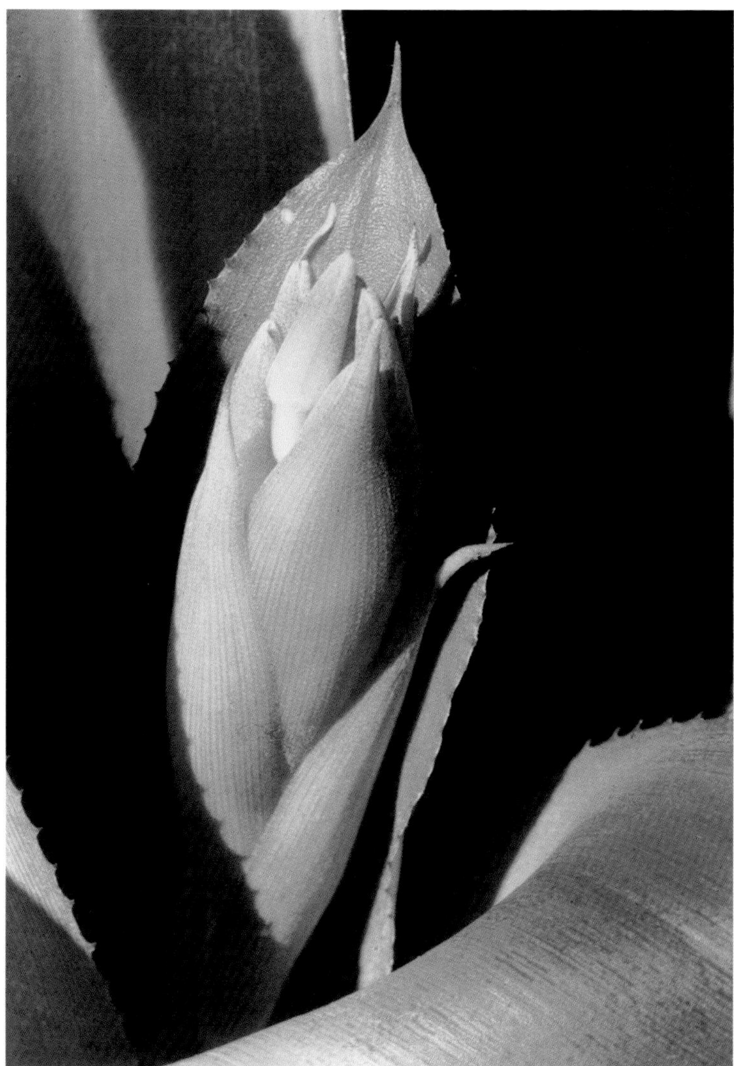

Imogen Cunningham (American, 1883–1976)

Exploding Bud (Billbergia), 1925

Gelatin silver print; 31.1 x 20.9 cm (12 ¼ x 8 ¼ in.)

Polaroid Foundation Purchase Fund 1973.302

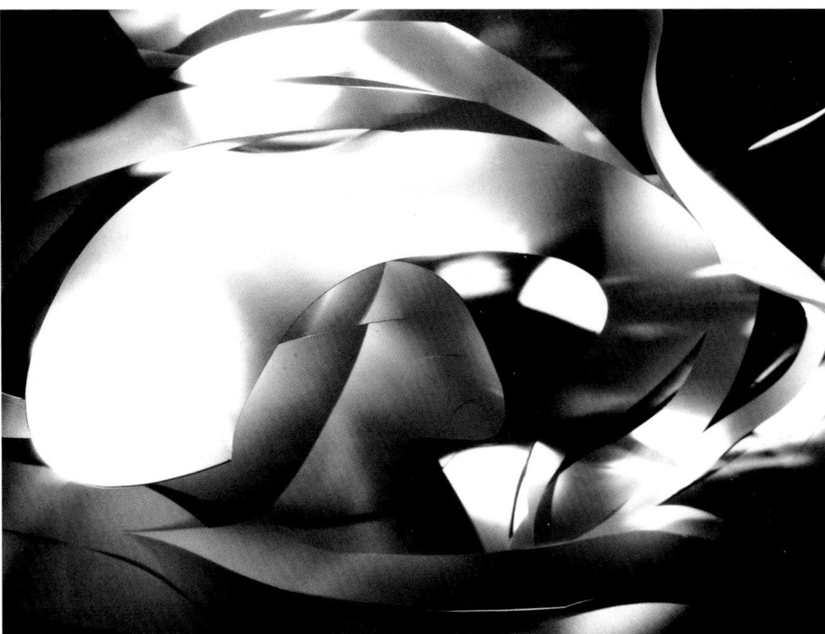

Francis Bruguière (American, 1879–1945)

Cut-Paper Abstraction, about 1926

Gelatin silver print; 20.3 x 25.4 cm (8 x 10 in.)

Sophie M. Friedman Fund 1986.585

The trend toward photographic abstraction that emerged in the 1920s is illustrated in these two photographs. This current paralleled the evolution of a strict realism to counter the Pictorialism that had prevailed early in the century. László Moholy-Nagy was a major figure in the development of modernist art and design in Europe and the United States, while Francis Bruguière, after an early Pictorialist phase, became an important influence on American avant-garde photography. Both men were pioneers in photographic experimentation.

Moholy-Nagy's innovative work at this time included the use of oblique angles, unusual points of view, photomontage, and the cameraless photographs known as photograms. Photograms are light drawings made by placing objects in direct, or near, contact with paper coated with light-sensitive chemicals. When exposed to light, the objects leave their impression on the paper, resulting in a unique image characterized by the immediacy of direct creation. Moholy-Nagy's bold and elegant 1939 example is made even more compelling by its large size. The identity of the objects is transformed into an abstract vision of overlapping, transparent planes floating in a void.

Bruguière experimented with multiple exposures, solarization, and the cut-paper abstractions for which he is so well known. His photographs of cut-paper designs, although not photograms, evolved out of experiments with using light alone to create abstract photographic forms. In this image, the cutout is photographed in strong, dramatic light, making its elaborate and graceful curves appear as a complex intertwining of light and shadow.

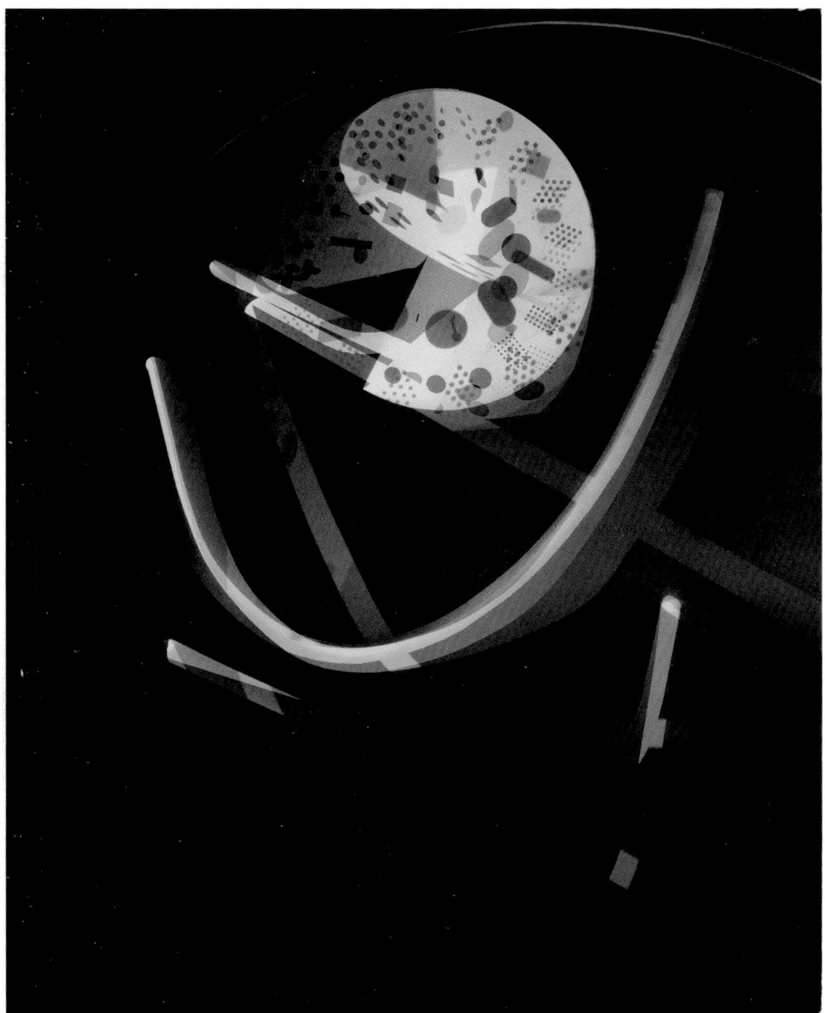

László Moholy-Nagy (American, born in Hungary, 1895–1946)

Untitled, 1939

Gelatin silver print; 50.5 x 40.3 cm (19 7/8 x 15 7/8 in.)

Museum purchase with funds donated by Virginia Herrick Deknatel 2001.10

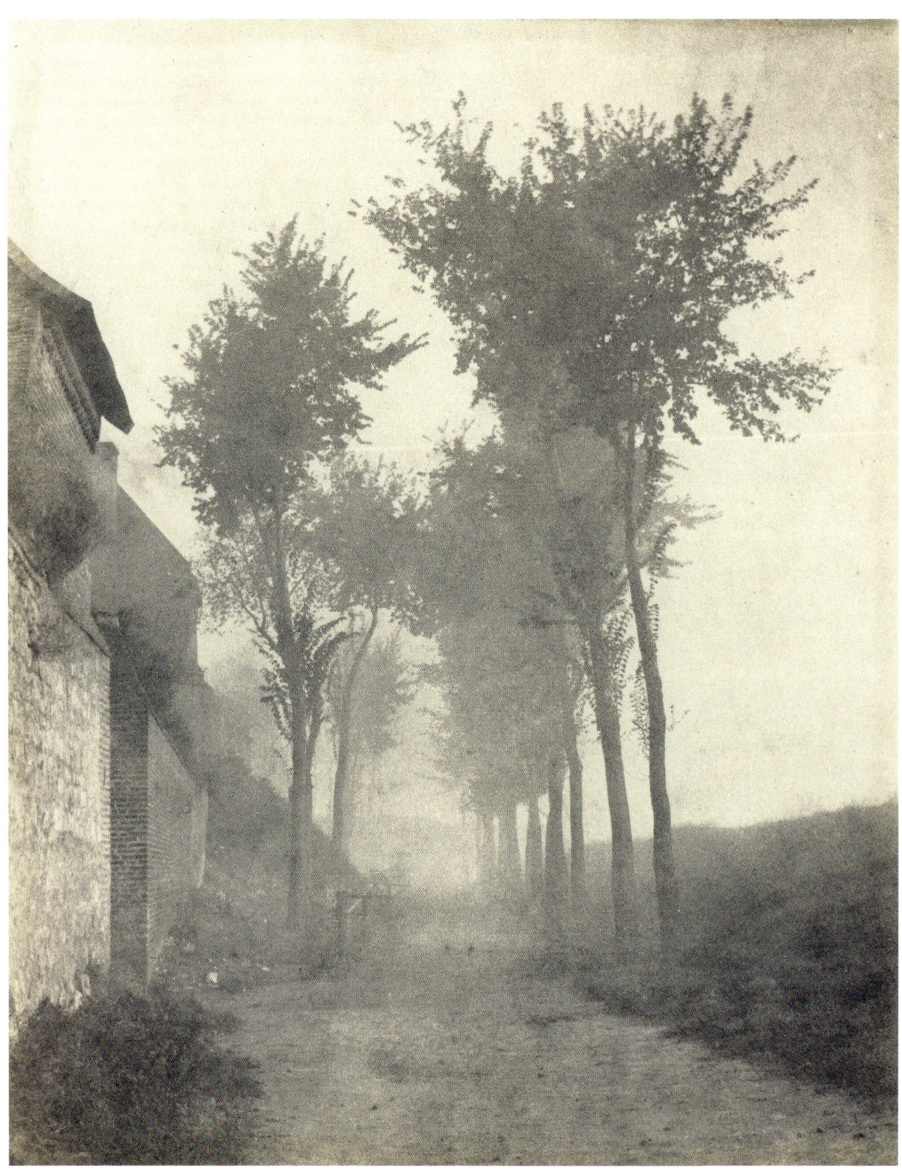

Eugène Cuvelier (French, 1837–1900)

Lane in Fog, Arras, 1860–65

Salt print from a paper negative; 25.7 x 19.8 cm (10 ⅛ x 7 13/16 in.)

Lucy Dalbiac Luard Fund 1989.21

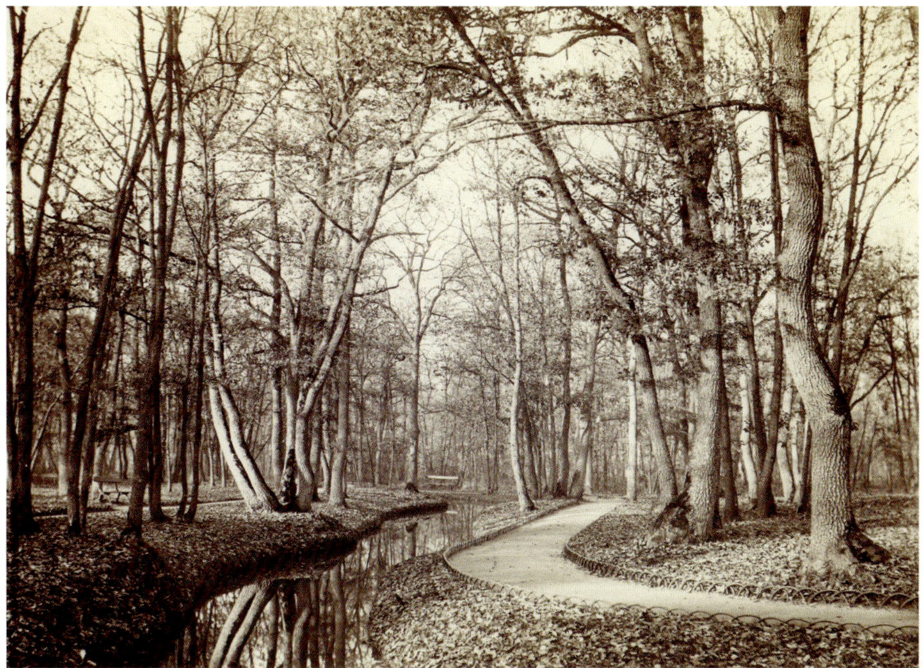

Charles Marville (French, 1816–about 1879)

Path in the Bois de Boulogne, 1858

Albumen print; 26.9 x 36.5 cm (10 9/16 x 14 3/8 in.)

Sophie M. Friedman Fund 1984.54

Eugène Cuvelier's poetic interpretation of a foggy lane in Arras is a markedly different vision of the French landscape than Charles Marville's crisp rendition of a woodland path in the newly redesigned Bois de Boulogne. Both men were trained as artists. Cuvelier grew up in Arras, near the Forest of Fontainebleau, where he became friends with many artists of the Barbizon school, the most inventive landscape painters of the day. Marville's career followed a commercial path. After youthful beginnings as an illustrator, by 1850 he had become a photographer specializing in landscape and architectural views. His work earned him important government commissions to record the transformation of the city of Paris that began in the 1850s.

The differences between these two images result in part from the photographers' choice of materials. For his *Lane in Fog, Arras*, Cuvelier used a paper negative, a material that had long before been superceded by the glass negative in photographic practice. The fibers of the paper muffled excessive detail, resulting in a soft rendering of the misty village byway that is reminiscent of contemporary works by the Barbizon painter Camille Corot. In his attention to the play of light and atmosphere, Cuvelier touched on ideas that would later become the major themes of Impressionism. For Marville, the glass negative was the logical choice for a documentary series on the new park. Its clear and detailed records were windows onto the artful design of the planned landscape, an urban forest playground for the citizens of the new Paris.

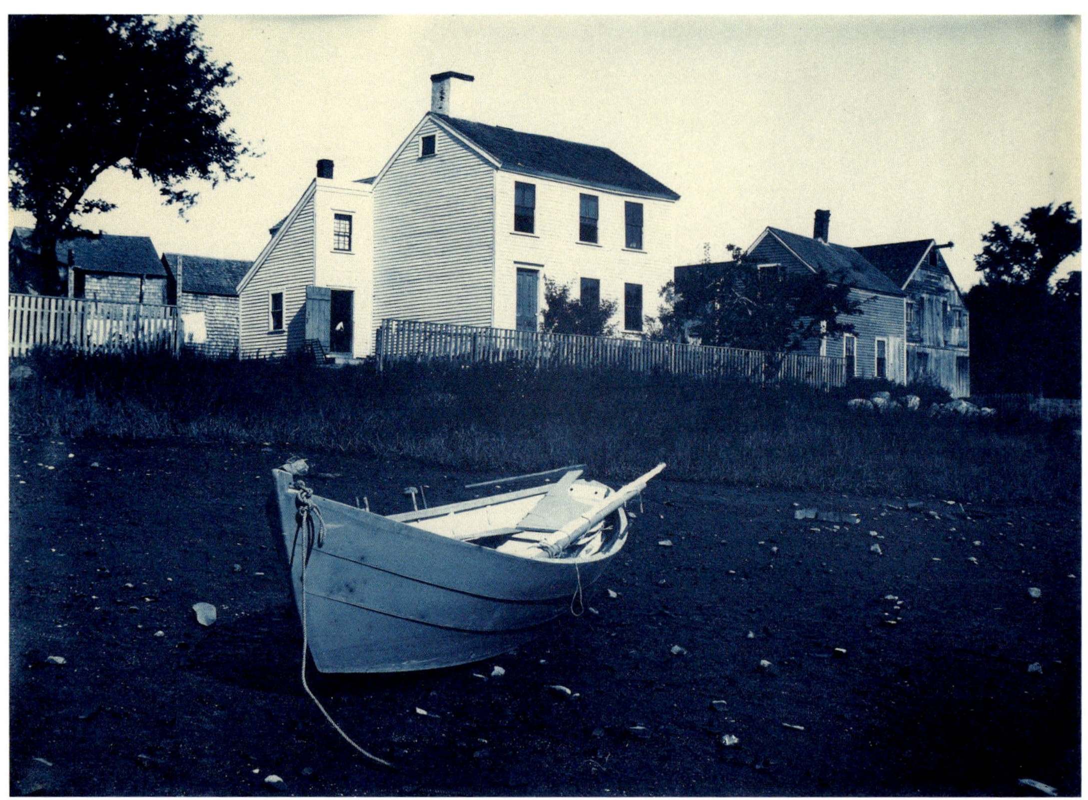

Arthur Wesley Dow (American, 1857–1922)

White Clapboard House and Dory, about 1900

Cyanotype; 15.3 x 20.4 cm (6 x 8 in.)

Gift of Philio Wigglesworth Cushing and Henry Coolidge Wigglesworth from the collection of their parents Frank and Anne Wigglesworth in memory of their love for Ipswich. M. and M. Karolik Fund and Charles H. Bayley Picture and Painting Fund 2006.1277.237

A number of photographers of the Arts and Crafts period sought to create images of rural simplicity infused with poetic atmosphere. One of these was Arthur Wesley Dow, an artist best known for his prints and paintings, who found inspiration in the Japanese print collection at the Museum of Fine Arts, Boston, where he worked in the 1890s. In response to prints by Hiroshige, Hokusai, and others, Dow developed aesthetic principles of design that focused on the flat, formal relationships of compositions and emphasized a harmony of line, tone, and color. Through his teaching and his popular manual *Composition*, first published in 1899, Dow influenced American art for decades. In his experiments with photography, Dow particularly appreciated the cyanotype process for the ease with which prints could be made and for their decorative blue shade.

George H. Seeley, younger by a generation, was undoubtedly familiar with Dow's ideas. As an art instructor in the Stockbridge, Massachusetts, public

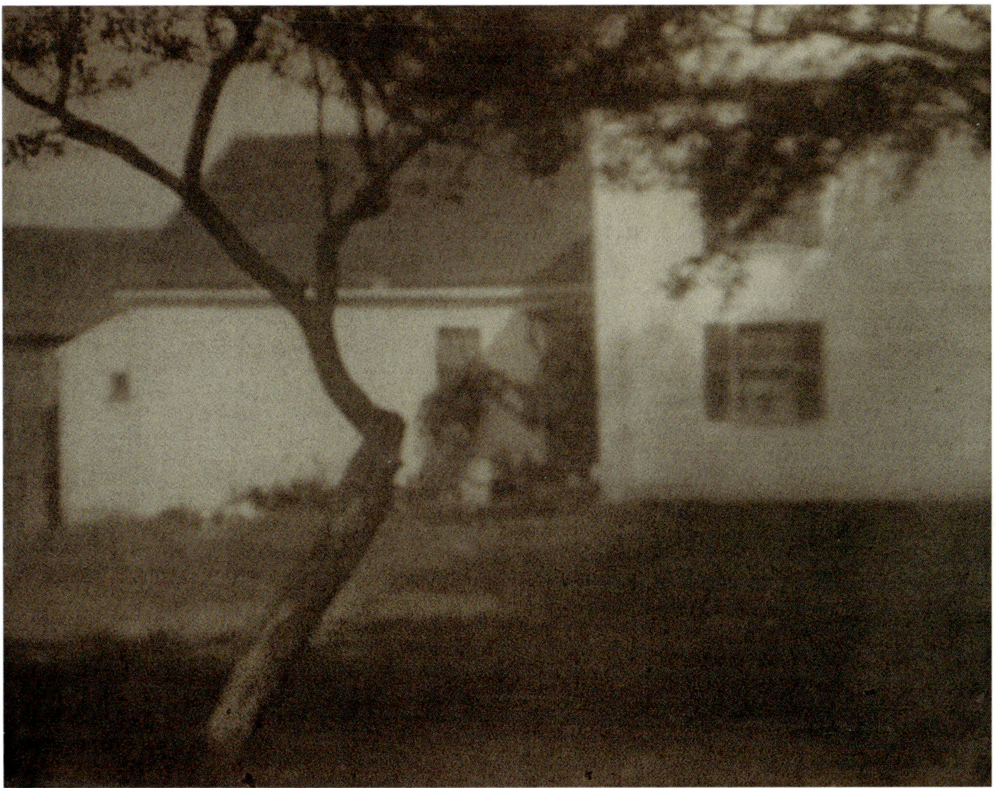

George H. Seeley (American, 1880–1955)

Apple Tree and House, 1914

Platinum and gum bichromate combination print

33.9 x 42.2 cm (13 3/8 x 16 5/8 in.)

Charles Amos Cummings Fund 1988.331

schools, he may have referred to the exercises in Dow's manual for his teaching. Seeley often printed his softly focused landscapes, still lifes, and portraits doubly, in platinum and gum bichromate, to enhance their tonal, impressionistic effect. The paring down of compositional elements and the emphasis on abstract shapes in this example and in the photograph by Dow can be seen as heralds of the modernist vision that was on the horizon.

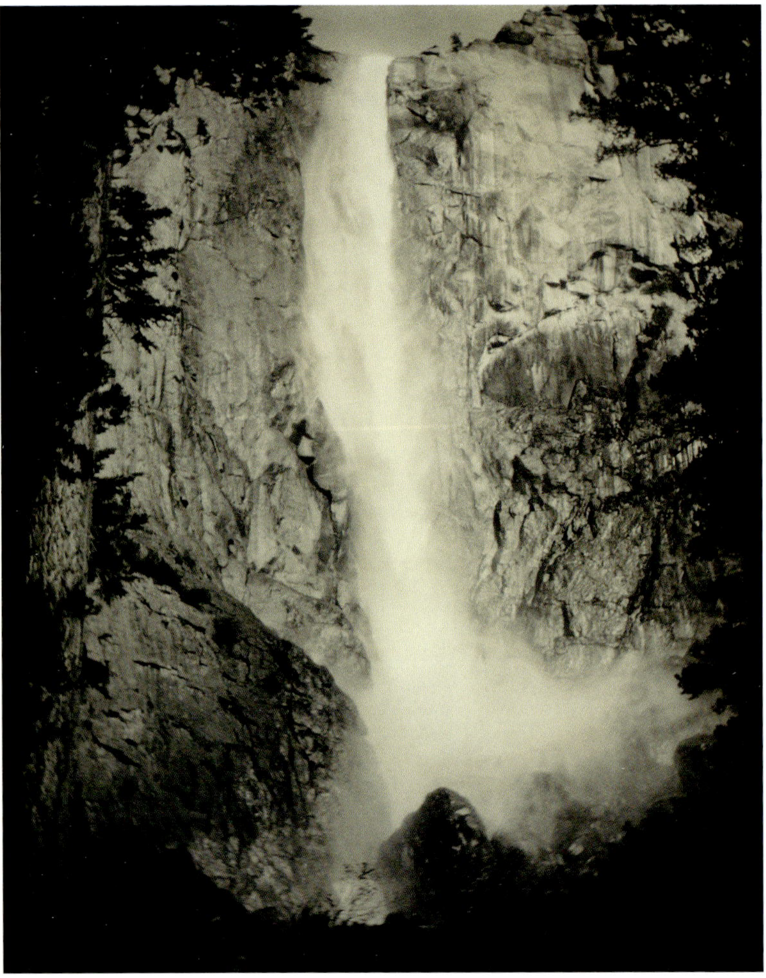

Alvin Langdon Coburn (American, 1882–1966)

Yosemite Falls, 1911

Platinum and gum bichromate combination print; 40.6 x 32 cm (16 x 12⅝ in.)

Sophie M. Friedman Fund 1981.146

These photographs of falling water by Alvin Langdon Coburn and Toshio Shibata represent diverse responses to nature. Coburn's *Yosemite Falls* is a Pictorialist vision of nature influenced by his teacher Arthur Wesley Dow's theories about harmony and tone, while Shibata's boldly formal work explores the tension between nature and the works of man, describing them as equal forces.

Coburn's images of the American West, although inspired by the pioneering photographers of California such as Eadweard Muybridge and Carleton Watkins, abandon the documentary purpose of his predecessors. His interpretation of Yosemite Falls is an impression, not a description, of lyrical beauty. The platinum process, combined with the painterly gum bichromate technique, produces a range of tones

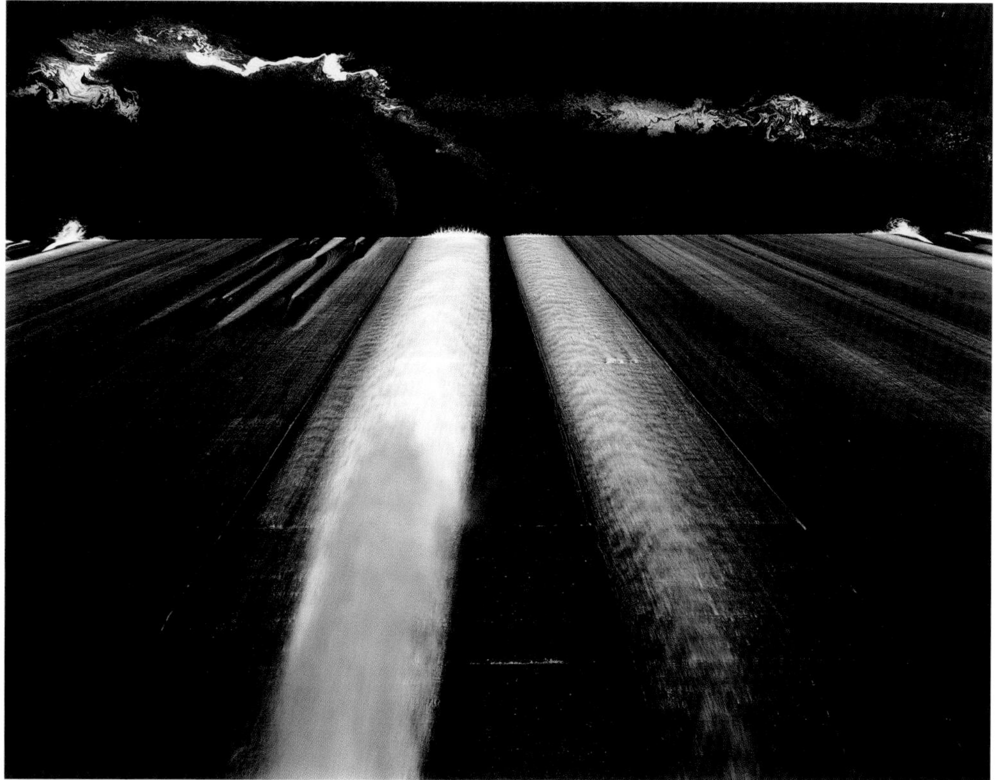

Toshio Shibata (Japanese, born in 1949)

Grand Coulee Dam, Douglas County, WA, 1996

Gelatin silver print; 104.5 x 128.9 cm (41 ⅛ x 50 ¾ in.)

Museum purchase with funds donated by John and Olivia Parker 1999.9

that is broad as well as deep: the velvety blackness of the surrounding trees frames the gray zones of the rocky escarpment, and the tonal progression culminates in the luminous white passage of the falls, softened almost to the point of abstraction by a long exposure.

In Shibata's *Grand Coulee Dam*, the dam itself, while powerfully present, is scarcely visible. Water flows over an immense surface in converging streams and columns, its inexorable rush in tension with the massive structure that holds it back. The vertiginous view is intentionally disorienting, with trails of foam easily misread as calligraphic clouds. The enormous size of the print showcases the confrontation between the natural and artificial worlds, reduced to an abstract idea of force and power.

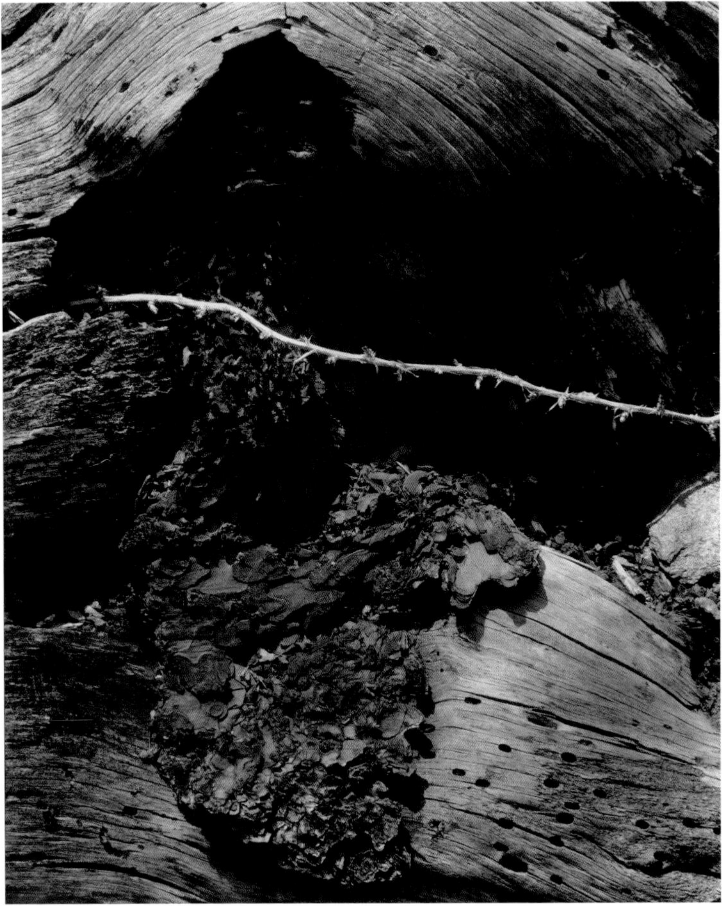

Paul Strand (American, 1890–1976)

Tree Stump and Vine, Colorado, 1926

Platinum print; 25.1 x 20.2 cm (9 ⅞ x 7 15/16 in.)

Sophie M. Friedman Fund 1977.781

American photographers Paul Strand and Harry Callahan both used their cameras to crop the great expanses of nature into ever smaller and more abstract images. During the 1920s, Strand began experimenting with close-up views of natural subjects, including mushrooms, rocks, and, in this case, a vine and tree stump. Working with a large-format camera in natural light and extremely sharp focus, Strand found in these intimate images fascinating microcosms of the larger world around him. Like Stieglitz's cloud pictures and Weston's photographs of shells from the same period, his close-up studies push the simplification of natural form to its limit without ever becoming purely abstract. Here, the artist seems to transform the branch of thorns into a vivid bolt of lightning and the weathered bark into the waves of a stormy sea.

Harry Callahan's 1970s view of Cape Cod shares with Strand's image a tendency toward almost complete abstraction. With its square format and perfect

Harry Callahan (American, 1912–1999)

Cape Cod, 1972

Gelatin silver print; 20.4 x 25.2 cm (8 1/16 x 9 15/16 in.)

Polaroid Foundation Purchase Fund 1975.337

balance between the expanse of glowing sky above and the rippled stretch of sand below, the image is stunning in its minimalism. Callahan had been drawn to photograph water for many years, especially at its edges and shorelines—first on Lake Huron and Lake Michigan and then during summers on Cape Cod. His goal was to capture in the most essential and economic way possible the subtle shifts of light and atmosphere at these ephemeral intersections where the sky ends and the earth and water begin.

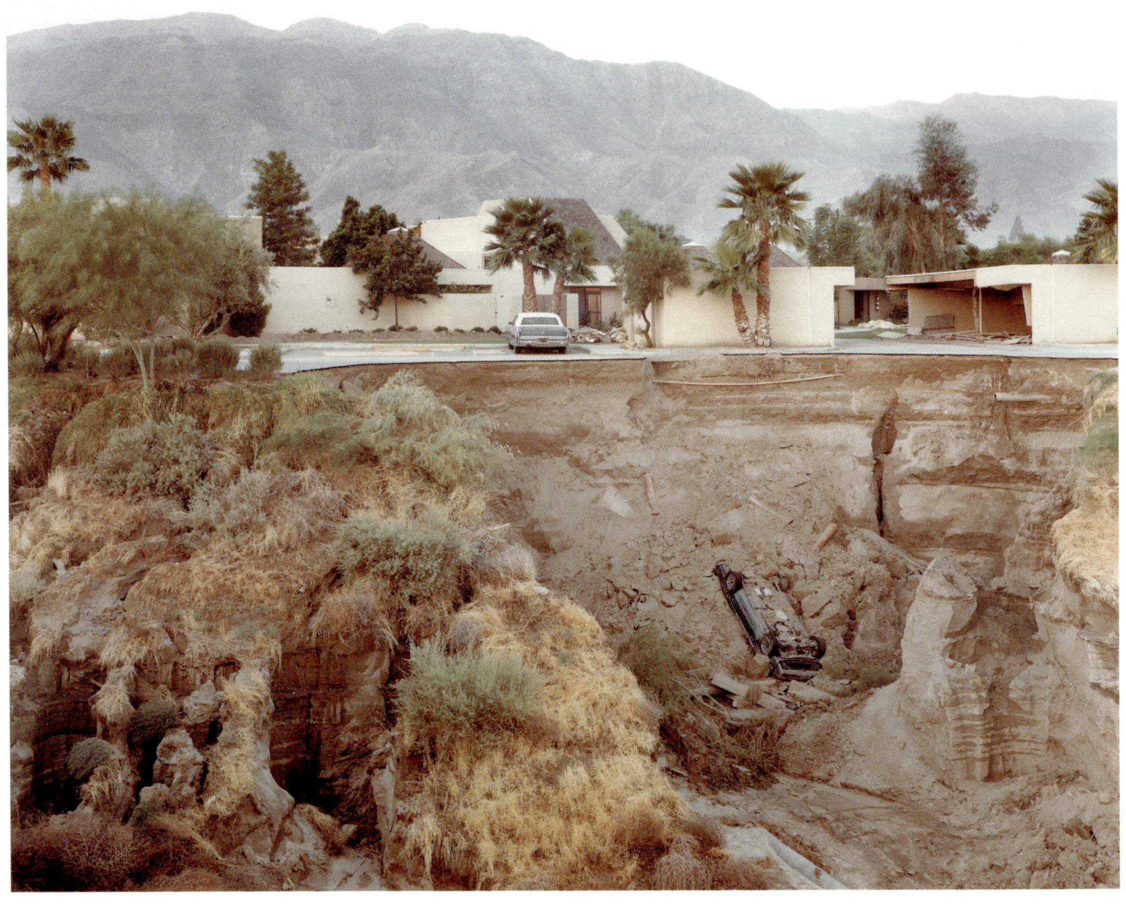

Joel Sternfeld (American, born in 1944)
After a Flash Flood, Rancho Mirage, California, July 1979
Chromogenic print (Ektacolor); 40.6 x 50.8 cm (16 x 20 in.)
Polaroid Foundation Purchase Fund 1982.529

During the 1970s, a growing number of American photographers, including Joel Meyerowitz and Joel Sternfeld, were linked by a newly dispassionate and less idealized approach to nature and culture. Sternfeld's photographs have a seductive beauty, even though they often focus on those places where the natural and man-made worlds come together in uncomfortable ways. In 1978, the artist began crisscrossing the country in a Volkswagen camper, working with a large-format camera and luminous color to create images that are frequently ironic or even humorous. His compositions appear simple but in fact are surprisingly complex and often unsettling. In this photograph of a suburban California neighborhood in the aftermath of a flash flood, the lovely

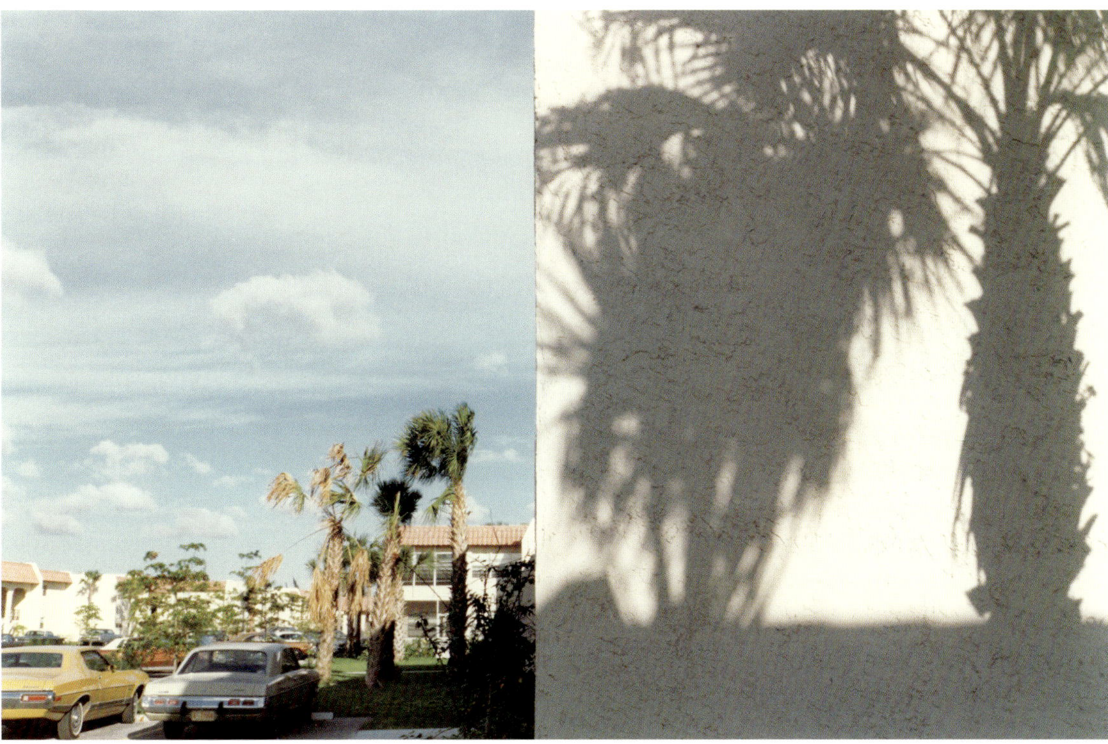

Joel Meyerowitz (American, born in 1938)

Florida, 1975

Chromogenic print (Ektacolor); 28 x 35.5 cm (11 x 14 in.)

Polaroid Foundation Purchase Fund 1975.372

monochrome tones trick us into not immediately seeing the car that has toppled into the gaping sinkhole or realizing that the buildings above could be on the verge of falling, too.

Joel Meyerowitz began as a street photographer in 1962, shooting at first in color and later in black-and-white. By 1974, he had turned completely to color, and in 1976 he started using an 8 x 10 view camera. Along with many photographers of his generation, Meyerowitz was drawn to the startling and strange aspects of everyday life and the visual challenges of the modern American landscape. His kaleidoscopic images from this period, like Sternfeld's, capture the collision of man and nature, but often from a more urban perspective. Here, the soft shadows of Florida palm trees fall on the stark surface of a wall, which bisects the image and creates a strange disconnect between near and far, artificial and real.

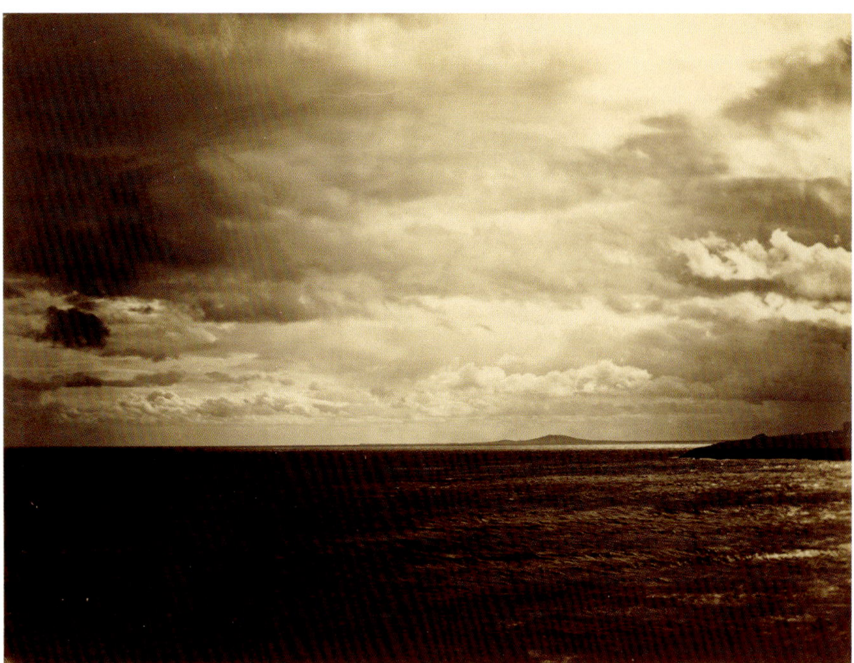

Gustave Le Gray (French, 1820–1882)

Cloudy Sky, Mediterranean Sea, 1857

Albumen print from two wet collodion negatives

31.1 x 39.7 cm (12¼ x 15⅝ in.)

Gift of Charles Millard in honor of Clifford S. Ackley 1997.241

Gustave Le Gray advanced the painterly aspects of early photography. A pioneer of photographic techniques and a sought-after teacher throughout his career, he is best known for the majestic ocean views that he made between 1856 and 1858. Printed on a scale that was large for its time, images such as this view of Mount Agde, taken along France's Mediterranean coast, have a visual power that brought Le Gray international praise. The project forced him to deal with the varying tonal intensities of the clouds and sea, which were difficult to record with the available technology. He skillfully circumvented the problem by using two negatives, which he unobtrusively joined at the horizon line during printing.

Like Le Gray, the Japanese photographer Hiroshi Sugimoto has captured breathtaking views of the sea, but his perspective is rooted in conceptual art. Sugimoto, who studied art in California in the early 1970s and who divides his time between Tokyo and New York, merges traditional Eastern ideas about the creative process with a 1960s Western minimalist approach. In much of his work, he contrasts light and darkness, void and substance. Sugimoto's seascapes, for which he has traveled around the world, are precisely planned: the horizon appears at dead center and all details of the place are avoided (he includes no land, no ships, no bird in the sky). The artist has said that his aim, in this series, is to evoke the emotional response of early man when he first encountered the vast open sea.

Hiroshi Sugimoto (Japanese, born in 1948)

Ionian Sea, Santa Cesarea I, 1990

Black Sea, Ozuluce, 1991

Gelatin silver prints; 48.3 x 60.3 cm (19 x 23¾ in.) each

Gift of Sylvan Barnet and William Burto in memory of Yasuhiro Iguchi

1992.212, 1992.214

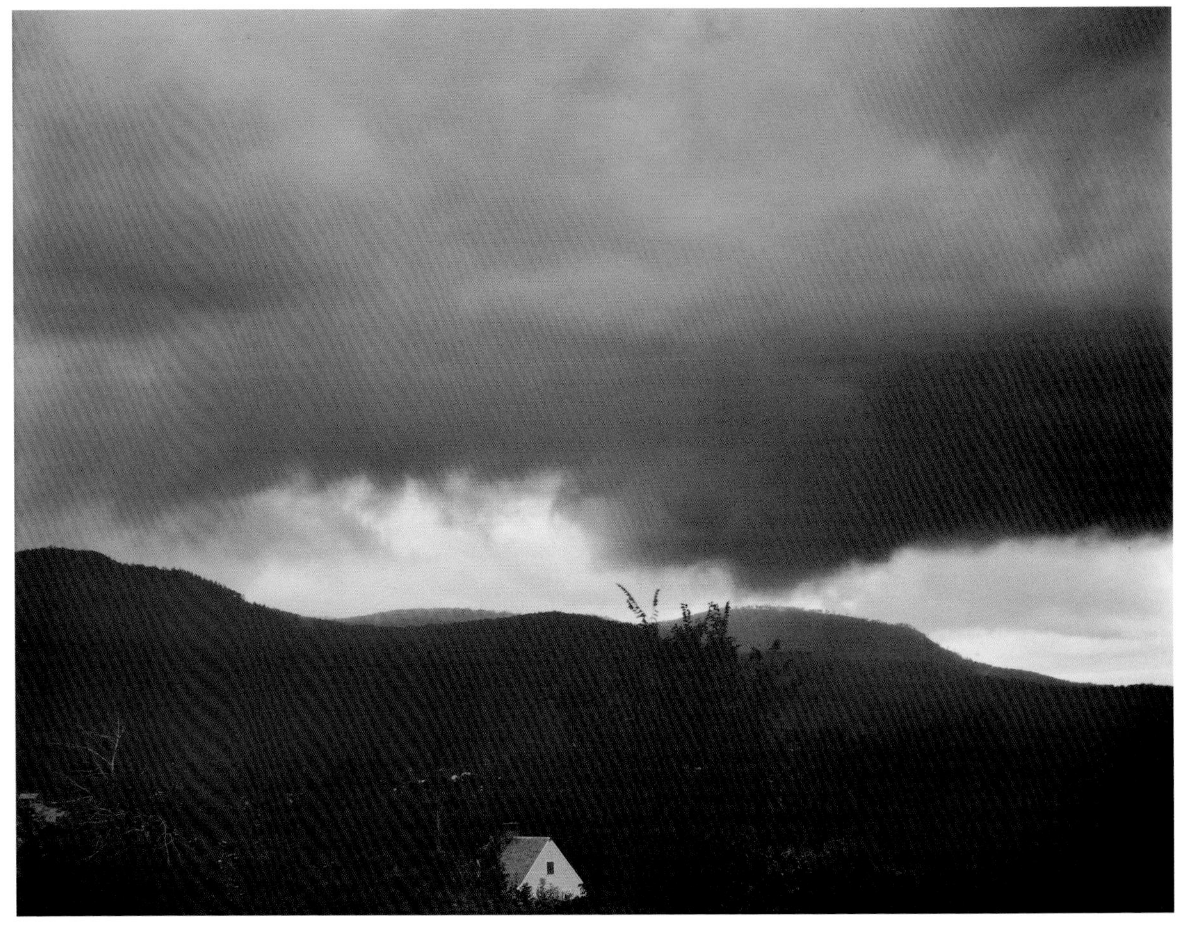

Alfred Stieglitz (American, 1864–1946)

Music: A Sequence of 10 Cloud Photographs, No. 1, 1922

Gelatin silver print; 19.1 x 24.1 cm (7 ½ x 9 ½ in.)

Gift of Alfred Stieglitz 24.1732

In this photograph, Alfred Stieglitz kept detail to a minimum, isolating a lone white house in a composition of overall darkness that is dramatically torn into two zones as the impending storm chases away the remnants of clear sky. The title of the work suggests that the image could be understood as a visual symphony, an equivalent of musical sound. Made at a time of personal turmoil in Stieglitz's life, the photograph had emotional resonance, as well. It is an important precursor to his celebrated images of clouds, titled the *Equivalents*, in which he developed his concept of photographs as metaphors for inner feelings. Stieglitz ultimately believed that through clouds he could express his philosophy of life.

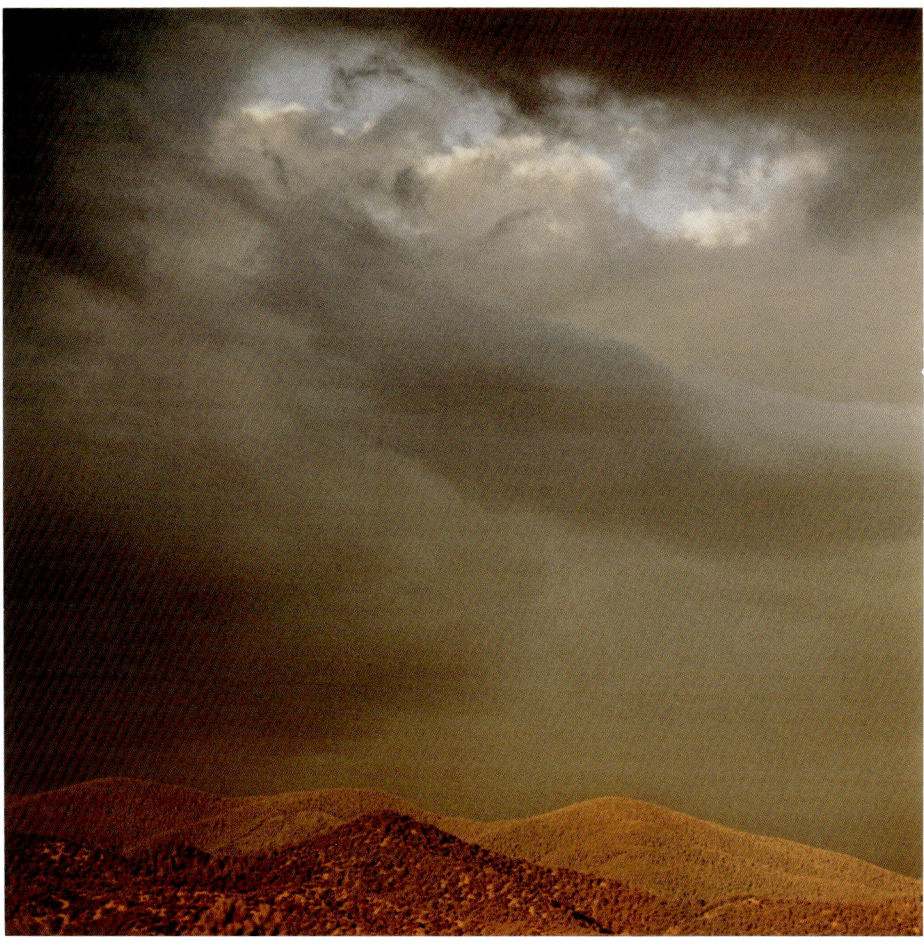

Eliot Porter (American, 1901–1990)

Sangre de Cristo Mountains at Sunset, Tesuque, New Mexico, 1958

Dye transfer print; 21.9 x 21.5 cm (8⅝ x 8 7/16 in.)

Sophie M. Friedman Fund 1984.148

Eliot Porter's nature photographs have been instrumental in both the growth of the environmental movement throughout the world and the increased acceptance of color photography as an artistic medium. A pioneer in color landscape photography, Porter was committed to the dye transfer process, a complex craft that allows extensive control over image color in all its subtle variations. His photograph of a blue-gray cloud mass over the orange hills of the Sangre de Cristo range is both a literal translation of a particular time and place and an artistic vision, worthy of a Baroque painter, of clouds parting onto blue and white heavens.

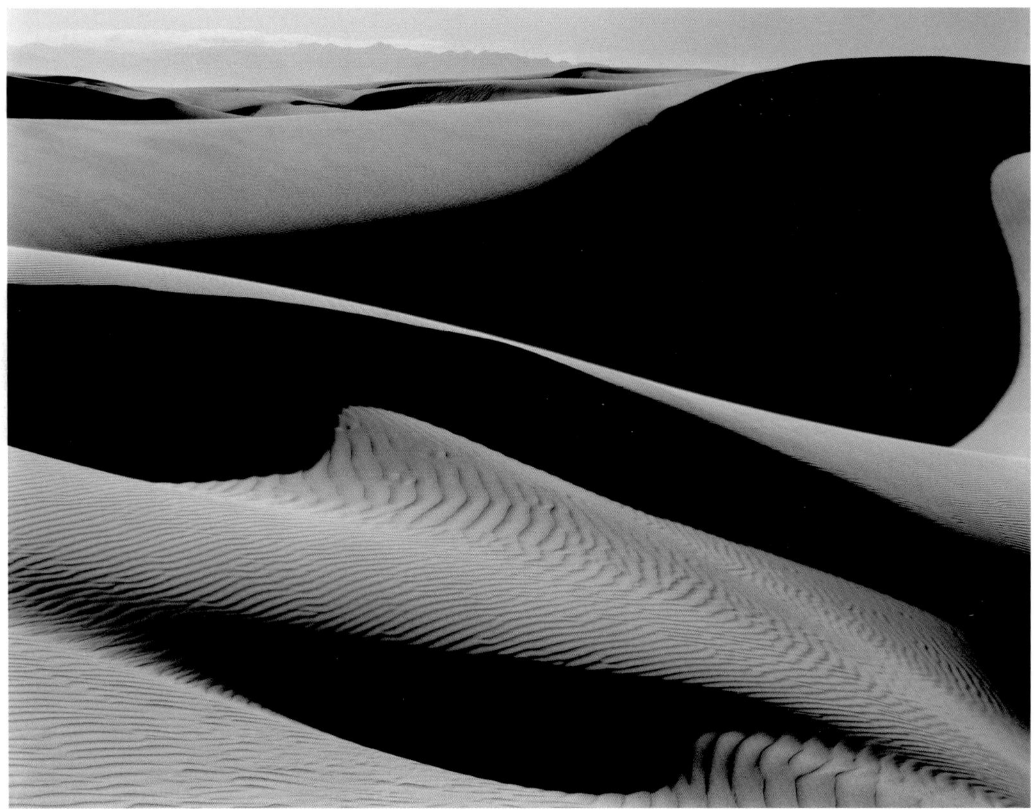

Edward Weston (American, 1886–1958)

Sand Dunes, Oceano, California, 1936

Gelatin silver print; 19 x 24.2 cm (7 ½ x 9 ½ in.)

Sophie M. Friedman Fund 1983.169

Toni Schneiders's and Edward Weston's photographs isolate abstract forms and patterns found in nature. In 1949, Schneiders and a number of other German photographers formed the Fotoform group, which spawned the Subjektive Fotografie movement of the 1950s and 1960s. His image of a bicyclist on a serpentine stretch of road is characteristic of the group's emphasis on daring black-and-white images that verge on almost total abstraction. Schneiders was clearly fascinated by the tendency of the aerial view to simplify the details of the landscape into graphic patterns and turn the distant figure into a dark speck on the bright ribbon of pavement.

Weston's extensive 1936 series of the dunes in Oceano, California, similarly focuses on line and pattern, in this case the sinuous lines and rolling shapes created by the wind and tides on the sand. He and his fellow Bay Area photographers were early proponents of the large-format cameras and small aperture settings that produced maximum image sharpness and great depth of field. As a result, Weston's contact prints of his Oceano views possess a sparkling clarity in the highlights and a tonal richness in the shadows that transform the flowing topography into a stunning visual puzzle that is at once highly detailed yet very abstract.

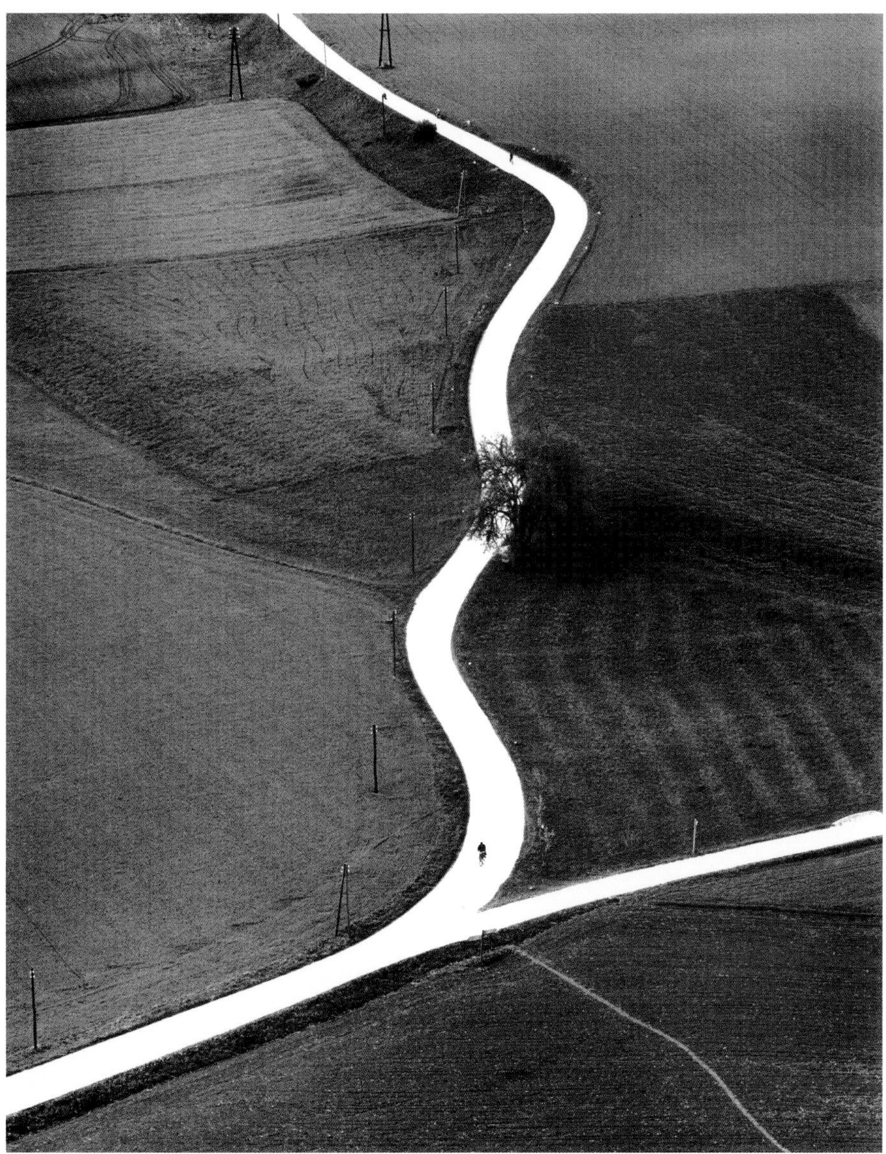

Toni Schneiders (German, born in 1920)

Landscape with Road, Kärnten, Austria, 1957

Gelatin silver print; 39.1 x 29.5 cm (15⅜ x 11⅝ in.)

Sophie M. Friedman Fund 2000.661

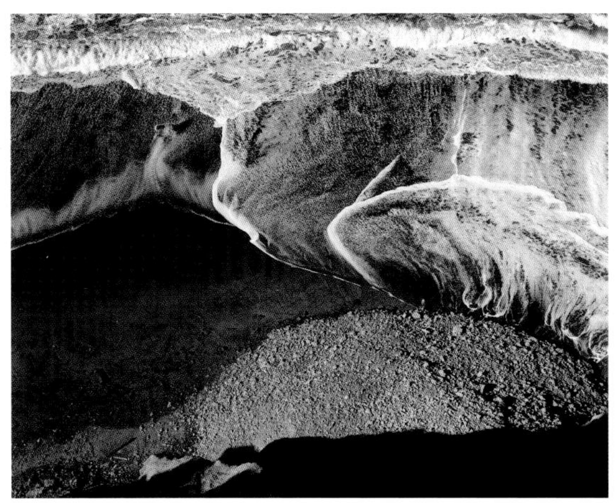

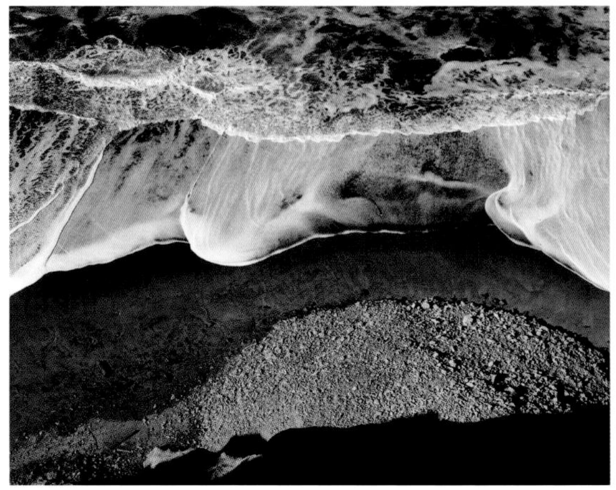

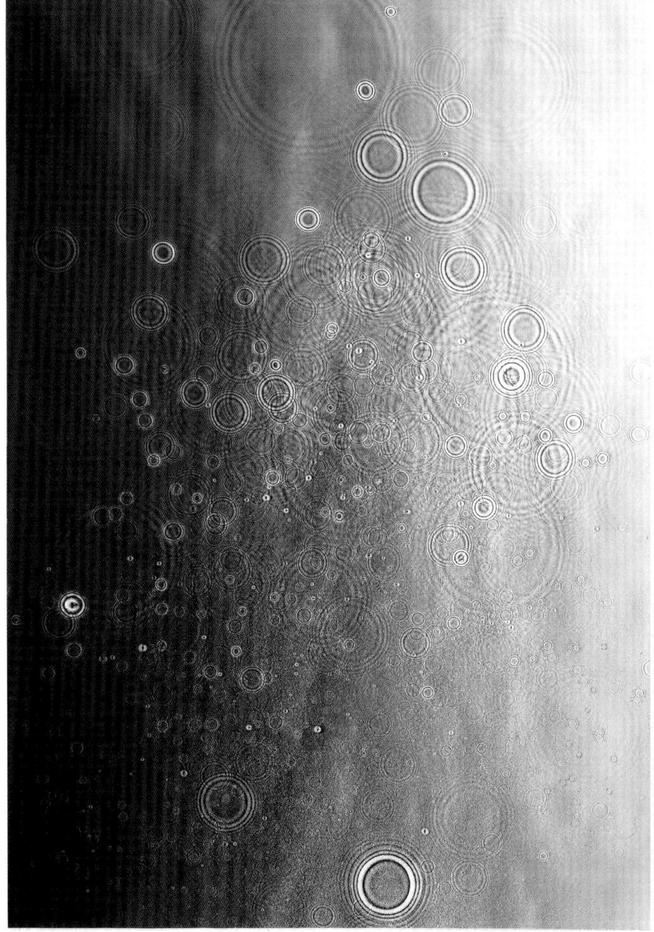

Adam Fuss (English, born in 1961)

Untitled, 1997

Photogram, unique gelatin silver print

169.9 x 118.4 cm (66 7/8 x 47 5/8 in.)

Sophie M. Friedman Fund 1999.8

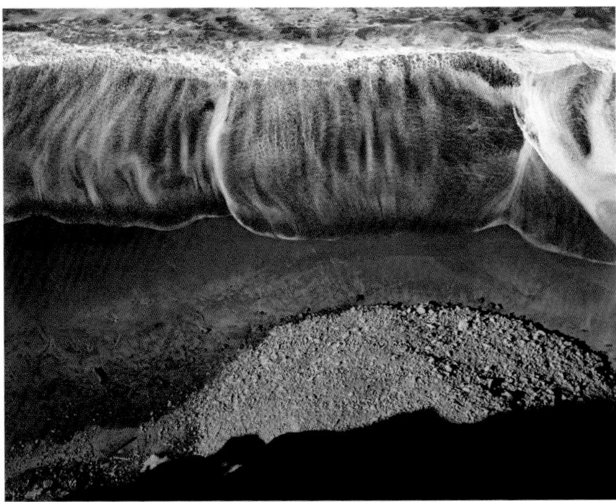

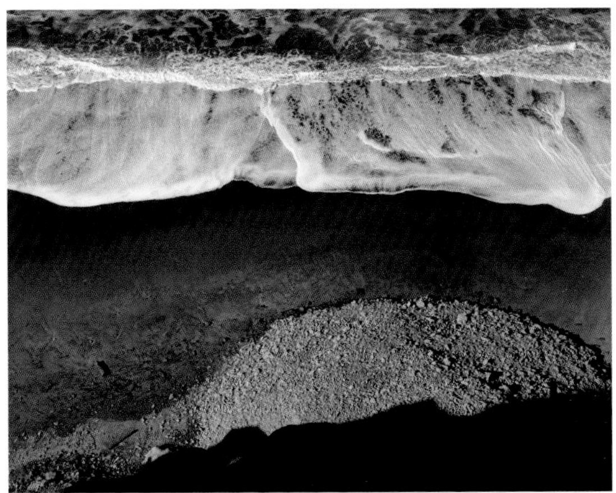

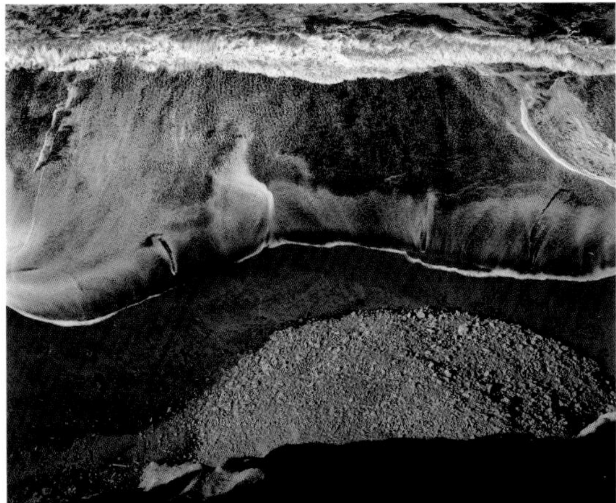

Ansel Adams (American, 1902–1984)

Surf Sequence, 1940, printed in 1973

Gelatin silver prints

26.2 x 32.2 cm (10 5/16 x 12 11/16 in.) each

Gift of Saundra B. Lane in honor of Clifford S. Ackley 2002.880

Water is the shared inspiration for these works by Ansel Adams and Adam Fuss, which explore varying levels of abstraction. Adams shot the five images of his *Surf Sequence* in 1940 during a drive along the Pacific Coast in California, returning from a visit to his friend Edward Weston in Carmel. Stopping along the highway overlooking the ocean, the photographer was taken by the lacy patterns that the waves created, and he made several exposures on the spot. The resulting photographs beautifully captured both a sense of movement and the passage of time, as the sun gradually moved across the sky and the shadows lengthened while he worked. These nearly abstract ocean views suggest the idea of themes and variations that Adams, trained as a concert pianist, appreciated in classical music. Early examples of his serial imagery, they have proved to be some of his most influential work.

In Adam Fuss's case, the representation of water was made without a camera. Like much of his work, this unique photogram captures a fleeting and ephemeral subject on light-sensitive paper and transforms it into something else: drops cascading into a tray of water become an abstract image of silvery concentric circles. Whether Fuss's cameraless images record snakes slithering through white powder, a child's christening gown transparent and glowing, or ghostly columns of smoke, they are at once familiar and strange. Using early photographic techniques, Fuss creates very modern, revelatory pictures.

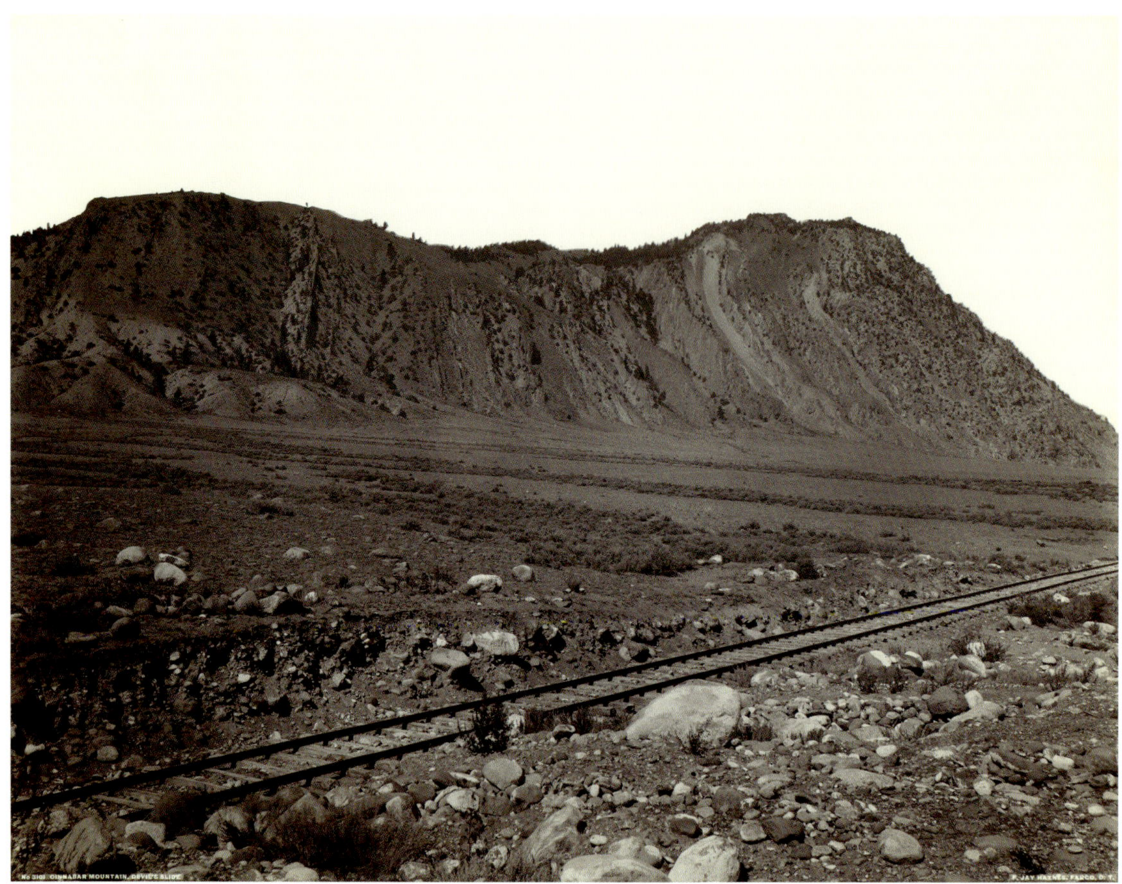

Frank Jay Haynes (American, 1852–1921)

Cinnabar Mountain, Devil's Slide, about 1890

Albumen print; 43 x 54.3 cm (16 15/16 x 21 3/8 in.)

Ernest Wadsworth Longfellow Fund 1999.10

The landscape of the American West has been a favorite subject of photographers since the invention of the medium. Frank Jay Haynes was among the second generation of photographers who worked for the railroads and on government surveys of the West during the last quarter of the nineteenth century. He was appointed the official photographer of Yellowstone in 1884 and opened a concession there to supply landscape views to the growing numbers of tourists to the park. Named for its distinctive dark red color, Cinnabar Mountain had been painted by artists such as Thomas Moran, who admired its dramatic shape and proximity to the scenic Yellowstone River. Haynes's image, in contrast, does not include any such picturesque elements, focusing instead on the railway tracks in the foreground and the eerie desolation of the site.

Nearly one hundred years later, photographer Len Jenshel likewise fell under the spell of the western landscape's great expanse. Having first discovered the region as a young child, Jenshel returned as an adult to document—with irony and a sense of

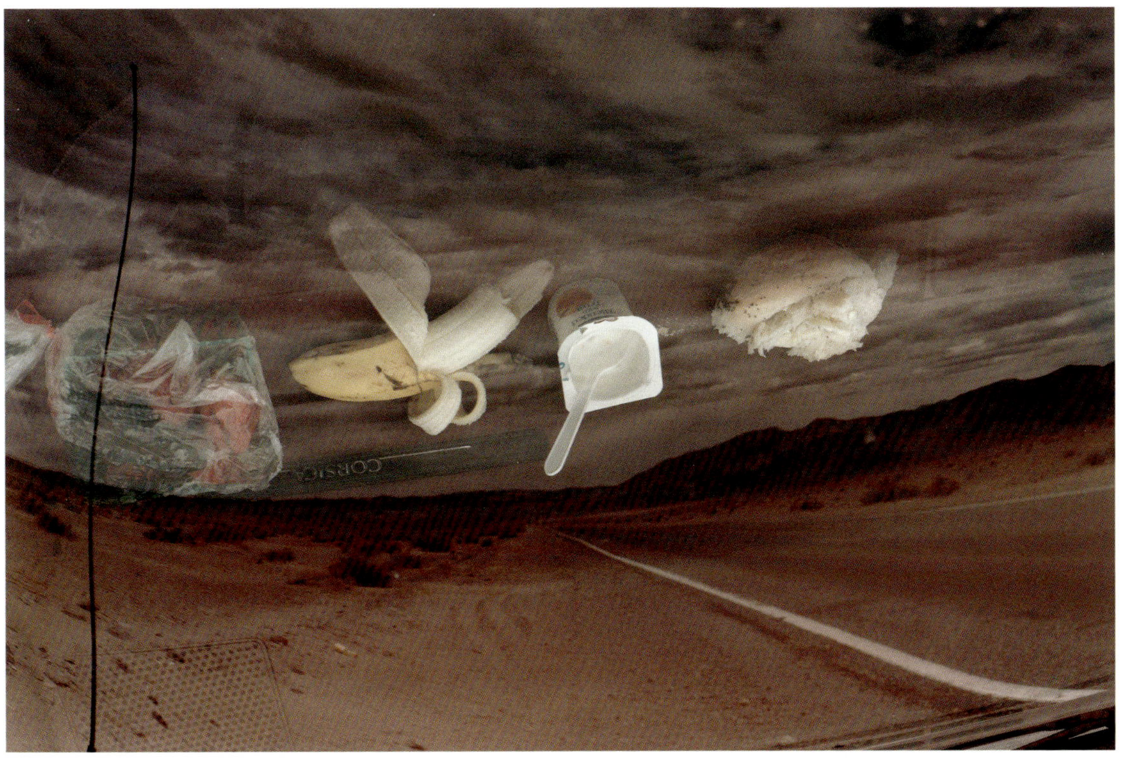

Len Jenshel (American, born in 1949)

Route 127 near Death Valley National Monument, California, 1990

Chromogenic print (Ektacolor)

50.8 x 60.9 cm (20 x 24 in.)

Sophie M. Friedman Fund 1992.67

humor—the impact of tourism and the automobile on the country's national parks. He had long admired the hallucinatory detail and unpeopled views of his nineteenth-century predecessors, but his large-scale color photographs also include signs of man's encroachment on even our most protected wilderness spaces. Here, for example, Jenshel captures a wry panoramic view of Death Valley complete with a topsy-turvy reflection of his lunch in his car's windshield.

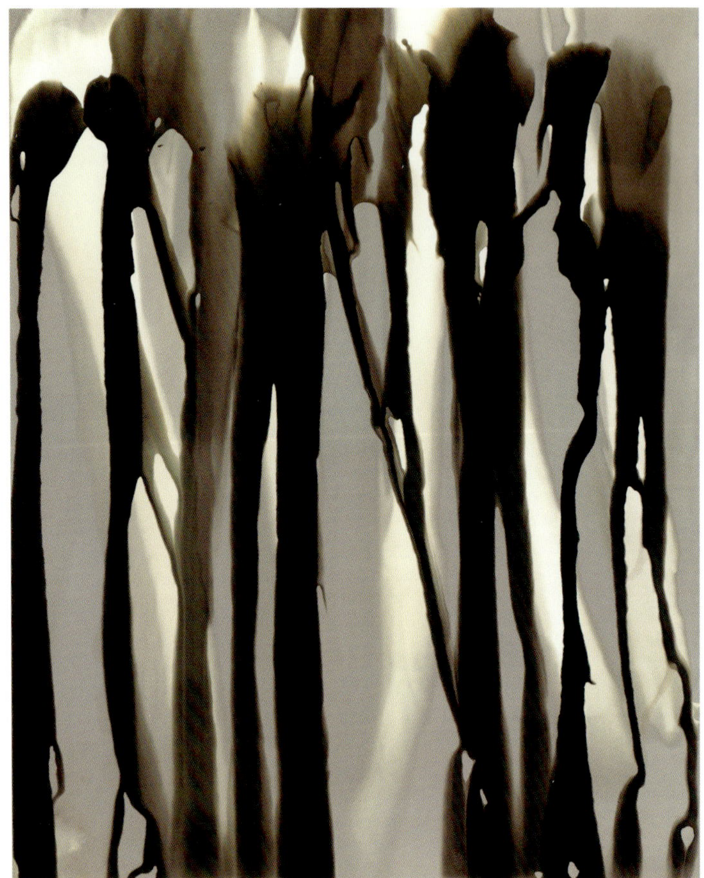

Kilian Breier (German, born in 1931)
Chemigraphik Oxydationsprozess,
about 1953–55
Gelatin silver print; 39.4 x 30.5 cm (15 ½ x 12 in.)
Museum purchase with funds donated
by John and Olivia Parker 2000.777

These two abstract images share a painterly sensibility and an experimental approach to photography. Kilian Breier's chemically produced photograph is an example of the type of unique cameraless pictures for which he is known, beautifully balancing expressive freedom on the one hand and mechanical control on the other. Created in the darkroom by flowing layers of developer on a piece of photographic paper, it is reminiscent of the delicate veil-like drips in the stain paintings of his American contemporaries Helen Frankenthaler and Morris Louis. Breier was a member of the so-called Subjektive Fotografie movement, which emphasized using experimental techniques to make graphic black-and-white pictures such as this that straddle the line between objective representation and abstraction.

Anselm Kiefer is a painter whose canvases are known for their complex layering of materials and of meaning, often featuring themes from mythology and German history. He first introduced photography into his work beginning in the late 1960s, producing images that are manipulated, painted, and written on. The title of this example refers to a scene from Wagner's epic opera *The Ring of the Nibelung*. Like many of Kiefer's works from the 1970s, it depicts a dark and mysterious landscape—in this case, a model staged in the studio out of sand, straw, and broken glass, along with a bottle and mushrooms meant to suggest the magic potion taken by the hero Siegfried, causing him to forget his love for Brünhilde.

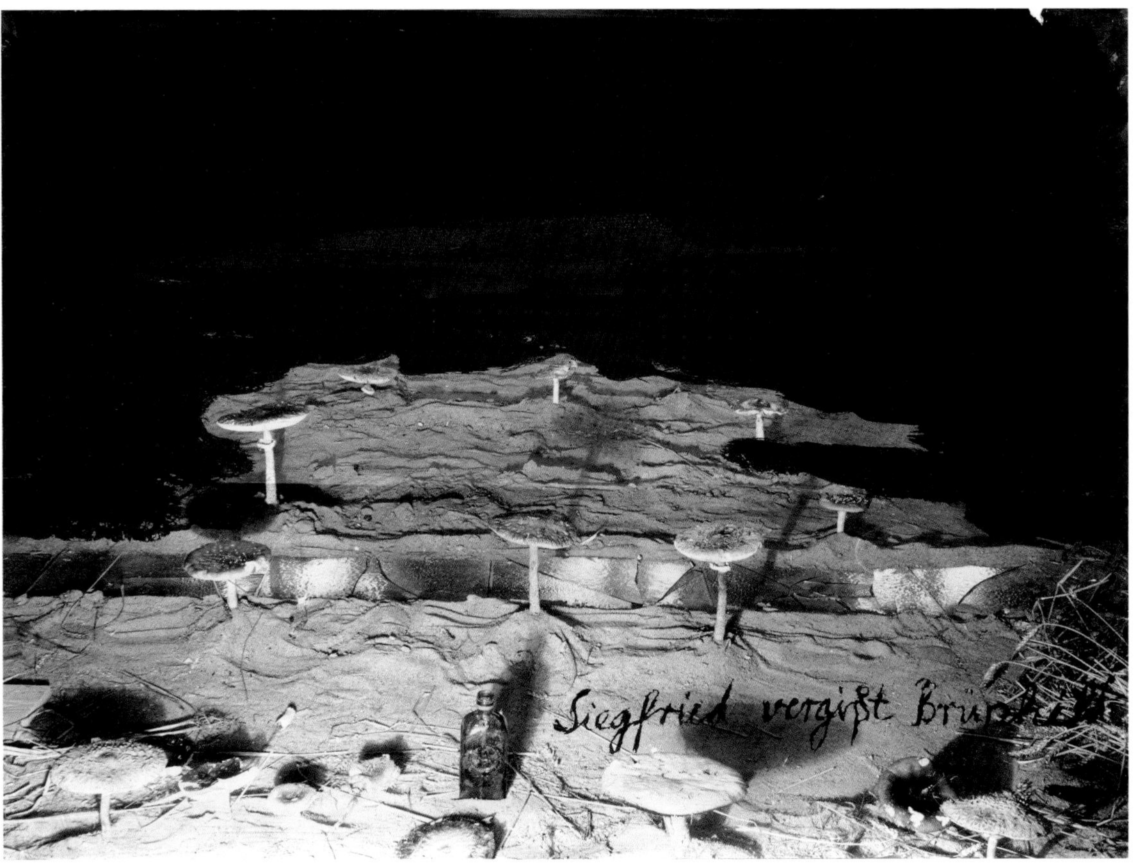

Anselm Kiefer (German, born in 1945)

Untitled (Siegfried Forgets Brünhilde),

about 1975–80

Gelatin silver print with hand additions in black acrylic paint and clear gel; 45 x 60.5 cm ($17\frac{11}{16}$ x $23\frac{13}{16}$ in.)

Gift of Mr. and Mrs. Theodore E. Stebbins in memory of Stephen D. Paine 1998.102

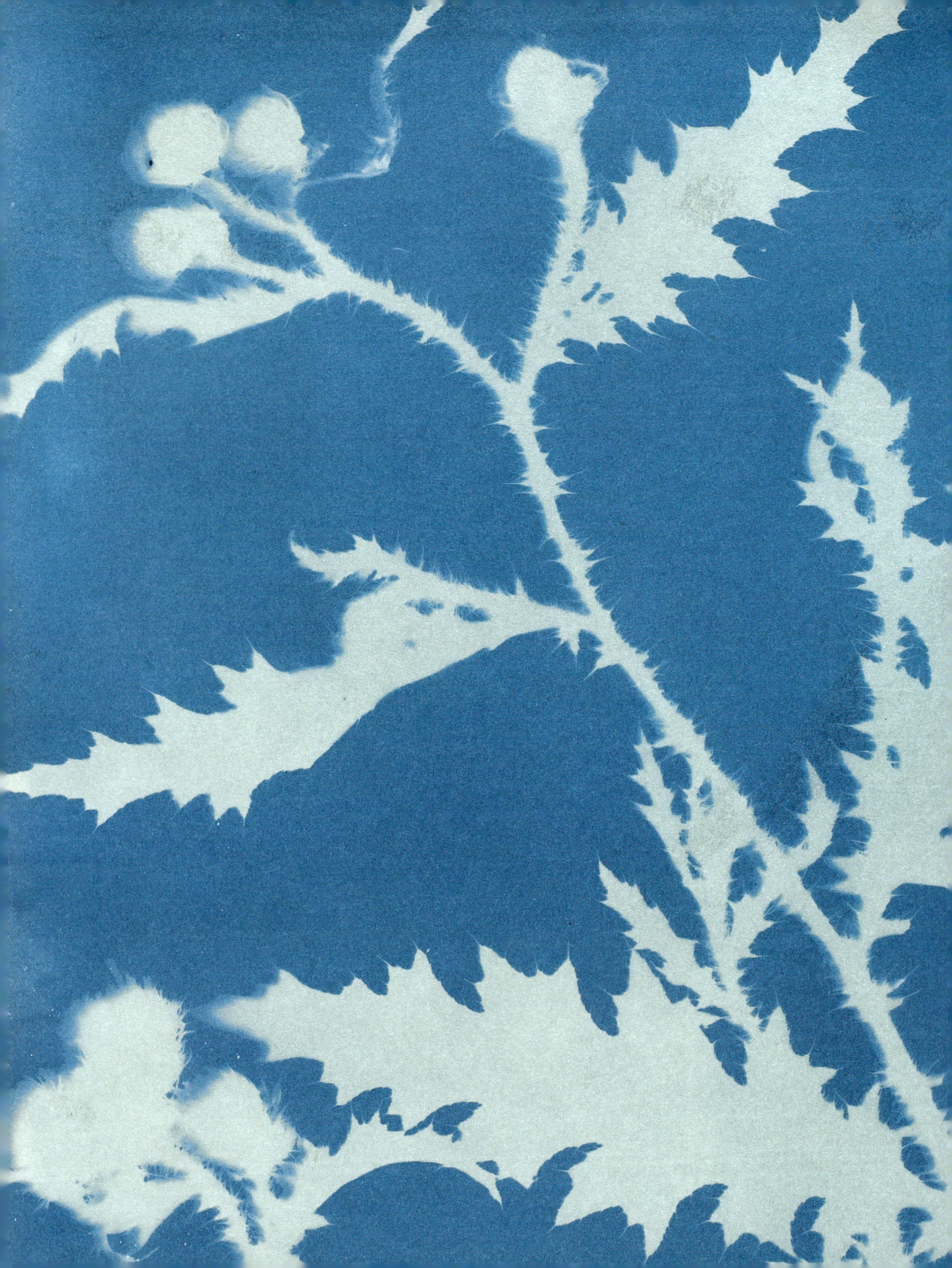

Glossary

albumen print. A photographic print characterized by an albumen (egg-white) coating containing light-sensitive silver salts applied to thin paper. Multiple images can be contact-printed from either a **glass-plate negative** or **calotype** using daylight. Commercially popular 1850s–1890s.

autochrome. The first color photographs, these unique three-color, transparent images on glass were made from red-, green-, and blue-dyed potato starch grains separated into layers and then coated with varnish and light-sensitized gelatin. They must be held up to light or projected in order to be viewed. Manufactured 1907–1933.

bromoil print. Based on the principle that oil and water repel each other, a gelatin silver-bromide print (a type of **gelatin silver print**) is chemically altered to retain only the gelatin matrix, which is then dampened in water, coated with a greasy ink, and used to transfer the ink to another paper surface in a printing press. The resulting bromoil print is less detailed than the original image, and its painterly effect can be enhanced by using a range of ink colors. Commercially popular 1910–1930s.

calotype. A term often used to refer to both a paper negative and a **salt print.** Calotype negatives are made by applying a series of chemical solutions to paper, rendering it light-sensitive. The sensitized paper is exposed in a camera to produce a latent image of reverse tones that is developed; the resulting negative, sometimes waxed to improve transparency, is then contact-printed with another light-sensitized paper in daylight to produce a printed-out photographic print. Commonly used 1840s–early 1850s.

camera lucida. From the Latin for "lighted room," this apparatus facilitates drawing by providing a reflected image for an artist to trace. The tool is comprised of a multifaceted prism secured to a vertical rod that can be clamped to a drawing board. Although clumsy to use, it was more portable than the earlier **camera obscura**.

camera obscura. From the Latin for "dark chamber," this tool—a box containing an angled mirror and an adjustable-focus lens—allows an artist to reproduce a subject by flattening it from three-dimensions into two and inverting it so that it appears in its true orientation.

carbon print. A print produced by a photomechanical process typically used for book illustration, in which carbon tissue is coated with gelatin, contact-printed on a negative, and processed in a series of additional steps to produce a pigmented image with continuous tone and excellent stability. Commercially popular 1870–1910; occasionally made today.

carbro print. A print created by a process similar to that used to make a **carbon print**. Three-color (also called tricolor) carbro printing entails the use of three prints of one subject (photographed through red, green, and blue filters) to produce individual negatives, bromide prints, and then pigmented layers of gelatin tissue, which in turn are transferred, one atop the other in alignment, to create a full-color image. Invented in 1868 and used until the early twentieth century.

carte-de-visite. A specific format for a mounted photograph, typically a portrait, that is attached to heavyweight cardstock of standard size, with outer dimensions of 4½ x 2½ inches.

chromogenic print. The most common type of color photographic print. During development of a chromogenic print, the silver salts and color-dye chemicals layered within the emulsion interact to produce a single full-color image. Despite improvements in the technology of dye stability, fading can occur in both light and dark environments. Invented around 1910 and still in use today.

cliché-verre. A print that combines aspects of photography and printmaking. The camera-less image is produced by drawing on a glass plate coated with an opaque substance (selectively removing the coating by scratching, scraping, etc.). The prepared plate is then used as a negative that is contact-printed on light-sensitized paper by exposure to light, producing a photographic drawing. In use by 1835 and still used today.

combination print. A photographic image resulting from the use of more than one negative to create a single composition. The technique was used in early landscape photography, for example, to compensate for the different exposure times required when employing the albumen process to record the varying tonal densities of land and sky. A combination print can also be comprised of more than one photographic printing process, such as platinum and gum bichromate.

contact print. A positive print that is the same size as the negative, created by placing the sensitized paper and negative in direct contact with each other in a print frame and exposing them to light.

cyanotype. A blue (or cyan) image produced by a photo-chemical process that relies on the light sensitivity of iron salts. The simple and inexpensive process can be used to contact-print photographic negatives or to create images of objects placed directly on light-sensitive paper, and was used for architectural blueprints. Invented in 1840 and occasionally produced 1840–1880; most popular 1880–1920 and still made today.

daguerreotype. The first commercially viable type of photograph, a daguerreotype is a unique photograph on a silver-plated copper support with a mirror-like surface. Because of its delicate surface, a daguerreotype is often protected within a hinged case. Invention announced in 1839; most popular 1839–1850s and still made by a few photographers today.

double exposure. A print resulting from a second exposure of a negative within the camera. Sometimes this happens accidentally when film does not advance in a camera as it should. Certain photographers exploit this technique intentionally.

dye-diffusion transfer. A method for creating unique prints or transparencies in which all image-forming layers (both dyes and developers) are present in one packet and are mixed by being squeezed together in the camera. Polaroid is the most common type. Viable process first noted in 1850s; more practical experimentation began around 1940, and "one-step" cameras became commercially available in 1947.

dye transfer. This particularly stable color photographic print process begins with a subject being photographed three times, through red, green, and blue filters, to produce three negatives. The negatives are used to make three gelatin relief matrices holding dyes, which are then transferred to a sheet of gelatin-coated paper, creating a full-color image. Invented in 1870s but not marketed by Kodak as "dye transfer" until mid-1940s; production of materials ceased in mid-1990s.

ferrotyping. A finishing technique in which the image side of a gelatin silver photograph is dried in direct contact with a highly polished surface, resulting in a glossy appearance. The technique is becoming obsolete as paper manufacturers produce high-gloss papers that do not require ferrotyping.

gelatin silver print. The most common type of black-and-white photograph, created by coating paper with a mixture of light-sensitive silver salts suspended in a gelatin emulsion. Gelatin silver prints typically display a full range of values from white to black. Commercial papers are available in a variety of surface textures, matte and gloss finishes, image tonalities, and degrees of contrast. Introduced in 1873 and in wide use by 1880s, replacing albumen papers by 1895; still in use today.

glass-plate negative. Generic term describing a negative created by applying a light-sensitive emulsion to a plate of glass. Such negatives typically produce sharper and more detailed images than **paper negatives** and are most often used in the creation of **albumen prints**. The glass can be prepared using collodion (wet plate negative, in use 1855–1880) or gelatin (gelatin dry plate, commercially popular after 1880).

gum bichromate print. A print created by coating paper with a mixture of gum arabic, pigments, and a solution of light-sensitive chemicals. When this prepared paper is exposed through a negative, the coating selectively hardens in relation to the amount of light it receives. Areas that do not harden are washed away, leaving less pigment and creating highlights, while hardened areas create the image. The resulting print appears soft and painterly. Introduced in 1894 and popular through the 1920s; occasionally used today.

Lambda print. A high quality, continuous tone photographic print with superlative clarity and color saturation derived from a computer source. The image is created by a laser beam comprised of three colors (red, green, blue) that exposes the photographic material in a single pass; no negative is required.

palladium print. Like a **platinum print**, except the final image material is palladium. Introduced in 1916 and popular after World War I; the scarcity of the metal has made the technique obsolete.

paper negative. See **calotype**.

photogenic drawing. The first (imperfect) photographic process to use a paper support and allow the possibility for creating multiple prints by the use of a negative. The method was problematic, as it took many hours to produce a faint image that remained light-sensitive; a viable chemical fixative had not yet been discovered. The images resulting from this pioneering technology are very rare and must not be exhibited, since they will continue to develop upon light exposure until the paper is darkened overall. Invented in 1834 and evolved by 1840 into the **calotype** process.

photogram. A cameraless photographic print made by placing objects on a sheet of light-sensitive paper or film, exposing the assembled materials to light, and fixing the image to wash away residual chemicals.

photomechanical printing. Any photographic-looking process in which the final image is not produced by means of light-sensitive materials. For example, an image that has been transferred by photographic means to a metal plate, silkscreen, or lithography stone and then printed on paper using printer's ink.

platinum print. Like a **palladium print**, except the final image material is the more expensive metal platinum. For this type of photographic print, a mixture of light-sensitive iron salts and a platinum compound is used to coat the paper, which is then contact-printed with a negative. The resulting print has a matte surface and excellent tonal scale. Invented in 1873; commercial papers available 1878–1937; some handmade platinum papers still prepared today.

salt print. See **calotype**. This printed-out photographic image derives from the use of table salt to sensitize the paper to light. The final image appears to stain the paper fibers, since there is no glossy binder layer. Invented in 1840; commonly used 1840s–1850s.

solarized print. A photographic print that has been intentionally exposed to light for creative effect after the process of developing it in a sequence of chemical baths has begun. The term solarization describes the characteristic lightening of dark backgrounds and unnatural dark halos surrounding shapes in the manipulated image. The expressive effects of the phenomenon were especially appreciated by modernist photographers working in the 1920s.

toning. A chemical means of changing the image color, tone, stability, or contrast of a photographic print, either during the development process or following it. Toning can produce a wide range of color effects ranging from warm purple to near neutral hues to red-brown or yellow-brown.

wet collodion process. A truly "wet" process that necessitates coating, sensitizing, exposing, and developing the prepared support material (glass plate or metal) before the collodion dries. When executed outside the studio, the process requires a portable darkroom. By the mid-1850s, a less frequently used dry collodion process was developed, which did not entail exposing a wet negative and eventually replaced its predecessor. Invented in 1848; commonly used 1850s–1870s.

Further Reading

As the literature on the history of photography is vast, this list is limited to a variety of general sources, many of which have extensive bibliographies.

Ackley, Clifford S. *Photographic Viewpoints: Selections from the Collection*. Boston: Museum of Fine Arts, 1984.

Baldwin, Gordon. *Looking at Photographs: A Guide to Technical Terms*. Malibu, CA: J. Paul Getty Museum, 1991.

Davis, Keith. *An American Century of Photography: From Dry-Plate to Digital*. 2nd ed. New York: Harry N. Abrams, 1999.

———. *The Origins of American Photography, 1839–1885: From Daguerreotype to Dry-Plate*. New Haven, CT: Yale University Press, 2007.

Frizot, Michel, ed. *The New History of Photography*. Cologne: Könemann, 1998.

Greenough, Sarah, Joel Snyder, David Travis, and Colin Westerbeck. *On the Art of Fixing a Shadow: One Hundred and Fifty Years of Photography*. Washington, DC: National Gallery of Art; Chicago: Art Institute of Chicago, 1989.

Hambourg, Maria, Pierre Apraxine, Malcolm Daniel, Jeff L. Rosenheim, and Virginia Heckert. *The Waking Dream: Photography's First Century; Selections from the Gilman Paper Company Collection*. New York: Metropolitan Museum of Art, 1993.

Hayworth-Booth, Mark. *Photography: An Independent Art*. Princeton, NJ: Princeton University Press, 1997.

Lenman, Robin. *The Oxford Companion to the Photograph*. Oxford: Oxford University Press, 2005.

Marien, Mary Warner. *Photography: A Cultural History*. New York: Harry N. Abrams, 2002.

Sontag, Susan. *On Photography*. New York: Farrar, Straus, and Giroux, 1977; New York: Anchor Books, 1990.

Szarkowski, John. *Looking at Photographs: 100 Pictures from the Collection of the Museum of Modern Art*. Boston: Little, Brown, 1973; New York: Bulfinch Press, 1999.

———. *Photography until Now*. New York: Museum of Modern Art, 1989.

Figure Illustrations

p. 12, fig. 1
William Henry Fox Talbot (English, 1800–1877)
Entrance Gate, Abbotsford, 1844, from *Sun Pictures in Scotland* (1845)
Salt print from a paper negative
16.5 x 20.7 cm (6½ x 8⅛ in.)
Charles Amos Cummings Fund 1984.436

p. 17, fig. 2
Benjamin Brecknell Turner (English, 1815–1894)
Hawkhurst Church, Kent, 1852
Albumen print from a paper negative
28.8 x 36.8 cm (11 5/16 x 14½ in.)
Charles Amos Cummings Fund 1981.173

p. 18, fig. 3
Gustave Le Gray (French, 1820–1884)
Portrait of Victor Cousin, about 1856
Albumen print
20.1 x 15.5 cm (7 15/16 x 6⅛ in.)
Gift of Charles Millard in honor of Sue Welsh Reed 2005.272

p. 18, fig. 4
Charles-Hippolyte Aubry (French, 1811–1877)
Poppies, about 1864
Albumen print
34.3 x 26 cm (13½ x 10¼ in.)
Sophie M. Friedman Fund 1990.603

p. 20, fig. 5
Carleton E. Watkins (American, 1829–1916)
Mount Starr King, Yosemite, No. 69, 1865–66
Albumen print
50.8 x 41 cm (20 x 16⅛ cm)
Ernest Wadsworth Longfellow Fund 2006.847

p. 21, fig. 6
Peter Henry Emerson (English, 1856–1936)
A Rushy Shore, 1886, from *Life and Landscape on the Norfolk Broads* (1886)
Platinum print
19.1 x 28.4 cm (7½ x 11 3/16 in.)
Lucy Dalbiac Luard Fund 1977.182

p. 22, fig. 7
William Herman Rau (American, 1855–1920)
Main Line West of Cove, about 1893
Gelatin silver print
43.5 x 54.3 cm (17⅜ x 21⅜ in.)
Ernest Wadsworth Longfellow Fund 1997.104

p. 23, fig. 8
Charles Jones (English, 1866–1959)
Pear, Beurre Superfine, 1895–1910
Gelatin silver print
10.8 x 15.2 cm (4¼ x 6 in.)
Museum purchase with funds donated by John and Olivia Parker 2004.2186

p. 25, fig. 9
Paul Strand (American, 1890–1976)
Rebecca's Hands, 1923
Palladium print
24.7 x 19.6 cm (9¾ x 7 11/16 in.)
Sophie M. Friedman Fund 1977.780

p. 26, fig. 10
Albert Renger-Patzsch (German, 1897–1966)
Trees in Winter, 1926
Gelatin silver print
37.7 x 27.5 cm (14 13/16 x 10 13/16 in.)
Sophie M. Friedman Fund 1981.298

p. 28, fig. 11
Marta Hoepffner (German, 1912–2000)
Glasses with Rose, 1956
Color carbro print, solarized
29.2 x 23.4 cm (11½ x 9 3/16 in.)
Lucy Dalbiac Luard Fund 2005.595

p. 28, fig. 12
Brassaï (Gyula Halász) (French, born in Hungary, 1899–1984)
Sleeping Tramp in Marseilles, 1935
Gelatin silver print
23.6 x 17.6 cm (9 5/16 x 6 15/16 in.)
Sophie M. Friedman Fund 1986.594

p. 29, fig. 13
Paul Outerbridge, Jr. (American, 1896–1958)
Still Life: Mask with Shells and Pearls, 1936–38
Color carbro print
40.1 x 32.9 cm (15 13/16 x 12 15/16 in.)
Graham Gund Photography Fund 1979.617

p. 29, fig. 14
Berenice Abbott (American, 1898–1991)
New York at Night, 1932
Gelatin silver print
15.3 x 12.4 cm (6 x 4⅞ in.)
Gift of Mrs. Jeanne Kanton Landon 1973.524

p. 31, fig. 15
William Klein (American, born in 1928)
Simone + Nina, Piazza di Spagna, Rome, for *Vogue*, 1960, printed later
Gelatin silver print
50.4 x 40.4 cm (19 13/16 x 15⅞ in.)
Ernest Kahn Fund 2006.1393

p. 32, fig. 16
Ivan Mikhaylovich Shagin (Russian, 1904–1982)
A Stratostat before Take-Off into the Stratosphere, 1933
Gelatin silver print
31.4 x 47.5 cm (12⅜ x 18 11/16 in.)
Ernest Wadsworth Longfellow Fund
2007.447

p. 33, fig. 17
Weegee (Usher Fellig) (American, born in Austria, 1899–1968)
Frank Pape, Sixteen-Year-Old Boy Who Strangled a Four-Year-Old Child to Death, 1944
Gelatin silver print
24.9 x 32.2 cm (9 13/16 x 12 11/16 in.)
Sophie M. Friedman Fund 2001.814

p. 35, fig. 18
Shomei Tomatsu (Japanese, born in 1930)
Prostitute, Nagoya, 1958, printed in 2003
Gelatin silver print
35.2 x 25.7 cm (13⅞ x 10⅛ in.)
Horace W. Goldsmith Foundation Fund
2006.1179

p. 36, fig. 19
Diane Arbus (American, 1923–1971)
Woman with a Veil on Fifth Avenue, NYC, 1968
Gelatin silver print, printed by Neil Selkirk
50.2 x 40.6 cm (19¾ x 16 in.)
Polaroid Foundation Purchase Fund
1976.40

p. 38, fig. 20
Marie Cosindas (American)
Ellen, 1965
Dye transfer color print from a Polaroid original
17.5 x 13.3 cm (6⅞ x 5¼ in.)
Gift of the Polaroid Corporation 1977.143

p. 38, fig. 21
Martin Parr (English, born in 1952)
Dakar, 2001
Lambda print
105 x 150.5 cm (41 5/16 x 59¼ in.)
Gift of Jessie H. Wilkinson—Jessie H. Wilkinson Fund 2006.1957

p.39, fig. 22
Robert Rauschenberg (American, born in 1925)
The Razorback Bunch (Etching IV), 1967–69
Photoetching printed from five plates
120.7 x 80 cm (47½ x 31½ in.)
Lee M. Friedman Fund 1982.156

p. 41, fig. 23
Abelardo Morell (American, born in Cuba in 1948)
Camera Obscura Image of the Empire State Building in Bedroom, 1994
Gelatin silver print
50.5 x 62 cm (19⅞ x 24 in.)
Sophie M. Friedman Fund 1995.17

p. 43, fig. 24
Alfred Stieglitz (American, 1864–1946)
The Steerage, 1907
Gelatin silver print
11.1 x 9.2 cm (4⅜ x 3⅝ in.)
Gift of Miss Georgia O'Keeffe 50.826

p. 44, fig. 25
Charles Sheeler (American, 1883–1965)
Criss-Crossed Conveyors—Ford Plant, 1927
Gelatin silver print
25.4 x 20.3 cm (10 x 8 in.)
The Lane Collection

p. 44, fig. 26
Yousuf Karsh (Canadian, born in Turkish Armenia, 1908–2002)
Winston Churchill, 1941
Gelatin silver print
97.2 x 75.3 cm (38¼ x 29⅝ in.)
Gift of Estrellita and Yousuf Karsh
1996.148

p. 45, fig. 27
Herb Ritts (American, 1952–2002)
Wrapped Torso, Los Angeles, 1989
Platinum print
56.8 x 46.1 cm (22⅜ x 18⅛ in.)
Gift of Herb Ritts 2000.885

Index

Credits

Grateful acknowledgment is made to the copyright holders for permission to reproduce the following works:

Abbott, *New York at Night*, © Berenice Abbott / Commerce Graphics Ltd., Inc., NYC

Adams, *Near Bolinas, California* and *Surf Sequence*, Photographs by Ansel Adams. Used with permission of the Trustees of The Ansel Adams Publishing Rights Trust. All Rights Reserved

Arbus, *Woman with a Veil on Fifth Avenue, NYC*, © 1971 The Estate of Diane Arbus, LLC

Auerbach, *The Temptation of St. Anthony*, © 2006 VG Bild-Kunst, Bonn / Artists Rights Society (ARS), New York

Avedon, *Robert Frank, photographer, and June Leaf, artist, Mabou Mines, Nova Scotia, July 17, 1975*, Photograph Richard Avedon. © 2008 The Richard Avedon Foundation

Bourke-White, *The George Washington Bridge*, furnished by the Estate of Margaret Bourke-White

Brancusi, *Eve and Shadow*, © 2006 Artists Rights Society (ARS), New York / ADAGP, Paris

Brandt, *Belgravia, London*, Bill Brandt © Bill Brandt Archive Ltd.

Brassaï (Gyula Halász), *Sleeping Tramp in Marseilles*, Photograph by Brassaï. © Gilberte Brassaï

Breier, *Chemigraphik Oxydationsprozess*, © Kilian Breier

Callahan, *Cape Cod* and *Eleanor*, © The Estate of Harry Callahan, courtesy Pace/MacGill, NY

Cosindas, *Ellen*, © 1965 Marie Cosindas

Coyne, *Untitled*, © Petah Coyne

Cumming, *Quick Shift of the Head Leaves Glowing Stool Afterimage Posited on Pedestal*, Art © Robert H. Cumming Jr. Living Trust / Licensed by VAGA, New York, NY

Cunningham, *Exploding Bud (Billbergia)*, Photography by Imogen Cunningham, © The Imogen Cunningham Trust

Drtikol, *Nude in Corner behind Disk*, © Ružena Knotková-Boková

Evans (Frederick H.), *Portrait of F. Holland Day*, By permission of Mrs. Janet Stenner, sole surviving granddaughter of F. H. Evans

Evans (Walker), *Man and Movie Poster, New Orleans*, © Walker Evans Archive, The Metropolitan Museum of Art

Fischli and Weiss, *Ehre, Mut, und Zuversicht*, © Peter Fischli / David Weiss, Courtesy Matthew Marks Gallery, New York

Frank, *Coffee Shop, Railway Station, Indianapolis*, © Robert Frank, from "The Americans"

Friedlander, *Atlantic City, New Jersey*, Courtesy Fraenkel Gallery, San Francisco

Funke, *Still Life*, Courtesy Miloslava Rupesová

Fuss, *Untitled*, © Adam Fuss

Gutmann, *The Beautiful Clown*, © 1998 Center for Creative Photography, Arizona Board of Regents

Henri, *Still Life with Pineapple and Cactus*, © Galleria Martini & Ronchetti, Genoa, Italy, www.florencehenri.com

Hoepffner, *Glasses with Rose*, © Estate Marta Hoepffner

Jacobson, *Song of Sentient Beings #1617*, © Bill Jacobson, 1995

Karsh, *Alexander Calder*, © 1965 Estate of Yousuf Karsh, and *Winston Churchill*, © 1941 Estate of Yousuf Karsh

Keïta, *Untitled*, © Seydou Keïta Estate. Courtesy J. M. Patras

Kertész, *Clochard and Posters, Paris*, Courtesy © Estate of André Kertész 2006

Kiefer, *Untitled (Siegfried Forgets Brünhilde)*, © Anselm Kiefer

Klein, *Simone + Nina, Piazza di Spagna, Rome*, © William Klein / Courtesy Howard Greenberg Gallery, New York

Koudelka, *Czechoslovakia*, © Josef Koudelka / Magnum Photos

Kühn, *Untitled (Still Life: Interior with Horse Chestnuts, Lamp, and Tea Kettle)*, Courtesy Galerie Johannes Faber, Vienna

Laughlin, *The Spectre of Coca-Cola*, Courtesy of The Historic New Orleans Collection, accession no. 1981.247.1.1373

Levitt, *New York*, © Helen Levitt

Lux, *Dorothea*, © Loretta Lux, Courtesy of Yossi Milo Gallery, NY

Man Ray, *Untitled* (1926) and *Untitled* (1932), © 2006 Man Ray Trust / Artists Rights Society (ARS), NY / ADAGP, Paris

Meyerowitz, *Florida*, © Joel Meyerowitz, Courtesy Edwynn Houk Gallery

Model, *Running Legs, New York*, © The Lisette Model Foundation, Inc. (1983), by permission of the Foundation

Modotti, *Worker's Hands, Mexico*, Courtesy of Throckmorton Fine Art

Moholy (Lucia), *Florence Henri, Paris*, © 2006 Artists Rights Society (ARS), New York / VG Bild-Kunst, Bonn

Moholy-Nagy (László), *Untitled*, © 2006 Artists Rights Society (ARS), New York / VG Bild-Kunst, Bonn

Morell, *Camera Obscura Image of the Empire State Building in Bedroom* and *Toy Blocks*, © Abelardo Morell / Courtesy Bonni Benrubi Gallery, NYC

Morris, *Abandoned House*, © 2003 Center for Creative Photography, Arizona Board of Regents

Nachtwey, *Kabul, Afghanistan*, © James Nachtwey / VII

Namuth, *Jackson Pollock Painting*, © 1991 Hans Namuth Estate

Nixon, *Bebe, Cambridge*, © Nicholas Nixon, courtesy Fraenkel Gallery, San Francisco

Outerbridge, *Saltine Box* and *Still Life: Mask with Shells and Pearls*, © 2008 G. Ray Hawkins Gallery, Los Angeles, CA

Parker, *Vessel*, Olivia Parker © 1993

Parks, *Rose Cleaning Bathtub*, © Gordon Parks

Porter, *Sangre de Cristo Mountains at Sunset, Tesuque, New Mexico*, © 1990 Amon Carter Museum, Fort Worth, Texas

Rauschenberg, *The Razorback Bunch (Etching IV)*, Art © Robert Rauschenberg / Licensed by VAGA, New York, NY

Renger-Patzsch, *Trees in Winter*, © 2006 Albert Renger-Patzsch Archiv / Ann u. Jürgen Wilde, Zülpich / Artists Rights Society (ARS), New York

Ritts, *Wrapped Torso, Los Angeles* and *Versace Dress, Back View, El Mirage*, © Herb Ritts Foundation

Ruff, *Portrait*, © 2006 Artists Rights Society (ARS), New York / VG Bild-Kunst, Bonn

Sander, *Painter Heinrich Hoerle*, © 2006 Die Photographische Sammlung / SK Stiftung Kultur—August Sander Archiv, Cologne / ARS, NY

Schneiders, *Landscape with Road, Kärnten, Austria*, Toni Schneiders / PhotoArt. Reproduced with permission

Shagin, *A Stratostat before Take-Off into the Stratosphere*, RIA Novosti

Shibata, *Grand Coulee Dam, Douglas County, WA*, © Toshio Shibata

Steichen, *Dana* and *Three Pears and an Apple*, Permission of Joanna T. Steichen

Sternfeld, *After a Flash Flood, Rancho Mirage, California, July 1979*, Copyright © Joel Sternfeld, Reproduction Courtesy Luhring Augustine Gallery

Strand, *Rebecca's Hands* and *Tree Stump and Vine, Colorado*, © Aperture Foundation Inc., Paul Strand Archive

Sudek, *Milena* and *Third Courtyard of the Castle, Prague*, © Anna Fárová

Sugimoto, *Black Sea, Ozuluce* and *Ionian Sea, Santa Cesarea I*, © Hiroshi Sugimoto

Tomatsu, *Prostitute, Nagoya*, © *Prostitute, Nagoya*, 1958, Shomei Tomatsu, Courtesy of Tepper Takayama Fine Arts

Weegee (Arthur H. Fellig), *Frank Pape, Sixteen-Year-Old Boy Who Strangled a Four-Year-Old Child to Death*, © Weegee / International Center of Photography / Getty Images

Wegman, *Intirely*, © William Wegman

Every effort has been made to contact copyright holders of images not listed. Any oversight in this regard is purely unintentional.